# FRAMING PIECES

# FRAMING PIECES

## Designs of the Gloss in Joyce, Woolf, and Pound

*John Whittier-Ferguson*

New York    Oxford
OXFORD UNIVERSITY PRESS
1996

Oxford University Press

Oxford    New York

Athens    Auckland    Bangkok    Bombay
Calcutta    Capetown    Dar es Salaam    Delhi
Florence    Hong Kong    Istanbul    Karachi
Kuala Lumpur    Madras    Madrid    Melbourne
Mexico City    Nairobi    Paris    Singapore
Taipei    Tokyo    Toronto

and associated companies in
Berlin    Ibadan

Copyright © 1996 by John Whittier-Ferguson

Published by Oxford University Press, Inc.,
198 Madison Avenue, New York, New York 10016

Oxford is a registered trademark of Oxford University Press

Library of Congress Cataloging-in-Publication Data
Whittier-Ferguson, John.
Framing pieces : designs of the gloss in Joyce, Woolf, and Pound /
John Whittier-Ferguson.
p.    cm.
Includes bibliographical references and index.
ISBN 0-19-509748-3
1. English fiction—20th century—Criticism, Textual.
2. Modernism (Literature)—Great Britain.    3. Joyce, James,
1882–1941—Criticism, Textual.    4. Woolf, Virginia, 1882–1941—
Criticism, Textual.    5. Pound, Ezra, 1885–1972—Criticism, Textual.
6. Joyce, James, 1882–1941—Technique.    7. Woolf, Virginia,
1882–1941—Technique.    8. Pound, Ezra, 1885–1972—Technique.
9. Fiction—Technique.    10. Poetics.    I. Title.
PR888.M63W48    1996
823'.91209—dc20        95-17101

1 3 5 7 9 8 6 4 2

Printed in the United States of America
on acid-free paper

O52296-3960K8

Grateful acknowledgment is given to Harcourt, Brace for permission to quote from the following copyrighted work of Virginia Woolf.

Excerpt from *The Diary of Virginia Woolf*, Volume 2: *1920–1924*, copyright © 1978 by Quentin Bell and Angelica Garnett, reprinted by permission of Harcourt, Brace & Company.

Thanks also to The New York Public Library for Woolf, Virginia. [Anon.] Holograph, unsigned and undated, 9p.; 13p.; 15p.; 9p. Henry W. and Albert A. Berg Collection. The New York Public Library. Astor, Lenox and Tilden Foundations.

Grateful acknowledgment is given to New Directions Publishing Corporation and Faber & Faber Ltd. for permission to quote from the following copyrighted works by Ezra Pound.

*ABC of Reading*. All rights reserved.
*The Cantos*. Copyright © 1934, 1937, 1940, 1948, 1956, 1959, 1962, 1963, 1966, and 1968 by Ezra Pound.
*Confucius: "The Great Digest," "The Unwobbling Pivot," "The Analects"* (Copyright © 1947, 1950 by Ezra Pound).
*Correspondence*
Pound/Zukofsky (Copyright © 1981, 1987 by the Trustees of the Ezra Pound Literary Property Trust).

*Guide to Kulchur* (Copyright © 1970 by Ezra Pound).
*Jefferson and/or Mussolini* (Copyright 1935, 1936 by Ezra Pound; renewed 1963 by Ezra Pound. Used by permission of the Liveright Publishing Company).
*Literary Essays* (Copyright © 1918, 1920, 1935 by Ezra Pound).
*The Rome Broadcasts: "Ezra Pound Speaking"* (Copyright © 1978 by the Trustees of the Ezra Pound Literary Property Trust).
*Selected Letters, 1907–1941* (Copyright 1950 by Ezra Pound).
*Selected Prose, 1909–1965* (Copyright © 1960, 1962 by Ezra Pound; Copyright © 1973 by the Estate of Ezra Pound).
*The Spirit of Romance* (Copyright © 1968 by Ezra Pound).

Previously unpublished material by Ezra Pound Copyright © 1991 by the Trustees of the Ezra Pound Literary Property Trust; used by permission of New Directions Publishing Corporation, agents.

*Ezra Pound's Poetry and Prose: Contributions to Periodicals* (Copyright © 1991 by the Trustees of the Ezra Pound Literary Property Trust).

*For my parents*
*Joanne O'Kelly Ferguson and Oliver Watkins Ferguson*
*who taught me to read and write*

# ACKNOWLEDGMENTS

This study has been framed—its pieces more firmly bound together than they otherwise would have been—by friends and colleagues. A. Walton Litz has presided over my work from its inception. I first read much of the poetry and prose I discuss here in his courses at the Bread Loaf School of English and at Princeton University. The topic of modernist glosses took shape under his inspired and inspiring supervision. His generous guidance and support have extended well beyond the bounds of this book.

Robert Spoo and Ronald Bush have contributed enormously to whatever is best in this study. Both have proved to be the most gracious, searching, critically encouraging readers imaginable.

It is my pleasure to record here my debts to my colleagues at the University of Michigan: George Bornstein, Michael Schoenfeldt, and the late James Gindin provided me with repeated, sustained, and invaluable assistance over the past few years. Others at Michigan—Leonard Barkan, Jonathan Freedman, Laurence Goldstein, Juan Leon, Marjorie Levinson, Adela Pinch, Theresa Tinkle, and Robert Weisbuch—have given portions of this book helpful readings.

"And say my glory was I had such friends": my work has benefited and I have been blessed by a number of readers whose queries and suggestions have helped me to clarify both the dimensions and the details of this project. They are Kirk Ambrose, Carl Dolan, Charles Ferguson, Sandra Gilbert, Janet Gray, Wallace Jackson, David Kramer, David Lamotte, Frank Lentricchia, Gail McDonald, Mary Pat O'Kelly, Omar Pound, Allen Reddick, Richard Tarlov, Keith Taylor, and Charles Wheeler. I am grateful to James Longenbach for both general counsel and particular advice. Victor Luftig offered me direction and inspiration at a crucial point in this manuscript's revision. I wrote always in anticipation of Bruce Redford's response, and continue to learn much from the example he sets in his own scholarship.

I wish to express my appreciation to the Mrs. Giles Whiting Foundation and Princeton University for a Whiting Fellowship in the Humanities at an early stage of this project. I have also received welcome support in the form of faculty grants from the Office of the Vice President for Research and the Horace H. Rackham Graduate School at the University of Michigan. The staffs of the Morris Library at Southern Illinois University at Carbondale; the Firestone Library at Princeton University; and the Beinecke Library at Yale University have all been most helpful.

I would like to thank Elizabeth Maguire, my editor at Oxford University Press, and her assistant, Elda Rotor, for their expeditious assistance throughout. I have been fortunate, too, in having Amanda Heller for my copy editor.

Frames do not merely contain; they can also support. It is in the sense of providing shape and meaning that Gale has framed this book. Henry and Margaret daily expand the dimensions and the significance of that frame.

# CONTENTS

# ABBREVIATIONS

| | |
|---|---|
| *ABCE* | Pound, Ezra. *ABC of Economics*. In *Selected Prose: 1909–1965*. Edited by William Cookson. New York: New Directions, 1973. |
| *ABCR* | Pound, Ezra. *ABC of Reading*. Norfolk, Conn.: New Directions, 1951. |
| "Anon" | Silver, Brenda, ed. "'Anon' and 'The Reader': Virginia Woolf's Last Essays." *Twentieth Century Literature* 25 (1979): 356–441. |
| *C* | Pound, Ezra. *The Cantos of Ezra Pound*. New York: New Directions, 1981. |
| EP, *Letters* | Pound, Ezra. *The Letters of Ezra Pound: 1907–1941*. Edited by D. D. Paige. New York: Harcourt, Brace, 1950. |
| *FW* | Joyce, James. *Finnegans Wake*. Corrected ed. New York: Viking Press, 1958. |
| *GK* | Pound, Ezra. *Guide to Kulchur*. New York: New Directions, 1970. |
| Gorman | Gorman, Herbert. *James Joyce*. New York: Farrar and Rinehart, 1939. |
| Gorman galleys | Galleys for Herbert Gorman, *James Joyce*. Herbert Gorman Papers. The Croessmann Collection, Morris Library, Southern Illinois University at Carbondale. |
| "HR" | Pound Ezra. "How to Read." In *Literary Essays of Ezra Pound*. Edited, with an introduction, by T. S. Eliot. Norfolk, Conn.: New Directions, 1954. |
| *JJ* | Ellmann, Richard. *James Joyce*. Rev. ed. New York: Oxford University Press, 1982. |
| JJ, *Letters* | Joyce, James. *Letters of James Joyce*. Vol. 1. Edited by |

Stuart Gilbert. Vols. 2, 3. Edited by Richard Ellmann. New York: Viking Press, 1957, 1966.

*JJA* 46     Joyce, James. *Finnegans Wake, Book I, Chapters 4–5: A Facsimile of Drafts, Typescripts, & Proofs.* Edited by David Hayman, Danis Rose, and John O'Hanlon. New York: Garland, 1978.

*JJA* 52     Joyce, James. *Finnegans Wake, Book II, Chapter 2: A Facsimile of Drafts, Typescripts, & Proofs.* Vol. 1. Edited by David Hayman, Danis Rose, and John O'Hanlon. New York: Garland, 1978.

*JJA* 53     Joyce, James. *Finnegans Wake, Book II, Chapter 2: A Facsimile of Drafts, Typescripts, & Proofs.* Vol. 2. Edited by David Hayman, Danis Rose, and John O'Hanlon. New York: Garland, 1978.

*JJA* 62     Joyce, James. *Finnegans Wake, Book III: A Facsimile of the Galley Proofs.* Edited by David Hayman, Danis Rose, and John O'Hanlon. New York: Garland, 1978.

*OE*          Beckett, Samuel, et al. *Our Exagmination Round His Factification for Incamination of Work in Progress.* Paris: Shakespeare and Company, 1929. Reprint. New York: New Directions, 1972.

*P*            Woolf, Virginia. *The Pargiters: The Novel-Essay Portion of "The Years."* Edited and Introduced by Mitchell A. Leaska. New York: New York Public Library and Readex Books, 1977.

*PE*          Pound, Ezra. *Polite Essays.* Norfolk, Conn.: New Directions, 1940.

*P/Z*        Pound, Ezra. *Pound/Zukofsky: Selected Letters of Ezra Pound and Louis Zukofsky.* Edited by Barry Ahearn. New York: New Directions, 1987.

*ROO*      Woolf, Virginia. *A Room of One's Own.* New York: Harcourt Brace Jovanovich, 1929.

*RS*          *"Ezra Pound Speaking": Radio Speeches of World War II.* Edited by Leonard W. Doob. Westport, Conn.: Greenwood Press, 1978.

*SP*          Pound, Ezra. *Selected Prose: 1909–1965.* Edited by William Cookson. New York: New Directions, 1973.

*t*             Jolas, Eugene, ed. *transition* 1–27 (1927–1938).

*TG*         Woolf, Virginia. *Three Guineas.* New York: Harcourt Brace Jovanovich, 1938.

*U*           Joyce, James. *Ulysses: The Corrected Text.* Edited by Hans Walter Gabler, with Wolfhard Steppe and Claus Melchior. Preface by Richard Ellmann. London: Bodley Head, 1986.

VW, *Diary* — Woolf, Virginia. *The Diary of Virginia Woolf.* 5 vols. Edited by Anne Olivier Bell. New York: Harcourt Brace Jovanovich, 1977–1984.

VW, *Letters* — Woolf, Virginia. *The Letters of Virginia Woolf.* 6 vols. Edited by Nigel Nicolson and Joanne Trautmann. New York: Harcourt Brace Jovanovich, 1975–1980.

*Waves* — Woolf, Virginia. *The Waves.* New York: Harcourt, Brace, 1931.

*WL* — Eliot, T. S. *The Waste Land.* In *The Complete Poems and Plays: 1909–1950.* New York: Harcourt Brace Jovanovich, 1971.

# FRAMING PIECES

# INTRODUCTION

*It's all rubbish to pretend that art isn't didactic. A revelation is always didactic. Only the aesthetes since 1880 have pretended the contrary, and they aren't a very sturdy lot.*

Ezra Pound to Felix Schelling, 8 July 1922, in *Letters*

The subject of this book—the gloss, the apparatus, authors' commentaries on their own lives or work—is always in danger of growing beyond proportion, finally comprising everything a given author wrote, or of dwindling until it includes only a handful of footnotes. "Framing pieces" can designate scraps loosely assembled around the peripheries of a poem, an essay, a novel; or the phrase can point to the elaborate construction of a textual border substantial enough to gather under a single title the scattered pieces of a broken text. Any collection of glosses may perform both functions sequentially or simultaneously. Eliot advises us at one moment in his "Notes on 'The Waste Land'" to "cf. *The Tempest*, I, ii" (*WL*, 52.192);[1] six notes later he offers us his crucial, gnomic characterization (perhaps the single most discussed gloss in twentieth-century literature) of Tiresias as the "most important personage in the poem, uniting all the rest" (*WL*, 52.218). And, depending on a particular reader's particular convictions, the most unobtrusive of Eliot's notes may stand transfigured on the page, the briefest reference to Dante or Webster or Weston suddenly revealing a way to set this tangled poem in order.

"Framing pieces" also names an activity that Joyce, Woolf, and Pound pursue, most energetically during the 1930s, in various but related ways— self-consciously creating an exegetical tradition into which they place their lives, their poetry, their prose, and their own glosses. The notes, marginalia, critical essays, and longer prose works with which these authors surround their complex art illuminate and obscure aspects of the annotated texts themselves. The apparatus also addresses and helps to create the conditions for the reception of the framed texts. In the first of his Charles Eliot Norton lectures (1932), Eliot characterizes "modern poetry as being extremely critical [since] the contemporary poet, who is not merely a composer of graceful verses, is forced to ask himself such questions as 'what is poetry for?'; not merely 'what am I to say?' but rather 'how and to whom am I to say it?'"[2] Our century's writing, given its fractured and vaguely demarcated audiences, must construct its contexts and the rules for its reading, must recall the traditions from which it springs, must carry with it selected crucial portions of those traditions for readers who would otherwise fail to discern the appropriate ancestors in its lineaments. And, sharing a related complex of anxieties about those plural audiences, Joyce, Woolf, and Pound often labor with equal care to discriminate among readers. Enlightenment and clarification by no means necessarily take precedence in the offices performed by modernist annotation. Exclusion plays a central part as well—the glossed text placed, like the potent goblet in Frost's carefully baffling "Directive," "under a spell so the wrong ones can't find it." Close to Eliot's questions at the beginning of the 1930s about the function and reception of poetry lies a related field of questions about the social power granted to the artist by a decade that will not allow aesthetic grace alone to justify the pursuit of art.[3] Whether and how an author might discover the authority to issue directives; whether those directives might take openly sociopolitical turns or might, with equal if less obvious political import, spurn engagement with the particular brutalities of the day; and whether even the most straightforward trailblazing is warranted or could be successful are issues that matter profoundly to Pound, Woolf, and Joyce. Each writer offers complex, frequently contradictory answers to Eliot's difficult questions—answers that will change along with the import of the questions themselves as we focus on annotated texts.

The glosses I discuss are often immediately recognizable as such. Joyce heavily annotates three margins of the pages of the "Lessons" chapter (II.2) in *Finnegans Wake*. Woolf adds footnotes to *A Room of One's Own*, composes a set of expository essays to accompany the fictional narrative of *The Pargiters*, and appends a wide-ranging set of "Notes and References" to *Three Guineas*. Pound's *ABC of Reading* collects a set of "EXHIBITS" with commentary. But I am equally concerned with less obvious scaffolding. Joyce stands behind his authorized biography, Herbert Gorman's *James Joyce*, and the first exegeses of *Ulysses* and *Finnegans Wake*, a covert manipulator of his public's perceptions. Planning far greater objectives for his guides and adamantly opposed to adulterating his Cantos with a key, Pound devotes himself in his poetry and prose of the 1930s to the enormous task of fashioning a culture suited to support and receive his own work. The sordid conditions of Western civilization, the incompetence of politicians, and the complacency of the public have forced him to postpone his exalted creative enterprise for a labor he considers secondary but essential: "Quite simply," he tells his readers in 1928, "I want a new civilization."[4] It might seem that no writing that furthers this grand ambition can accurately be labeled annotation; but from the late 1920s through the early 1940s Pound clearly views himself as waging a pedagogical campaign by means of instructive commentary on history and the troubled world—a duty that leads him astray from the poetic work for which he is best suited. I follow

Pound's own description of his work from this period when I place it in the category of scaffolding.

But Pound continually confesses exemplary doubts about the instability of this category—doubts that Joyce and Woolf also entertain. Lee Patterson's introduction to an issue of the *South Atlantic Quarterly* titled "Commentary as Cultural Artifact" succinctly expresses the tendency of glosses for any text, from the Bible to *Pale Fire*, to upset

> the assumption that there is a difference between the text and [the gloss] itself ... [since] without warning we discover that [the gloss] has itself become a text or—more unsettling still—moved from the margins into the center to become an indistinguishable part of that to which it was originally merely a submissive addition.[5]

The differences between "scaffolding" and "temple," to use a figure of Pound's for apparatus and text, invariably prove impossible to capture in a definition, and I have deliberately avoided attempting to propose a general theory of the gloss or its function, preferring instead to open each chapter of this book by framing the domain I will survey, and then moving to a discussion of the particular effects of each author's apparatus in its local habitation.[6] The footnote, tied by number to a specific point in a specific text, encourages us to recognize the crucial fact that all apparatus can be discerned and can do its work only in context, however ambiguous and perpetually changing that context may be. My study thus depends on close readings that attend to important but now often concealed or forgotten frames: the periodicals, for example, in which these writers' first readers encountered texts that now come to us in anthologies or books, stripped of their earlier associations. I have also found it useful to examine archival materials—drafts, notes, diaries, letters—that constitute private but no less relevant contexts for the works I study. I turn to public and private apparatus with the awareness that I can only assemble germane contexts but cannot thereby presume to know how each of Woolf's readers would have interpreted the photographs in the first edition of *Three Guineas*, or exactly what the subscribers to the *New York Herald Tribune Books* would have made of Pound's "How to Read," or whether the followers of "Work in Progress" would have taken the time to read the manifestos and exegeses surrounding Joyce's text in *transition*. But the imponderables vexing all discussions of reader response and authorial intention should not discourage us from efforts at discovering as fully as possible what it was that readers might have responded to and following even the most tentative or contradictory records of the evolution of an author's designs for a work.

Eliot's notes to *The Waste Land* offer a perfect illustration of apparatus that has grown so thoroughly familiar that we can scarcely read it apart from the earnest additions and endless elucidations of subsequent editors. This still growing body of notes nevertheless stands in its original shape as a characteristically elaborate and ambitious instance of modernist gloss. In the notes themselves, and in his later pronouncements about this unwieldy addition to his poem,

Eliot addresses the poet's construction of his art and his audience, answering in the most deliberately ingenious fashion the questions he later declares all poets must confront: How and to whom am I to say it? I can think of no more effective introduction to the complexities of twentieth-century apparatus, and no better illustration of how glosses can embody an author's thoughts concerning the creation and dissemination of a work, than to examine Eliot's production of framing pieces for his poem.

*The Waste Land* was published in book form with notes on 15 December 1922 (two months after it was printed without annotations in the *Criterion* and the *Dial*).[7] Eliot's last Norton lecture (1933) furnishes an apposite gloss on the effect of his addition to the poem. He gently chastises modern poetry's "ordinary reader," whose failings are at least in part a cause and a consequence of *The Waste Land* and its apparatus:

> Instead of beginning, as he should, in a state of sensitivity, he obfuscates his senses by the desire to be clever and to look very hard for something, he doesn't know what—or else by the desire not to be taken in. There is such a thing as stage fright, but what such readers have is pit or gallery fright.[8]

It is not a fear that affects the more discriminating audience in the box seats. Calculated to induce unnecessary cleverness on the one hand and an uneasy sense of being "taken in" on the other, Eliot's notes instantly divide his public into distinct groups. Pound recalled in 1940 that "the immediate reception of [*The Waste Land*] even by second rate reviewers was due to the purely fortuitous publication of the notes, and not to the text itself."[9] Pound's condescension reveals the catch in the notes: to spend too much time chasing Eliot's references or to rely too obviously on his thematic guides is to confess oneself a "second rate reviewer"— unable to read the poem without its author's help, prone to "pit or gallery fright" in the face of challenging art.

When confronted with an author's annotations, the critic will always be similarly threatened. Harriet Shaw Weaver perfectly exemplifies the trap with her perverse solution to the obscurity of Joyce's "Work in Progress." "Would it be utterly against the grain, your convictions and principles," she asks Joyce in November 1926, "to publish (when the day comes), along with an ordinary edition, also an annotated edition (at double or treble price, say?) I throw this out as a mere suggestion" (*JJ*, 584). Weaver proposes two editions for two separate audiences, and yet the "ordinary" text would presumably be intended for the uncommon few who did not require Joyce's notes. The trebly expensive special edition would be needed by every common reader. Or else one is to purchase both editions, perhaps hiding the annotated copy, since its appearance on the shelf is a confession that here is another hapless reader who cannot go it alone.

Once Eliot's notes were in print, essayists dutifully summarized Weston, nodded to Frazer, and mumbled a few words about Tiresias and the tarot deck, but they disliked spending time with Eliot's appended prose instead of working with the poem itself. That this distinction between crib and art immediately became impossible to maintain contributed substantially to reviewers' irritation.

Conrad Aiken makes a typical objection in his review essay of 1923. The notes give us aid, he admits, but

> if the precise association is worth anything, it is worth *putting into the poem*; otherwise there can be no purpose in mentioning it. . . . [T]he key to an implication should be in the implication itself, not outside of it. We admit the value of esoteric pattern: but the pattern should itself disclose its secret, should not be dependent on a cypher.[10]

Aiken's charges still beset virtually every text I discuss in this study and are made by students and critics alike. Richard Poirier, in *The Renewal of Literature*, looks disapprovingly on the merely "difficult" modernist text as opposed to the admirably "dense," commenting that "maybe with the help of notes and annotations" we can "master the 'difficulty'—[but we] cannot in the same sense master 'density.'"[11] It is a fine irony that a number of modernists themselves, Eliot and Pound above the rest, are in large part responsible for making these charges against apparatus carry such weight and that they accomplish much of this devaluing of explanation in the apparatus itself. But Aiken the reviewer, looking not unreasonably for tighter, more conventional connections between the lines of poetry and their glosses, declares that *The Waste Land* is not a self-sustaining, self-disclosing artifact. Eliot has unnaturally forced obscure material into his misshapen poem, following arcane structural principles known only to the poet. His poem possesses scaffolding but no skeleton. Its form is willed rather than organic.

The notes made doubly irate those reviewers inclined toward hostility. It was presumptuous for a modern poem to come before readers flaunting what appeared to be scholarly apparatus. *The Waste Land*, with its numbered lines and pages of explanatory material, looked overdressed: an immodest young man wearing his academic gown when street clothes would do. To make matters worse, Eliot had only half kept the promise of illumination held out by his glosses. His cryptic hints prompted antagonistic reviewers to single out the notes as an irresistible target. In the words of one such reader:

> [A] poem that has to be explained in notes is not unlike a picture with 'This is a dog' inscribed beneath. Not, indeed, that Mr. Eliot's notes succeed in explaining anything, being as muddled as incomplete. What is the use of explaining 'laquearia' by quoting two lines of Latin containing the word, which will convey nothing to those who do not know that language, and nothing new to those who do? What is the use of giving a quotation from Ovid which begins in the middle of a sentence, without either subject or verb, and fails to add even the reference? And when one person hails another on London Bridge as having been with him 'at Mylae,' how is the non-classical reader to guess that this is the name of a Punic sea-fight in which as Phoenician sailor, presumably, the speaker had taken part?[12]

In our century the note is often assumed to be a democratic addition to the text, encouraging rather than exclusive, and more accessible than the annotated material. This assumption regularly runs counter to the nature of apparatus, which lends itself to elliptical or abstruse commentary addressed to a smaller audience than is the text proper.[13] Because Eliot's notes reach a comparatively large and diffuse audience, one that makes genuine, extensive demands for clarification, they cannot wholly succeed as a game among insiders or even as a gathering of materials already familiar to the few who know Virgil, Ovid, and Greek history. Ironically, Eliot's display of erudition—less serious, less single-minded than that of the earnest critics who upbraid him for writing a poem requiring notes—spurs reviewers to augment the objectionable glosses. In the angry passage just quoted, F. L. Lucas, fellow of King's College, Cambridge, demonstrates his knowledge of Latin syntax and faults the poet for not including information on a "Punic sea-fight," thereby proving himself an annotator at heart and weakening his case against explanations of poetry. The subtext of Lucas's complaint is that he can explain allusions in *The Waste Land* more competently than Eliot. He represents "muddled" readers without joining their undesirable company. The notes provide him with a convenient platform from which he can observe the middlebrow audience congregated in the pit below.

Even under heavy fire, Eliot waited until 1956, in a lecture titled "The Frontiers of Criticism," to brand the notes "bogus scholarship."[14] Eliot's gloss on his glosses, his offhanded dismissal of his "scholarship," has, for the most part, been taken seriously by later critics of *The Waste Land*, who assume "license therefore to ignore" the apparatus, or who use isolated notes simply to confirm interpretations of the poem.[15] Ideally, "The Frontiers of Criticism" would be heard instead of read: Eliot delivered his lecture to a crowd of 14,000 people assembled in a baseball stadium at the University of Minnesota in Minneapolis.[16] Before this heterogeneous audience, gathered to see a celebrity and not to follow an intricate theoretical argument, Eliot sounds nothing like the formidably cerebral author of *The Waste Land*. He has become a wry, wise, candid elder statesman of the arts.

Eliot has watched the development of the academy in our century with a knowing smile: "I have been somewhat bewildered to find, from time to time, that I am regarded as one of the ancestors of modern criticism, if too old to be a modern critic myself."[17] At the conclusion of his talk, he reassures his fans that the intellectual elite are not to be taken quite as seriously as they take themselves: "These last thirty years have been, I think, a brilliant period in literary criticism in both Britain and America. It may even come to seem, in retrospect, too brilliant. Who knows?"[18] The quiet, comic turn against critics' ingenuity is an important component of Eliot's comments on his own encouragement of excessive critical brilliance. A former adversary of simplicity, he pleads guilty to a past violation of his readers' innocence:

> Here I must admit that I am, on one conspicuous occasion, not guiltless of having led critics into temptation. The notes to *The Waste Land*! I had at first intended only to put down all the references for my quotations, with a view to spiking the guns of critics of my earlier poems who had accused me of plagiarism.[19]

Not Eliot but his troublesome critics, carping if he failed to mention sources, generated the apparatus.[20] Eliot's exclamation mark stands for a philosophic sigh that so much commotion arose from such an insignificant gesture. *The Waste Land* itself seems slight from this distant perspective:

Then, when it came to print *The Waste Land* as a little book—for the poem on its first appearance in *The Dial* and *The Criterion* had no notes whatever—it was discovered that the poem was inconveniently short, so I set to work to expand the notes, in order to provide a few more pages of printed matter, with the result that they became the remarkable exposition of bogus scholarship that is still on view to-day.[21]

It is improbable that Eliot and his publishers suddenly "discovered" the length of *The Waste Land* in print, and even more doubtful that Eliot would casually have added filler to a poem that he had revised with such painstaking care.[22] But in Minnesota in 1956 the established poet urbanely distances himself from the younger Eliot, heir of the meticulous symbolists, who weighed every word for its effect. His story of the notes constitutes a revisionary glance at the scrupulous aesthetics of modernism, well after those aesthetic principles have triumphed in the academy.[23]

Equally evasive is his comment that the notes "became the remarkable exposition" of scholarly dead ends. Had he desired, the author could have supplied us with more lucid references, just as the printer could have remedied the poem's "inconvenient" brevity by making adjustments in the book's design. By publishing the notes after the poem's first appearance, Eliot ensured that the book published by Boni and Liveright would present the public with an obviously new edition of his poem.[24] He also manufactured an intriguing amount of mystery and confusion before producing his "solution." He prepared the way for his guides well while giving the first printing of the unannotated *Waste Land* time to impress the audience with its austerity.

Eliot grows increasingly colloquial in "The Frontiers of Criticism," as he describes a possible cleansing of *The Waste Land*: "I have sometimes thought of getting rid of these notes; but now they can never be unstuck. They have had almost greater popularity than the poem itself—anyone who bought my book of poems, and found that the notes to *The Waste Land* were not in it, would demand his money back."[25] How many of the 14,000 in the stands shifted uneasily at this disarmingly friendly attack on the philistines who prefer teaching aids to texts, who want their money's worth from art? Eliot pauses momentarily, in what has become a subtly damning assessment of his poem's inadequate readers, and contrasts his scaffolding with that of another modern poet: "As for Miss Marianne Moore, *her* notes to poems are always pertinent, curious, conclusive, delightful and give no encouragement whatever to the researcher of origins."[26] Of course, Moore's notes, consisting largely of sources for her poems, also provoke research. Eliot's effusive praise is genuine as it springs from an intelligent, appreciative reader of Moore's poetry (one who has no need of notes to admire her art) and ironic as it suggests how his own annotations might have been received. Readers like Moore suffered no harm from his notes, Eliot concludes. He does penance for those less able to keep their heads when tempted with a gloss: "It was just, no doubt, that I should pay my tribute to the work of Miss Jessie Weston; but I regret having sent so many enquirers off on a wild goose chase after Tarot cards and the Holy Grail."[27] Eliot has mounted an agile defense masked as an apology, a confession equally compounded of frank dissatisfaction with his notes' effect on the interpretation of his poem and disdain for clumsy "enquirers" sure to bungle any task of analysis. We shall see Joyce, Woolf, and Pound exhibiting comparably complex attitudes toward their apparatus and their critics.

Eliot's ambivalence, manifested in his rhetorical agility before the Minnesota audience, does not derive from thirty-four years of misreadings. From the outset, in his stylistically and structurally assorted collection of notes, he entertained contradictory impulses to satirize, assist, and mislead students of *The Waste Land*. Apparatus regularly seems to inspire authors to play diverse roles, to propose a succession of approaches to the annotated text. Clive Bell, in his memoir, *Old Friends*, recalls that Eliot's glosses were never straightforward. According to Bell, Roger Fry urged Eliot "to elucidate the text of *The Waste Land* with explanatory notes," but Fry could not have been altogether satisfied with the response: "Eliot met him half-way: he supplied notes, but whether they are explanatory is for others to decide."[28]

And yet Eliot could not make his long poem less fundamentally troublesome no matter how sincerely he wanted to—a fact that should be evident to every reader of modernism's keys and guides. His notes, although a great deal more varied in style and approach, make contributions to our understanding comparable to Roland McHugh's *Annotations to Finnegans Wake* or Carroll Terrell's *Companion to the Cantos of Ezra Pound*. This is not to impugn McHugh or Terrell, both of whom would acknowledge that they have assembled primers for books beyond the scope of annotation. Having sifted any of these collections of glosses for items we find relevant, we must still wander into texts where words and phrases often look only half familiar. Eliot's apparatus demonstrates how "completely separate [are] the man who suffers and the mind which creates."[29] They leave us puzzling over the unmeasurable distances between the hooded god returning from the dead—"Who is the third who walks always beside you?"—and the note on Shackleton's expedition to the Antarctic; between the "dead sound" of bells and the dry gloss on that awful sound (in which Eliot advises us that he has "often noticed" this "phenomenon"); between the poem's endless internal echoes and "Cf. Part I, l. 37, 48." The tone of the annotations to the anguished *Waste Land* suggests a man who has in fact suffered very little. Throughout his critical career Eliot insists that this is precisely the kind of paradox that art engenders. Following the crooked logic of creation, the biographical notes to a perfect poem would be entirely irrelevant: "[T]he more perfect the artist . . . the more perfectly will the mind digest and transmute the passions which are its material."[30] Eliot's notes express his profound skepticism concerning the critic's labor, particularly when the critic evaluates his own creation.[31]

He announces his doubts frequently. "The Function of Criticism," printed in the *Criterion* nine months after publication of *The Waste Land*, clearly describes what he finds objectionable in "interpretation." The quotation marks are Eliot's, a literal sign of his distrust of analysis that strays from the straightforward amassing of facts germane to the work. To "interpret" is to entertain subjective impressions of an author's life and work, and "it is difficult," Eliot warns, "to confirm the 'interpretation' by external evidence."[32] Thirty-three years earlier, Oscar Wilde celebrated exactly what Eliot writes against—interpretive criticism: "the purest form of personal impression, . . . more creative than creation, as it has least reference to any standard external to itself, and is, in fact, its own reason for existing." Wilde welcomes the critic's consequent freedom, with "all interpretations true and no interpretations final."[33] Even as he knows that his work must always be received by twentieth-century incarnations of Wilde's vagrant critic, Eliot fears for and is afraid of the deserted and busily interpreting reader, left with no sturdy bridge between the poem and another's sense of that poem :

> Instead of insight, you get a fiction. Your test is to apply it again and again to the original, with your view of the original to guide you. But there is no one to guarantee your competence. . . . We must ourselves decide what is useful to us and what is not; and it is quite likely that we are not competent to decide.[34]

The alternative to this anxious, solitary weighing of personal fiction and inaccessible original, however, is to study what Eliot calls simply "fact." At the end of his essay, Eliot admits that the term is too volatile for use.[35] The supposedly solid foundations of responsible reading crumble under the onslaught of qualifying, dependent clauses: "[I]f any one complains that I have not defined truth, or fact, or reality, I can only say apologetically that it was no part of my purpose to do so, but only to find a scheme into which, whatever they are, they will fit, if they exist."[36]

And even before we reach this impasse, Eliot teaches us that following the elusive fact is a severely limited pursuit: "[A]ny book, any essay, any note in *Notes and Queries*, which produces a fact even of the lowest order about a work of art is a better piece of work than nine-tenths of the most pretentious critical journalism."[37] We rummage through the variously worthy pieces at the end of *The Waste Land* and fully comprehend the impossibility of finding the poem's essence in any one. "Certain references to vegetation ceremonies" is a preposterously inadequate clue to meaning, but the author cannot lead us much farther without becoming an intrusive, untrustworthy interpreter. None of us, including Eliot, can avoid assuming this role as we work at reading, but it is equally certain that none can communicate his or her findings in satisfactory richness or depth to another. Jeffrey Perl has written eloquently on the extent of Eliot's skepticism, his "scrupulous relativism," regarding all acts of interpretation. "From the outside" of any individual's perspective, Perl comments, "there is no answer; from the inside there is no question. For the insider, there is nothing to explain."[38] Eliot is not competent to analyze his deeper indebtedness to Joyce and the symbolists or to exhume the psychic material that lies beneath the poem. Weston and Frazer earn their prominent place in the opening note precisely because they do not come from the poem's heart. In "The Function of Criticism," Eliot names this unsatisfying deployment of fact "comparison and analysis" and summarizes its advantages over interpretation in a figure at once grim and hilarious: "Comparison and analysis need only the cadavers on the table; but interpretation is always producing parts of the body from its pockets, and fixing them in place."[39] The subject's death must be assumed from the outset. We merely choose whether we will study a corpse or create a monster. Eliot's notes, as he acknowledges in "The Frontiers of Criticism," filled the pockets of incorrigibly inventive critics, and yet his apparatus is in itself also a model of the limitations of interpretation. Reading the notes, we circle the periphery of *The Waste Land*, wondering at what blossomed from this inhospitable soil.

In 1933, as Eliot sternly assumes the "role of moralist" in *After Strange Gods*, meting out charges of heresy to Pound, Yeats, Lawrence, Mansfield, and other writers of his time, he conceives of a severely truncated instance of apparatus: his lucid, uncompromising essay is followed by a dour "Appendix" that proves emblematically different from the mercurial, many-voiced collection of notes that accompany *The Waste Land*. The brief addition of an appendix to *After Strange Gods* is motivated by Eliot's certainties that humanity, obsessed by a simplistic urge to cultivate the merely personal, lacking deeply understood or fervently embraced moral standards, is becoming "more and more vaporous" and that, in the political realm, "a soul destitute of humility and filled with self-righteousness, is a blind servant and a fatal leader."[40] The spiritual and social consequences of botched interpretation are thus unimaginably large — the progress of our disease is best measured by our failures to conceive of its effects — and instead of encouraging us in meditations on poetic origins and the impossibilities of comprehensive readings, Eliot provides us with an opportunity to begin rehabilitating our occluded sense of what evil looks like: "I had thought of supplementing [the essay] by a graduated Exercise Book, beginning with very simple examples of heresy, and leading up to those which are very difficult to solve; and leaving the student to find the answers for himself."[41] Our first assignment consists of subjecting four quotations to moral rather than literary analysis. (Eliot has already demonstrated at length, in the body of his essay, how we are to read as moralists.) We are assisted in our task by his guarantee that each example is somehow tainted: he leaves us less to our own interpretive devices in 1933 than he did in 1922. This is, after all, as the subtitle to *After Strange Gods* proclaims, "A Primer of Modern Heresy." There would be little point, in our benighted century, of working up a text for advanced students.

Primers occupy a central position in my study, primarily because Joyce, Woolf, and Pound are largely concerned during the 1930s with teaching us how to read — themselves, their texts, their cultures, the political crises of their time — and because the pedagogical impulse expresses itself naturally in annotation. That the decade and the impulse coincide in each author's work indicates urgencies that all share regarding an increasingly dispersed and heedless audience and global political turmoil that threatens the cultural foundations on which each constructs a world. Of course Joyce, Woolf, and Pound commence building frames with their earliest ventures into print. But all three, from the late 1920s until the Second World War, pursue projects for which the gloss, in a dazzling variety of forms, proves critically important. I do not maintain that it is only during the 1930s that these artists turn toward a world outside the preserve of the aesthetic; and yet during these troubled years each author spends more and more time brooding about contexts and communities, about the adequacies and the failings of the frames that further and frustrate understanding.

I have used the word "political" twice in the preceding paragraph. It is a vague word that today often commands an enormous amount of unearned authority, particularly as it is used in opposition to an equally indefinite something denominated "modernism."[42] The larger purpose of chapter 1, which takes Joyce as its subject, is to offer a polemical illustration of how we might talk carefully about political aspects of modernist texts. That care can best be signaled at the start by focusing our discussions assiduously on particular moments—in texts, in time—and querying, though not eliminating, the impulse to generalize from those moments. I choose two such moments, both involving politically resonant frames for Joyce's work that either bear evidence of his design or contribute to the potential political impact of his "Work in Progress": Joyce's attempt in mid-1939 to clarify his politics for his first biographer, Herbert Gorman; and the more diffuse but equally complex ideological gestures that fill the final issue of *transition*, published in the spring of 1938 (containing, as was regularly the case, an installment from Joyce's "Work in Progress"). In studying these frames, we discover Joyce taking principled stances, at a time when a second world war seems increasingly inevitable, against what constitutes political practice in our century. We also witness Eugene Jolas, the editor of *transition* and resourceful promoter of Joyce's difficult last book, assume similarly thoughtful positions in the intermittently hopeful, fundamentally pessimistic pages of the final number of his journal.

Readers encountering "Work in Progress" in *transition* would have had substantial opportunities to consider connections between Joyce's text and its textual surroundings even before 1935, when they came on the portion of *Finnegans Wake* (II.2) intimately encumbered with numerous marginalia and lengthy footnotes. In chapter 2, I discuss this heavily annotated piece in detail, but first I examine the nature of two closely related larger frames for Joyce's "Work." Not only are exchanges between "Work in Progress" and *transition* explicitly and implicitly political, but also almost every installment from Joyce comes framed by manifestos (which frequently seem written with Joyce's experiment in mind) and essays that offer equivocal assistance to Joyce's readers. In 1929 the first guidebook to "Work in Progress" was published: *Our Examination Round His Factification for Incamination of Work in Progress.* Consisting almost entirely of selections from *transition*, this framing piece is by turns antic and pedantically helpful. *Finnegans Wake* initially appeared at the center of a heterogeneous collection of avant-garde projects and acrobatic interpretations—its expansive language both generating and caught in innumerable reflections in the surrounding pages of *transition* and in the curious "Exagmination" staged just beyond the journal's borders. To discuss the text's internal and external glosses is to inquire into the dynamics of reading and writing, the relations between author and audience, at the heart of Joyce's *Wake.*

Woolf's experiments with apparatus, like Joyce's, unsettle the spurious authority of the single voice, though she breaks the frames of her books for more expressly tendentious reasons. I study, in chapter 3, a cluster of three annotated books, all inspired by public speeches for political ends. The notes and expository essays that complicate the pages of *A Room of One's Own, The Pargiters*, and *Three Guineas* only appear to be more orthodox than the glosses Joyce adds to "Work in Progress." Woolf sometimes cultivates this appearance, reassuring a restive audience at various points in her annotated texts that her arguments are founded solidly on footnoted facts, that her attack on orthodoxies of every description is based, like the retrograde documents she regularly cites, on meticulous attention to history and contemporary life in the form of precedent and current texts. But sustained scrutiny of her apparatus reveals how thoroughly she demolishes this comfortable, dangerous acceptance of the authority of annotation and how tightly she ties certain forms of textual assertion to political tyranny. She provides us instead with her protean version of the gloss—its formal variety every bit as remarkable as the more famous aesthetic innovations in her fiction of the 1920s—its intent different although equally complex: she would participate in the social and political debates that grow more furious, more consequential, less productive throughout the 1930s, but she refuses to sacrifice the integrity of her position by contributing to those debates in a manner sanctioned by tradition. Debates customarily conducted have, in Woolf's startling perception, led always to the same closely related ends: domestic repression, the silencing of others' voices in texts, and the abjection of populations by governments. Whether anyone will hear her differently pitched contribution is a question that harrows her throughout the decade.

Pound generally masks his uncertainties during the 1930s with shrill proclamations of the world's disease; but as we read his textbooks from the period, we encounter his fears—comparable to Woolf's—that he has fruitlessly assumed his role as educator of a recalcitrant public. Chapter 4 is devoted to Pound's instructional apparatus: "How to Read" (1929), the *ABC*s of economics (1933) and reading (1934), three volumes of Cantos (1934, 1937, 1940), the *Guide to Kulchur* (1938), and the broadcasts made for Radio Rome (1941–1943) during the Second World War. This body of work, commencing as a comparatively modest set of notes on texts and concepts Pound deems important, expands with the poet's mounting sense of isolation to include a fantastic variety of material. If his is virtually the only voice teaching lessons that will save the world, those lessons must become correspondingly more ambitious.

Isolation marks the art of all three authors I discuss, and its consequences are particularly visible in their apparatus—troubled points at which the writer assesses the extent of his or her public. In the last of his Norton lectures (1933), Eliot offers one revealingly baroque solution to the sense of solitude and irrelevance that haunts so many artists in the 1930s. "Every poet," he confesses, "would like . . . to be able to think that he had some direct social utility."[43] The use of poetry, then, depends, to a greater extent than he would have admitted ten years earlier, on readers: "I believe that the poet naturally prefers to write for as large and miscellaneous an audience as possible, and that it is the half-edu-cated and ill-educated, rather than the uneducated, who stand in his way: I myself should like an audience which could neither read nor write."[44]

That startlingly radical last sentence poses a riddle and a fantasy few but Eliot could invent: that only illiterates will fully understand the modernists' notoriously literary productions. But Eliot goes on to say that he once solved his riddle in a way that "cut across all the present stratifications of the public — stratifications which are perhaps a sign of social disintegration." He experi-mented with a play that, like Shakespeare's plays, would work on "several levels of significance," offering, in ascending order of importance to ascending intel-lectual classes of readers, the satisfactions of "plot," "character," "words and phrasing," "rhythm," and, ultimately, "a meaning which reveals itself gradually." There was to be one character in particular who would seem to address the "material, literal-minded and visionless" figures onstage (surrogates for the play's unlettered, easily satisfied spectators), but who would also always be talking to "a small number" in the audience who would experience the simul-taneous and contradictory sensations of knowing that they were participating in a socially useful public spectacle and that they were caught up in a form that took as its founding principle the inevitable isolation of the intelligentsia, the failure of art to express its greatest power in "direct social utility."[45]

The apparatus of Joyce, Woolf, and Pound stand in a similarly mediative relation to their work as this mysteriously polyvocal figure in Eliot's imagined play stands to his two audiences: those onstage and those in the theater. Posi-tioned indeterminately between text and context, their address always plural as they measure and create a space for the text they accompany, the glosses we shall study are invariably meditations on who is likely to open the book before us and how that book will be understood.

# 1

# JAMES JOYCE
# REFRAMING THE
# POLITICAL

*But the attitude expressed by the word "indifference" is so complex and
of such importance that it needs even here further definition.*
Virginia Woolf, *Three Guineas*

Although never so famous a promoter of self and projects as Pound or Eliot,
James Joyce worked, sometimes openly, often deviously, throughout his career
to establish contexts for the reading of his books and for the assessment of his
life. He pursued his framings with increasing conviction and effect as he aged
and as the shape and significance of his oeuvre came under what, by the end of
the 1930s, must already have begun to seem endless scrutiny. His efforts at
elaborating the ways in which he and his books were to be understood have
been variously addressed but never sufficiently considered in the aggregate as
parts of a lifelong attempt to summon a fit audience, to teach that audience how
to read, and to place his art in precise relation to the surrounding and complexly
included world. These efforts, which I collect under the commodious terms
"apparatus" and "gloss," manifest themselves in a wide range of forms. There
are, for example, the carefully circulated schemata to *Ulysses* and analogous,
though less fully systematized, cribs to the *Wake*. There are the guidebooks to
Joyce's work by, among others, Herbert Gorman (1924), Stuart Gilbert (1930),
Frank Budgen (1934), and the fourteen contributors to *Our Exagmination
Round His Factification for Incamination of Work in Progress* (1929), each of
which bears witness to the attentions of its most interested reader. There is
Herbert Gorman's biography, *James Joyce* (1939), not simply authorized but in
part actually authored by its subject.[1] Although Joyce registers his interpretive
preferences less pervasively and with less control in *transition*—the forum for
much of "Work in Progress"—virtually every installment of Joyce's gnomic text

appeared in the company of defenses, apologies, manifestos, and counterattacks to delight and edify the convert and to sway or shame the skeptic.

These instances of apparatus obviously lie at different distances from Joyce's shaping hand. At its farthest remove from the author, what I call apparatus might also be designated "context"—the author's design present only in his awareness of the textual environment in which readers will encounter his work (Joyce's knowledge of the other contributions and the editorial statements in *transition*, for example). The boundaries between categories grow uncertain, too, when one turns to a given gloss intending to determine whether it is peripheral or central to the annotated text. Joyce himself explores the perpetually changing compass of apparatus in the heavily annotated "Lessons" chapter of *Finnegans Wake* (II.2). Instead of proposing a set of characteristics essential to the phenomenon of the gloss and absent from the glossed text or proposing a formula by which we might ascertain at what point the author's involvement transforms mere context into apparatus, I intend in this and the following chapter to discuss Joyce at work and being worked upon within a variety of contexts over which he wields varying degrees of authority, in which he exercises varying amounts of choice. That authority may be relatively easy to discern, as when Joyce composes marginalia and footnotes for the *Wake* or writes on the galleys for Herbert Gorman's *James Joyce*: "Try to rewrite this part all over again" (Gorman galleys, 81). It may prove harder to delimit, as in the case of the material accompanying "Work in Progress" in the pages of *transition*.[2]

Throughout my study I maintain that Joyce is an active, canny participant in the positioning of his life and work. His apparatus has too often and too easily been overlooked by readers who then christen him "modernist" or "avant-garde," "political" or "apolitical," "revolutionary" or "reactionary," while dismissing his own careful negotiation of the issues encompassed by these and related terms. The fact that Joyce is often refined out of existence by his critics, as though he remained relatively oblivious to or careless about the ideological tides surrounding his words, becomes particularly ironic when those same critics set out to redeem his art as culturally engaged, politically potent work. In her important, wide-ranging book *Joyce's Anatomy of Culture*, for example, we find Cheryl Herr unnecessarily moving Joyce offstage in her introduction: "[W]e cannot take seriously Joyce's protests of his own apolitical nature."[3] Those "protests," by no means simple denials of the political, should not be excluded from the field of criticism that seeks to elucidate how "Joyce's major works . . . circle back on the cultural processes that shaped their composition as well as on the social realities inscribed by those operations."[4]

As she reconstructs sociological contexts for Joyce's fictions, Herr explains her decision to leave the author silenced in the wings by pointing critically at the "biographical approach to literary scholarship" exemplified in its useful but reductive form by Richard Ellmann and Dominic Manganiello.[5] In objecting to the limitations of source hunting, however, Herr (to some extent like Ellmann and Manganiello) fails to discriminate between the search for antecedents and influences and the examination of Joyce's adroit addressing of the cultural and aesthetic issues that continue to concern his readers. She refuses to accord Joyce's apparatus—his considerations of "cultural processes" and "social realities"—the rhetorical, aesthetic, and ideological sophistication that she allows in the fiction. Asserting that "Joyce's beliefs are not as important to our understanding as are his formal experiments," Herr overlooks the fact that Joyce's agile dissemination of keys for his works and clues to his convictions are themselves an important part of his "formal experiments" and repeatedly teach us that "beliefs" do not stand either neatly separable from or clearly linked to those experiments.[6] His reader's guides, alternately lucid and opaque, paradoxically and deliberately teach us also that the vexed, always changing relations among the artist, his words, and his readers cannot be mastered by an author's assertion of authority, and we must not congratulate ourselves for being the first to see political implications in Joyce's intentional subversion of mastery. Ironically, studies of Joyce that exclude his frames from their survey of cultural and textual intersections in his fiction give us a simplified portrait of the artist that resembles the invisible, socially remote, aesthetic God of whom Stephen Dedalus dreams: they leave us with a reflection, each detail reversed, of the formalists' purified texts.

But how are those political implications evident in the events of our century? How, if they cannot be clearly delineated, and if they remain tenuously or circuitously tied to political effects, do they avoid being counted as simply another trope, another merely textual gesture whose repercussions never echo beyond the boundaries of the book? These questions haunt all three writers with whom this study is concerned. By "politics" and "the political" I denominate what Joyce, Woolf, and Pound might also call public life—a category comprising the individual and collective acts that affect the internal and external affairs of states. And it should scarcely need saying that all three artists refuse to consider their work apart from this domain. It is equally important, however, to acknowledge Joyce's, Woolf's, and Pound's various, continually evolving insistences on the distinctions between, say, a speech delivered at Trinity College, Dublin, urging that Gaelic be taught to Irish youth and a quotation from that speech in *Ulysses*; a proposal for monetary reform in the *Cantos* and that reform voiced at a meeting of governmental ministers; or a suggestion in *Three Guineas* that the daughters of educated men should form an "Outsiders' Society" and that suggestion proposed to a public assembly of disenfranchised women. James Longenbach, discussing Wallace Stevens and Kenneth Burke, offers a cogent description of the terrain that lies between the hypothetically discrete poles of the directly political and the purely aesthetic—ground that has proved difficult to map in a century inclined to view its art and its politics dualistically. Stevens and Burke, says Longenbach,

> knew that their words made something happen, but they were simultaneously aware of the difficulty and the danger of defining that process conclusively. Unwilling to adopt Pound's prophetic voice (poetry is "the acknowledged guide and lamp of civilization") or Auden's reactionary diminution of that voice ("poetry makes nothing happen"), they occupied a middle ground that offered neither the consolation of certainty nor the support of like-minded colleagues.[7]

And we shall see, when we turn to Pound's work of the 1930s, that even he inhabits a middle ground, though he remains fundamentally vexed by his uneasy residence there. His assertion that poetry is society's "acknowledged guide and lamp" is more a wistful revision of Shelley's *Defence* than a confident assessment of reality. He, too, ponders the different parts played and the different powers exercised by poet and statesman—the distinctions as well as the connections between creation of the "timeless" and action in the "agora," as he expresses the opposition in his drafts for the *ABC of Reading*. Joyce, Woolf, and Pound frequently turn to measuring these disjunctions and intersections in their apparatus—liminal textual spaces that encourage considerations of the text's own mediate positions and largely unpredictable, undocumentable effects. Often implicit, sometimes explicit, in these glosses are versions of questions that Woolf asks as she proposes a society founded in opposition to traditional party politics, a "Society of Outsiders," a society that will include among its elusive members artists with an interest in political reform and a distrust of political practice. How will this association of the marginalized "work to any purpose?" (*TG*, 115). What are the sociopolitical effects of manifest indifference to a country's calls for patriotism? How might the "thoughts and actions" of individuals, brimming with "the intensity of . . . private emotions," change the course of contemporary history (*TG*, 142)? If poetry is in fact the lamp of civilization, how is its light reflected in a state's legislative processes, its tax laws, its educational institutions, its banking practices? Woolf significantly refuses to answer these questions in definitive terms. To present comprehensive descriptions of and agendas for the Outsiders as social agents would be to fall into yet another iteration of politics as usual.

Joyce, like Woolf, shuns overarching theories of the political effects of art and is more reluctant than she to propose even the most judiciously framed legislative reforms. He chooses instead to address the world largely by parallels and in parables; the concerns of his day find their place in a web of analogous narratives and their articulation in a language that, by the time of "Work in Progress," is literally alternative to the rest of the world's words. Pound, though temperamentally and politically inclined to construct general theories of the relation of art to the state—totalitarian treatises that bind artistic and political pursuits inseparably together—finds himself instead composing notes toward this ultimate synthesis. He pauses often in his glosses of the 1930s to insist that his summoning of yet another partial theory, yet another particular example of a praiseworthy or notorious political or artistic act, leads ineluctably toward an imminent synthesis of details. But none of these writers, in text or margin, ties politics and art together in a single, stable knot.[8]

The discussion that follows presents two politically charged instances of apparatus. Although the first comes directly from Joyce's pen and the second is a frame that Joyce knew intimately but did not compose, both force us to confront issues central to Joyce's politics. Both also urge us to reconsider related, tenacious critical myths that modernist artistic practice is culpably divorced from twentieth-century society or that modernist aesthetics finds its political expression in the totalitarian shaping of nations. Joyce and the editor of *transi-*

*tion*, Eugene Jolas, insist, in significantly comparable terms, that their aesthetic practice is fully grounded in cultural awareness, and that protests against politics are profoundly different from evasions of the political.

I first examine Herbert Gorman's *James Joyce*, focusing on the part Joyce plays in the creation of his image for the public. *James Joyce*, with its subject never far removed from its pages, constitutes one of the last public forums in which Joyce was covertly to declare and qualify his allegiances and beliefs. As we study this biography, we should keep in mind that Joyce was making his extensive revisions to Gorman's galleys during the spring, summer, and fall of 1939, immediately after adding his final corrections to the pages of *Finnegans Wake* (published on 4 May 1939) and coincident with the beginnings of the Second World War. It is not my aim to discuss the entire range of Joyce's effects on Gorman's supervised labor;[9] rather, I choose to look carefully at a particular moment where Joyce, making a crucial change to a page from the galleys of the biography, describes his sense of the artist's place in a fractured world. Our sense of Joyce's position (and the similar position occupied by Jolas and *transition*) is then further refined by an examination of the pages of an exemplary issue of *transition*, where "Work in Progress" reassumes an engagement with events and ideas of the 1930s never displayed in the entirely different frame of *Finnegans Wake*.

Joyce intervenes in Gorman's biography to offer a gloss on his political position in a century that demands, in an increasingly strident voice, that its artists take sides. I turn to that passage to demonstrate the importance of attending to Joyce's glosses and to provide a sample of the painstaking attention he gave to the terms of his reception by his readers. The deletions and additions on the typescripts and galleys of Gorman's biography of course constitute only one of Joyce's many annotative labors; no single project stands as a paradigm for Joyce's apparatus. At stake in this passage from the biography is a characterization of Joyce's politics during the years 1915 to 1919, while he lived in "the haven of neutrality" that was Zurich (Gorman, 231). Discussing the Easter rebellion, Gorman had written that

> Joyce, although he sympathized with the promoters of the rebellion from the theoretical Irish point of view, was convinced from the beginning that the move was ill-advised and doomed to failure. He continued to follow affairs in Ireland (as well as he could from his distance) and betrayed a keen sympathy with the struggle and was delighted when determined opposition in Ireland prevented the English from enforcing conscription there. (Gorman Galleys, 81)

Gorman gives us a man glad to be safely beyond the shambles of a botched rebellion but willing to cheer temporary triumphs from a distance. Joyce deletes the entire passage and inserts his profoundly different replacement on the back of the galley along with a criticism of Gorman's version. Joyce's revision describes a much more complex, more principled political dissociation. To declare him in sympathy with or opposed to "the struggle" in 1916 is to misconstrue his attitude at the time and to make the equally serious error of forcing him into an alignment almost certain to be misread in 1939. Joyce notes impatiently that his readers will find the vague gesture toward "the theoretical Irish point of view" "worth nothing." Who, he asks, assaying that divided country—more broken in 1939 than in 1916—would comprehend any reference to "the" view of Ireland's future? Nor, at the end of this fractious, polemical decade, will many grasp the meaning of Joyce's refusal to endorse even so much as the terms of political debate. The concept of neutrality itself offered little refuge, particularly when embraced by an Irish citizen in 1939, at a time when Eire's neutrality was suspiciously construed by Europe in a dozen different lights, all of them unfavorable.[10]

Joyce introduces his alternative description of his *non serviam* with a bitter comment to Gorman: "It is almost impossible in the present political state of the world of [*sic*] what was his political attitude if it can be dignified by such a term at this time." The two phrases "in the present" and "at this time" expose Joyce's wry certainty that nothing he or Gorman could write would satisfy the partisan readers of a Europe on the verge of war. He laments, in his sarcastic aside concerning the "dignity" of the practice called politics as he has witnessed it in our century, that his words will be interpreted, willy-nilly, according to simplistic rules represented perfectly by MacCann in *Portrait*, requiring all to be either friend or foe, signatory or enemy.

At the beginning of the 1930s Joyce had experienced how easily and destructively the nonparticipant could be named a traitor. In a 1931 essay much on Joyce's mind as he read proofs for Gorman's biography, Michael Lennon had accused Joyce of working for the "department of propaganda which the British government had established in Italy" during the First World War: "the British government appears to have been very satisfied with Joyce's services for which he was well remunerated."[11] Lennon adds that the crown gave Joyce, whom the article casts as a quintessentially shiftless and politically opportunistic Irishman, "sufficient cash in hand to be able to loll about for several months" in Paris after the war.[12] Joyce makes sure, in his notes on the galleys, that Gorman pronounces Lennon responsible for the "campaign which was organised by the Irish-Catholic elements in America against the proposed repeal of the ban [of *Ulysses*]" in the early 1930s. *Ulysses* suffered in America, Joyce tells Gorman, owing to Lennon's widely circulated charge that Joyce had aided England "at a time when the British Government was carrying on a war of its own against the nationalist forces in Ireland which culminated in the Easter Week rebellion" (Gorman galleys, 24; see Gorman, 257). Joyce believed with good cause that it was in part precisely his lack of public, politically uncomplicated commitment that left his life and his works subject to politicized manipulation, that kept his books from being printed, that kept him and his family under often hostile scrutiny.

Although Joyce knows the certainty of misreadings, he nevertheless replaces Gorman's inept, comparatively clear-cut political summary with two evocative parables, both of which express a rejection of the very idea of allegiance to a polity. Joyce frames his alternatives cautiously, fearful lest even parable be read as political dogma: "His political attitude . . . may be divined, perhaps, through two statements of his." Gorman includes this chary introduction and makes no changes to the "statements" that Joyce provides. The first of these "statements" forces us immediately from the lofty, undenominated, mythic space of "the rebellion" into a mundane, modern locale where politics pursues its dreary twentieth-century course along utterly bureaucratic lines. Joyce removes Pearse and Cuchulain from Dublin's General Post Office, as it were, leaving us merely with a building where mail is sorted. He reports an encounter with a bureaucrat enamored of an outworn, anachronistic nobility, a man who fancies himself in a romantic role:

> When leaving Trieste in 1915 he had to apply for a passport to the United States Consul there who had charge of British interests. Apparently this official, who seems to have been officious as well, was nonplussed by Joyce's bored replies and finally remarked that he himself was proud to feel that he was acting for the British Consul, "the representative of the King of England." Joyce said, "The British Consul is not the representative of the King of England. He is an official paid by my father for the protection of my person." (Gorman, 234)

The man playing opposite Joyce in this brief, pointed comedy remains completely ignorant of the part he momentarily assumes: an outsider to the ailing Commonwealth, a citizen of the United States mouthing a line that he imagines would come naturally to his British counterpart in the consulate. His facile invocation of the monarch—whether seen as a risky attempt to produce reverence from an Irishman in 1915 or an act of a colonialist bullying by proxy—betrays the requisite lack of historical and political awareness necessary for assent to political myth. And Joyce, bored before His Majesty's surrogate representative, is the same Joyce who explodes nationalist mythology in "Ireland, Island of Saints and Sages" (1907). There he finds in the period of Irish history before England's arrival not inspirational examples of Celtic power but "a veritable slaughterhouse." He insists, too, that England has "many crimes to expiate in Ireland" but maintains that it is "rather naive to heap insults on England for her misdeeds in Ireland" since the British have only pursued the conqueror's common if despicable course and since Ireland, in Joyce's damning analysis, has proved so readily complicitous with its colonizers.[13] In his portrait of his country he leaves no refuge for simple belief, turning "Ireland, Island of Saints and Sages" from a celebratory title into a debilitating cliché mumbled by backward-looking dreamers while "the double yoke [of England and Rome] wears another groove in the tamed neck."[14] He similarly breaks the consul's romantically fabricated link to the Crown, reminding him that the British consul is an employee bound to do the bidding of the king's unwilling Irish subjects.

Joyce's second instructive story, focused even more specifically on the evils of nationalism, is also more elliptical than his first: "When a questioner asked him if he did not look forward to the emergence of an independent Ireland[,] Joyce is reported to have counterqueried, 'So that I might declare myself its first enemy?'" (Gorman, 234). A reductive and I think mistaken interpretation of this barbed reply would attribute it simply to Joyce's lifelong resentment against

> This lovely land that always sent
> Her writers and artists to banishment
> And in a spirit of Irish fun
> Betrayed her own leaders, one by one.[15]

That reading neglects Joyce's stipulation that his statements display something larger, less purely personal—a "political attitude." Although this exchange occurs prior to Ireland's statehood, we should remember that Joyce volunteers it to the public after the Anglo-Irish War and the Irish civil war, after sixteen troubled years of the Irish Free State, after the Constitution of 1937—completely dominated, in its detailed and explicit social agenda, by the institution of the Catholic church—a constitution that delineated an "independent Ireland" ardently committed to defining and defending its cultural and political borders. Joyce directs his enmity against all that accompanies the building of a modern nation, grimly, comprehensively illustrated in the history of the Irish state as it had been constructed by 1939: external and internal armed conflict, stringent censorship, rampant xenophobia, social paralysis everywhere manifest—all cloaked by a dangerously seductive phrase, "an independent Ireland." In his deliberate juxtaposition of these two moments, Joyce balances his refusals to bow before examples of the imposing, correspondent fictions by which both England and Ireland claim dominion over their citizens.

Only distance from his country's cause allows Joyce to resist the siren's call for devotion and to maintain his rigorous inquiry into the dynamics of sociopolitical affairs. But preserving that enabling distance, as Joyce knows through repeated, galling experience, will rarely be considered politically responsible. He would leave the readers of his biography with no doubts about his support for Ireland. To Gorman's declaration that "Joyce, if anything, was an Irish Nationalist at heart," Joyce adds a clause specifying how he has practiced his nationalism: "if a lifelong and so far successful battle against English ideas merits that title" (Gorman, 186; Gorman galleys, 65). And yet we can already see the beginnings of an importantly different portrait of Joyce in Gorman's slightly altered preface to the parables we have just studied. Accepting Joyce's sneer regarding the "dignity" of anything portentously labeled a "political attitude," Gorman adds that Joyce holds only "the opinions of a man immersed in a vast literary endeavour to the practical exclusion of all else" (Gorman, 234). While elsewhere in the biography Joyce gives similar accounts of his aesthetically motivated aloofness, and while his silent approval sanctions this revision, its position at the head of these political vignettes subtly diminishes their impact. Gorman has moved his readers a small step closer to Richard Ellmann's *James Joyce*, where the American consul makes his appearance in an almost wholly comic scene that is separated from its counterpart concerning Irish patriotism. Rather than dwelling on the struggle for authority at the consulate, Ellmann chooses to emphasize the fiscal irresponsibility of the Joyce family, appending to Joyce's cool words for the consul the aside "(The notion of John Joyce paying taxes for any reason must have secretly entertained him)" and adding a footnote on James Joyce's refusal to pay taxes in Trieste (*JJ*, 385-86).[16] We look now with tolerant amusement on a man scheming to evade an obligation that defines the rest of us as civically accountable adults — an artist who thinks only of how he can slip from the social.

The construction that we place on the details of Joyce's life matters enormously, since our readings inevitably produce an interpretive frame for his fictions and contribute, on a larger scale, to a more or less theorized conception of modernism. The Joyce of Gorman's biography vacillates between his roles as a man who creates with absolute disregard for the sociopolitical and as an artist who lives deeply mired in contemporary enmities. Gorman is concerned (as is Joyce behind him) not simply with James Joyce but with the trials of sustaining a modernist practice of indifference. I deliberately choose "indifference" as my descriptive term because it carries the aestheticist freight placed on it by Stephen Dedalus ("refined out of existence, indifferent").[17] Yet Virginia Woolf also reveals to us a tremendously forceful political sense of the word; it is the word she uses to characterize the attitude of those belonging to the enigmatically active, circuitously engaged "Outsider's Society" that she proposes in *Three Guineas* (*TG*, 107). Joyce's practice fully comprehends both senses. Attempts to maintain this complex indifference were regularly attacked during the 1930s, and they remain profoundly difficult to understand or credit in our own time, when literary modernism is often called to the bar for evading the world beyond the page or for mistakenly insisting, with terrible consequences, that political matters admit of aesthetic solutions. But Joyce, like Woolf in *Three Guineas* (and unlike Pound in the late 1920s and the 1930s), scrupulously refuses to collapse the political and the aesthetic even as he demonstrates, in the *Wake* and in the portrait he helps to create in Gorman's book, that the spheres of art and politics are bound together by tangled and numberless ties and that the political effects of disinterestedness must always prove virtually indeterminable.

At the moment when he specified to Gorman how he had performed his nationalist duties for Ireland, we might already have detected Joyce's doubts about his political efficacy: the phrase that champions his "battle against English ideas" betrays in equal measures a sense of pride and futility, particularly when Gorman demonstrates so clearly the relentless cultural power of "the Moral English Printer" who refused to publish Joyce's books, and "the smug Philistines" who never stop their attacks on his work (Gorman, 275). The same complex alternation between assertions of magisterial, potentially revolutionary comprehension and rueful confessions of irrelevance marks Gorman's descriptions of Joyce in a neutral but politically frenzied Zurich during the First World War, where Joyce observes "with some irony the Gilbertian antics of the heterogeneous society that plotted, conspired, argued and propagandized all around him" (Gorman, 232). This entire chapter on Joyce in Zurich, culminating in an extensive discussion of the imbroglio between Joyce and Henry Carr, serves as a comic, thoughtful, and embittered survey of Joyce's situation during a time when "all the belligerents adopted the tactics of trying to justify themselves and their causes by intensive cultural and artistic propaganda" (Gorman, 243).

Joyce in Zurich stands determinedly outside, observing but ostensibly untouched by European events; his existence, Gorman tells us, "ran parallel with the Great War." Theoretically preserved from contamination by conflict, Joyce exclaims, "For God's sake, let things be finished and let men think of the arts again" (Gorman, 239, 241). He comes closest to commentary when he breaks into his parodic anthem to "Mr. Dooley," a song that he provided for both Frank Budgen and Gorman as each attempted to describe Joyce's politics.[18] Although Budgen prints only two lines and Gorman only a stanza, the song succinctly presents Joyce's case against war. He obviously considered it important enough to distribute to his portraitists. Making points that are, again, similar to Woolf's in *Three Guineas*, "Dooleysprudence" charges that governments mask the economic causes of war with "blatant bulletins" extolling patriotism; that religion actually contributes to each nation's bellicosity; that the ridiculous trappings adopted by heads of court and state ironically signal the inequities and perversions of justice on which those institutions are founded; that taxes unfairly force material allegiance on disenchanted individuals; that all "Noah's arks"—all political systems designed to redeem men and women awash in our stormy century—are themselves dangerously unsound conveyances (creators, even, of "the flood" they claim to master) and are best avoided by the skeptical citizen. Mr. Dooley's prudence, originally proclaimed during the years 1915 to 1919, would potentially have reverberated even more forcefully for readers hearing his philosophical song in the early 1940s.[19] If Gorman failed to print the entire piece, he did follow his quotation from "Dooleysprudence" with a summary paragraph that reinforces Joyce's proleptic wisdom during the Great War: "Questions settled by force were never settled for him. They were merely brutally silenced for the moment. Tomorrow the same question would be asked again" (Gorman, 241).

But, however ably Joyce demonstrates his prescience, however incisive his comic analysis proves to be, however energetically he shows us that indifference and carelessness are not synonyms, he requires that we recognize Europe's refusal to allow him to live by principles that mandate separation of the artist from all governments. Just when he believes himself to be fruitfully engaged in an enterprise for the arts, busily casting actors and actresses for Zurich's first production of *The Importance of Being Earnest*, along comes "a young man named Henry Carr, employed at the British Consulate" (Gorman, 251).[20] Joyce's explosive quarrel with Carr over what Carr felt was scandalously meager payment for playing the part of Algernon Moncrieff culminated in two lawsuits brought by Joyce—one for damages, one for libel—a countersuit for damages brought by Carr, and a distraint levied against Joyce for failure to pay court costs and damages in the libel suit.

Except for its brief telling in Budgen and its more substantial treatment in Gorman, the feud between Joyce and Carr has generally been taken to illustrate Joyce's litigious, even paranoid nature. Ellmann, Maddox, Cixous, and Stoppard all present it primarily as farce. Although nodding to the fact that behind Carr can "be discerned the whole of the British Empire and all its history of colonisation," none of these later biographers has fully grasped the significance that the story seems to have held for Joyce.[21] Ellmann finds the weight Joyce places on the incident "absurd" (*JJ*, 428); Brenda Maddox calls it a "farcical row."[22] Like the parable of the American consul, this narrative about politics and the artist dwindles, when removed from contexts materially under Joyce's control, into a detail illustrative of character rather than an episode that demonstrates the ways in which sociopolitical tensions impinge directly on the artist.

On the galleys of Gorman's account Joyce asserts at the outset that his decision to become involved with the formation of the English Players was largely motivated by a sense of indebtedness to one of his earliest and most compromised, compromising patrons, the British government, which had given him £100 in August 1916: "[I]t was conveyed to him unofficially but pretty plainly that he should officially do something in return for what had been done for him—*i.e.*, the gift from the King's Privy Purse" (Gorman, 251; Gorman galleys, 87).[23] Although Gorman maintains, as he records this gift, that "it did not destroy [Joyce's] attitude of neutrality" and that "Joyce remained what he had been for years, a Dubliner alienated by the paralysis and cruel inconsistency of the city of his birth," the very fact of this insisted-on independence suggests that Joyce has been ringed already by the subtle snares of political patronage (Gorman, 233). Within two paragraphs Gorman will be repeating the narratives concerning Ireland and the consul as supplied by Joyce; shortly before the Carr account will come Joyce's tributes to two other patrons, Edith McCormick and Harriet Shaw Weaver. The rhythm of this chapter consists of declarations and promises of independence quickly followed by meticulous enumerations of entanglement.

We make a mistake if we evaluate the conflict between Joyce and Carr solely on legal or social grounds. Budgen and Gorman acknowledge, in terms so similar that I am inclined to hear Joyce giving conversational cues to both men, that "the manifest objects over which the dispute was waged appear to be small," that "all this may sound a little like Gilbert and Sullivan."[24] Both writers follow their acknowledgments with the assurance that Joyce "did not fail to extract some humour" from the case (Gorman, 255), and both then quote his parody of "Tipperary," which transforms the encounter into song.[25] But Budgen also insists that "[t]he relation of one citizen to another is never a trifling matter, nor is the relation of the simple citizen to a department entrusted with authority a trifle."[26] And it is Gorman who enlarges the feud's domain further, so that it ultimately represents the subject of the artist's impossible neutrality. The purpose of this long recitation against Carr, Gorman declares, is not merely to furnish Joyce with further vindication, but to counter the "rumors of Joyce's activities during the Great War" spread by Michael Lennon in his attack of 1931 (Gorman, 257). I have previously glanced at one aspect of that attack—the allegation that Joyce, a secret employee of the English government, feigned neutrality during the war—and I have noted Joyce's assertion that Lennon's slurs affected the American reception of *Ulysses*. Having left their author, books find themselves quickly marshaled under banners they never chose, caught in battles they may likely not wish to fight—battles often conducted by altogether foreign (though, by 1939, all too familiar) rules of encounter. There is little space devoted to substantive aesthetic criticism in Lennon's broadside, for example, and there is nothing original in his objections:

Joyce's texts are indecent, incoherent, and pretentious jumbles; he can claim nothing more than a "gramaphonic" ability; that is, he "can reproduce what he has heard."[27] What concerns Lennon most are matters primarily outside the books' pages: that the shiftless, deluded, unprincipled John Joyce took a job as secretary of the Conservative Club ("of a Protestant and Anglophile outlook"); that James Joyce shamelessly broadcast "family intimacies" in *Portrait*; that he failed to "grant the protection of even a civil marriage" to Nora in 1904; that he contributed to his mother's early death by dashing her hopes for his success; and that the seedy spectacle of the Joyce family's progress derives naturally from flaws indigenous to the Irish people.[28]

Joyce, responding by way of Gorman to these particular attacks, forces the framing piece that is this biography to tell two very different stories, to serve opposite but intimately compatible ends. In this summary paragraph concluding the case against Carr and glancing angrily at Lennon, Gorman assures his pro-Irish readers that Joyce was "the best hated British subject (by British bureaucrats, of course) in the country" and follows that assurance with the familiar, more exalted refrain: "Joyce did not meddle in politics in any way. He was above the conflict as were all the wise unimpassioned minds of the time and his entire devotion and travail were concentrated on the development and perfection of his own art" (Gorman, 257).

The distance between Gorman and Joyce, between author and intrusive, concealed, annotating editor—a space that diminishes when we turn from published book to manuscript and that grows impossible to measure when we consider unrecorded conversational exchanges—allows Joyce to occupy Olympus and the marketplace, to write in the quiet tower, and to tread the public, politically active thoroughfare. His responses to consul and Irish patriot and Lennon, his more general responses to petitions and writers' congresses and the taking of sides, appear before his public in what is to some indeterminate extent another's voice. That same composite voice, belonging clearly neither to Gorman nor to Joyce, repeats over and over versions of what has largely come to be taken as the "high modernists'" high-formalist credo. Even when

> writing for the sake of one's self or one's art became *démodé* and propaganda and politics sucked up the vital forces of the majority of the younger men; still Joyce laboured. . . . By the 1930's he had lived in five distinct eras of history, every one of them differing from the other. . . . One will look in vain to find the thumb-prints of these varying stages of history on the work of Joyce. . . . Even attack, and he has never ceased to be attacked in certain quarters, moved him not at all. (Gorman, 339–40)

By this point in my discussion, though, I hope that Gorman's proclamation resonates with complexities that make it difficult to use the passage to gesture convincingly toward a formalist sanctuary in which Joyce comfortably takes refuge—exemplary modernist from beginning to end of his long career. Gorman has shown us in *James Joyce* an artist under siege in Zurich, the world's neutral center, and has shown us that artist's manifold responses: trenchant rejoinders, lawsuits, angry letters, satirical songs, the careful embedding of "cer-

tain names in *Ulysses*" (Gorman, 262). Gorman's manuscript has revealed both
authors' thumb prints, sometimes at precisely those spots where indifference is
advertised (I deliberately choose the passive voice). He—the pronoun should
float here between both authors—concludes the Zurich chapter with an
account of Joyce's loss of Mrs. McCormick's patronage; Joyce adds a long footnote in galleys pointing out the pattern of loss in his life.[29] Writing in the third
person, he muses on what I have already referred to as the rhythm of this
chapter: "[A]ll through his life he seems to have had admiration both in its spiritual and its material form spontaneously and suddenly offered him and subsequently just as suddenly transformed into passive or open hostility" (Gorman,
265; Gorman galleys, 91). As Joyce's intricate work with this biography demonstrates, there is no haven from context, no harbor where composition occurs
with only "one's self or one's art" to ponder.

But his glosses and Gorman's text also register why the struggle to maintain neutrality matters so dearly to Joyce. We abridge the complexities of Joyce's
stance, the subtleties of his own thoughts on art, its purpose, and its frames, if
we assume, as Margot Norris does in *Joyce's Web*, that Joyce, deeply attuned to
art's engagements, consequently turns against the aesthetic.[30] Norris's Joyce
elaborately constructs textual expressions of indifference and perfect formalist
designs in order to expose more fully their dishonest evasions in "narrative
maneuvers of self-repeal and sub-textual counterreadings that allow the Joycean
text to incriminate and indict itself—both for its aesthetic effects and its bourgeois values."[31] Norris proposes that "[a]n art like Joyce's . . . pretends to ideal-
istic status as the product of soul in order to expose the contradiction between
its institutional discourse and its commercial reality."[32] And that commercial
reality stands somehow closer to the real, the honest, the true than does the aesthetic: "In Joyce's texts . . . art lies about itself in order to tell the truth about its
lying."[33]

Whereas the merely aesthetic—embraced by Stephen at some moments,
and by Gabriel Conroy and Gerty MacDowell, for example, at others—crum-
bles insubstantially under Joyce's ironic gaze, and "bourgeois values" receive his
equally searching examination, the aesthetic means for Joyce a discipline for the
clear-headed analysis and construction of actual and possible worlds. It is not
simply a collection of socially equivocating, self-referential "effects," though
subsequent critics have often reduced it to such a limited category. Little Chandler, deciding how to add weight to his poems—"he would put in allusions"—strives for "effects," and Joyce reveals in awful detail how those timidly
artistic yearnings render his inarticulate young poet "a prisoner for life."[34] Joyce,
spending all day seeking "the perfect order of words" in a single sentence for
"Lestrygonians," may look as though he is engaged in a project comparable to
Little Chandler's, but allusions and meticulous syntactical achievements are not
inherently dishonest, automatically evasive.[35] Art paralyzes Little Chandler
because the fictional poet seeks in his sentimental, stillborn poetic figures an
anodyne for his stunted world; Joyce's fictions refuse this easy, illusory redemp-
tion of "the dull inelegance of Capel Street."[36] Nor is the formal refinement or
complexity of those fictions intrinsically more suspect ideologically than the

propagandistic cries surrounding Joyce throughout his life. And before we grow completely disenchanted by Joyce's considered refusals to join public causes, we might pause to survey the ill-conceived commitments chosen by any number of artists working during the 1920s and 1930s.

Norris is rightly unsatisfied with schematic portraits of modernism that juxtapose "the artistic and the social, the mundane and the sublime," but she mistakenly insists on Joyce's rejection of the aesthetic and unconvincingly offers a simplified, stable modernism against which Joyce's texts define themselves.[37] Following a theoretical line developed by Herbert Marcuse and more recently elaborated by Peter Bürger, Norris charges that art in our century "live[s] in untruth" whenever it embodies a "commitment to aesthetic formalism, to verbal craft and classical discipline."[38] By proclaiming "its autotelic constitution," modernist art in its formalist guise delusively suggests that the social wounds inflicted by modernity can be salved by an art that transcends "its social and economic degradations, at the very moment that capitalism and censorship, colonialism and world war, class struggle and revolution, inscribe themselves on its production, reception, and form."[39] Only the artistic avant-garde, since it turns against the institution of art itself, manages to avoid aesthetic dishonesty, and Norris singles out Joyce as a modernist who manages to surmount the bad faith of modernism by composing formally polished modernist texts that undercut themselves along avant-garde lines, that perform their own "ideological self-correction." Norris hopes "to show in the Joycean language an avant-garde intention (in Buerger's sense) of criticizing, rather than reinforcing, the autonomy, separatism, and ultimate transcendentiality of modern art."[40]

We have not escaped from the dichotomies that Norris wants to dissolve: the artistic maintains integrity only if it is undercut by the social. Ironically, though Norris seeks to liberate Joyce from the pernicious effects of canonization as an aesthete, she takes as a background for her portrait of the de-canonized Joyce a monochromatic modernism in which we can discern nothing more than the outlines of other canonical writers in our century, their complex struggles and fissured texts reduced to the socially conservative, aesthetically defensive gestures of those who willfully accept blindness to sociopolitical realities.[41] The subtitle of her book—*The Social Unraveling of Modernism*—reveals her inclination to see modernism as whole cloth that Joyce unravels. But the cloth that is modernist art always lay, always lies, already raveled, shot through with its ties to history and culture, rent by forces we gather haphazardly into an entity we name politics.[42]

I want to complicate, too, the division between modernism and the avant-garde—a division that is easiest to maintain on a purely theoretical plane.[43] With Joyce's work, the divide between modernist and avant-garde impulses grows increasingly difficult to discern as we study the thoughtfully engaged nature of his sociopolitical indifference. I trust that my chapters on Pound and Woolf will equally confound these categories. It is worth remembering, even before we examine those authors and their work of the 1930s, that the meanings gestured to in phrases such as "modern art," "aesthetic form," "political engagement," and "the anti-aesthetic" change radically throughout the period we call modernist precisely because those meanings are historically constituted. "Modernism" does not stay poised outside time or frozen in, say, 1922 while the avant-garde moves vigorously into contemporary confrontations. Woolf, for example, in 1929 addresses fascism in terms that focus predominantly on the aesthetic, though already, of course, the sentence carries significant political weight: "The Fascist poem, one may fear, will be a horrid little abortion such as one sees in a glass jar in the museum of some country town" (*ROO*, 107). By 1937 fascism evokes a more literal image: behind the fascist dictator, Woolf sees ruthlessly unfigurative "ruined houses and dead bodies — men, women and children" (*TG*, 142). The aesthetic now occupies another space, as does the political; the artist writes for different stakes and for an audience that has also changed; even similar gestures mean differently in an altered context, a different year. As we turn to the self-described avant-garde journal *transition* — the context, between 1927 and 1938, for approximately five-sixths of "Work in Progress" — we see from yet another angle how inadequate are schemata that link political, anti-aesthetic intervention to the avant-garde while dissevering an aestheticized modernism from the world. These categories and accompanying characteristics regularly break into confused freedom in each particular, heterogeneous issue of that journal.[44]

The disjointed pages of *transition* lie predominantly outside the sphere of Joyce's direct intervention. Other than providing various degrees of guidance to those critics whose explications of "Work in Progress" appeared in the journal — guidance I explore further in the next chapter — Joyce did not involve himself in editorial matters. Although he worked only on isolated portions of this particular frame for "Work in Progress," however, an expressive commerce exists between journal and unfolding text, and this commerce is obviously germane to any consideration of the aesthetic and political position his text occupied as it was being written and received. One of the many framing pieces for Joyce's enormous project is *transition* itself. Its editors, Eugene Jolas, Elliot Paul, and Robert Sage, were among Joyce's most committed defenders on the pages of their own journal and elsewhere; Jolas habitually and explicitly used Joyce's evolving text to gloss principles stated or exemplified in the journal; Joyce, along with Gertrude Stein, was the best known of the journal's authors; his readers turned to *transition* as their primary source for keys to his work; and Joyce's contributions were longer and more regular than those of any other contributor.[45] In the frame that is *transition*, Jolas will not allow "Work in Progress" to stand irrelevantly beyond the world's concerns. His journal, like the biography that Gorman and Joyce wrote, expresses comparably nuanced and quite similar understandings of how an artist's project might reform contemporary politics and of why taking sides in the late 1930s constitutes simply another goad to maddened governments. Jolas, rather than Joyce, dominates this final portion of my chapter because, in spite of his pivotal position in the dissemination and interpretive history of *Finnegans Wake*, he has received almost no serious attention from students of Joyce. Readers of our own day, if they return to the archives, have been more comfortable scrutinizing the frames that Joyce built or more explicitly blueprinted: the essays in *Our Exagmination*, the letters and recorded comments to friends and potential exegetes. But *transition* is too much of a hodgepodge, too curious to offer a ready way into the *Wake*.

Marvin Magalaner and Richard Kain provide a representatively derisive summary comment in 1956, finding Joyce's association with Jolas and the *transition* group "destructive to the dignity of the foremost Continental author of the time."[46] Hugh Kenner, with even greater venom for those surrounding the artist, paints an exhausted, long-suffering Joyce ("almost blind") who "needed a publishing arrangement for the new book that wouldn't strain his nerves. So he admitted the amazing Gene Jolas to his friendship, withheld comment while the jitterbugs of the night-world processed his reputation, and sardonically contemplated the creation of a legend."[47] Thirteen of the seventeen issues of *transition* in which Joyce published "Work in Progress" appeared before 1930, rather too early to diagnose Joyce as a wholly cynical, neurasthenic artist willing to endorse any arrangements for publication as long as he might be left alone. And his letters, from beginning to end of his career, reveal obsessive, active concern regarding every detail of the contexts in which his work appeared before the public. Furthermore, as we have glimpsed in the galleys of Gorman's biography and will see further in the next chapter, Joyce was never one to contemplate a legend's creation—particularly when he was at its center—without collaborating in the enterprise.[48]

Richard Ellmann more moderately allows that "Joyce was highly content to have this outlet for his work": if the journal can be defined as nothing more than mere "outlet," it cannot contaminate Joyce's transcendent text (*JJ*, 589). Dominic Manganiello makes no reference at all to *transition* in *Joyce's Politics*, in spite of the fact that every issue bristled with a wide range of political discussions, a number of them bearing directly on "Work in Progress." Dougald McMillan, author of a useful and extensive study of the journal, nevertheless perpetuates the image of *transition* as an asylum among periodicals for Joyce, a place where the author could retreat when the factions clamored too loudly around him: "*transition* also offered the advantage of political neutrality. . . . Joyce could publish . . . without giving up the apolitical stance so important to him."[49] Since we have attended in some detail to Joyce's concerned indifference, and since we have seen, in part because of Joyce's shaping of his biography, that there was no truly disengaged European space in which he could write or publish "Work in Progress," we may correctly suspect that political complexities lie behind the labels "apolitical" and "neutral." In fact, the ideological skirmishes on the pages of *transition*, repeatedly bracketed by insistences from Jolas and others that the era's warring coalitions must learn to reconceive their violently contested stakes, are perfectly suited as a frame for the pages of "Work in Progress," where mythopoeia gathers endless legendary, historical, and contemporary conflicts into a cluttered collection of patterns without resolution.

This composed discord, this community of antipathetic voices, is perfectly illustrated in the journal's last issue, published in 1938. The particular fragment from "Work in Progress" Joyce chose for this final number is the section in book 2, chapter 3, now familiarly called "How Buckley Shot the Russian General," a convoluted presentation largely concerned with martial prowess and rebellion against oppressive military power. When I turn to the episode's conclusion at the end of this chapter, Joyce's text should reverberate a little more fully with political implications, a little more as it might have to a reader of the piece in 1938. In *The Textual Condition*, Jerome McGann encourages us to attempt reconstructions of the various historically specific material contexts framing and shaping all literary texts.[50] Reading a sample of the interactions between *transition* and "Work in Progress" and beginning to read the politics of those interactions must require at the outset a more nuanced understanding of *transition*.

In the spring of 1938, Eugene Jolas began the journal's final issue with a retrospective survey of editorial policy over the previous decade. Since its first number in 1927, *transition* had

> faithfully adhered to a belief in the primacy of the creative spirit. Nor did it climb on the band-wagon, when a split occurred in the ranks of writers everywhere simultaneously with the world-depression in 1930, but took its stand on the side of a metaphysical, as opposed to a materialist-economic, interpretation of life. (*t* 27 [1938]: 9)

To stand among the relatively small number of intellectuals who pursued a "metaphysical" reading of life was, for Jolas, to stand outside a tightly confining political ring—to stand, at least, apart from all who trammeled their imaginative faculties in thoughts of particular social crises and possible solutions. Only from this remove could Jolas have made what was perhaps his most audacious declaration in ten years of writing manifestos: the title he chose for his closing survey characterized the years between 1927 and 1938 as the "Frontierless Decade" ( 7).[51]

For the "creative spirit," Jolas's title proclaims, the late 1920s and the 1930s have been years of endless expansion and discovery, years without national, psychological, or linguistic boundaries, in which the explorers associated with *transition* have uncovered "new words, new abstractions, new hieroglyphs, new symbols, new myths" (*t* 3 [1927]: 179). From a geopolitical point of view, however, it is difficult to conceive of a ten-year span in world history more obsessed with the maintenance, the violation, the expansion, the inadequacy and fragility of frontiers.[52] A couple of months before the publication of this last *transition*, Germany had completed the *Anschluss* of Austria; it had reoccupied the Rhineland two years earlier. This was the decade in which Italy annexed Abyssinia. As Jolas wrote, Japan was prosecuting its invasion of China, and Franco's Fascists were defeating the Republicans in a civil war that drew Russian, Italian, and German forces into Spain. Jolas was not unaware of these events.[53] They simply demonstrated how fruitless it was for artists to attempt direct intervention in political affairs, how recalcitrant those affairs had proved to any efforts at reform: "The bankruptcy of sociological literature and art," he adds in his retrospective, "should now be fairly obvious even to the most zealous activist of the arts" (*t* 27 [1938]: 9).

But that the world in 1938 remained largely heedless of metaphysical exploration was equally obvious and deeply disturbing. Also in this issue of *transition,* Jolas includes a tribute to Joyce's "Work in Progress," advertising the imminent publication of the "Book of Proteus" (175). McMillan, citing evidence of collaboration between Joyce and Jolas at a number of points in the tribute, calls Jolas's essay "the closest thing to a final summary statement by Joyce on *Finnegans Wake* that exists"—in effect an introduction to the *Wake* written by the foremost promoter of "Work in Progress" in consultation with the author.[54] In his "Homage to the Mythmaker," we discover Jolas wondering whether Joyce's book will find an audience: "We who have watched ["Work in Progress"] grow, hope that there will be ears to hear and rejoice at the fabulous new harmonies of this All-World Symphony!" (175).[55] Hyperbolic pronouncements partly conceal Jolas's anxieties about the limited scope of the rejoicing. He prophesies that the published text will "doubtless attract the attention of the inter-continental world with the electric shock of the thunder-word that epitomizes poly-syllabically one of its leit-motifs" (169).

The doubts in "doubtless" further manifest themselves in the violent language with which Jolas advertises Joyce's new work. The terms of the "Homage" exceed the rhetorical flamboyance common to many of the journal's editorial statements; the decade's brutality bleeds through phrase after phrase, as though Jolas cannot avoid describing the broken "inter-continental world" whose fierce confusion threatens to make Joyce's experiment beside the point. Joyce's readers hear "the ultimate note of a word mutilated in the nightmind" (169). His is a "tale of humanity's progress through the abyss of the ages" (169)—a "progress" that occurs entirely "in the abyss of time and space, in the world of phantoms, in the night-memory of the family—and of the human race" (171). Jolas emphasizes the conflict "that dominates [Joyce's] conception on the nocturnal stage" (170), "the inner scissions of an entire household, of mankind in general" (171). The elements of this story—a family divided against itself, struggling in the abyss, standing in that struggle for "the human race"—might well have resonated as political allegory to readers in 1938 and might, ironically, have compelled those readers to wonder whether life in the embattled abyss allowed them leisure to puzzle over the conundrums of "Work in Progress."

But Jolas adamantly maintains that the politically constructive power of Joyce's book originates precisely in its relative distance from the day's events, its tendency to reveal pattern where those trapped in their own time find nothing but specific provocations inciting them to war: "Only absolute indifference to the sociological habit of thought could make possible such a devotion to the purely creative *élan*. Joyce does not take sides. He tells the pessimistic story of mankind's internecine war with a smile of irony and sometimes pity" (174). Even when Jolas appeals to the materialists among his readers—following a line of promotion suggested to him by Joyce—he establishes more firmly than ever Joyce's theoretical position behind, beyond, or above the turmoil of 1938:

> [I]s it not a fact that all his characters—beginning with those in *Dubliners* and continuing through *Work in Progress*—are people of the lower social strata, the so-called proletarized lower middle-class, the poor white whose struggles in the

never changing world of Cain and Abel, or Shem and Shaun, he presents with the detachment of a whimsical understanding? The martial antinomies of life are the elements with which he deals. (174)[56]

Here is class outside history, a proletariat tracing its ancestry to Genesis rather than to nineteenth-century industrial economies. Here, too, is history marked not by evolution but by repetition. The impending war—nothing more or less than the latest expression of "the martial antinomies of life," its irremediable causes lying buried in human nature—will shift power from Shem to Shaun (or is it Shem's turn to win?) without altering in the slightest the dynamics that vex families and nations.

Writing from a perspective similarly affected by the mythic design of the *Wake*, Gorman repeatedly focuses his narrative on a particular moment only to sweep the details aside in a large gesture comprising vast expanses of time that yield pattern where a historian or a politician might simply see particulars:

> [Dublin] exists as a modern metropolis today, but yesterday it was a concentration point for heroic figures that now loom larger than life-size and for gestures, beautiful, savage, gnostic, that become epitomes of all history. In the mythos Howth is more than a hill and the Liffey is more than a river. (Gorman, 4)[57]

We find in Gorman's *James Joyce* and in Jolas's farewell blessing of "Work in Progress" the same careful refusal to recommend political parties or legislation that would bring the peoples and events of the late 1930s into symmetry with these ancient forces.[58] That alignment exists always: indeed, the "pessimistic story," as Jolas characterizes it, is pessimistic because of its repetitive nature. Particularly since he inclines to harmonic visions, Jolas consistently writes as a hopeful man inevitably destined to despair on the political level, a man who knows that every age, most certainly including his own, will build and then put itself to the sword. This same humane fatalism lies behind Joyce's comment to Budgen on the qualities of *Ulysses* that will make it unpopular with those "of violent beliefs," those who yearn for action, for intervention: "It is the work of a sceptic, but I don't want it to appear the work of a cynic."[59] Both Joyce and Jolas attempt to see rather than join, to record rather than aggravate, the contests that regularly force the world to redraw its maps.

Jolas himself knew much about the redrawing of maps; in this final issue of *transition* he briefly recalls his past and, in that recollection, clarifies the politics of his journal: "In the little border-town of Lorraine, where French and German civilizations sought and fled each other in a ceaseless tension, I spent my childhood before the World-War dreaming escape from the millenary struggle of languages and races" ( 243). The verb "dreaming," especially poignant in this last issue, hints at Jolas's awareness of the fragility of his vision. In his autobiography he describes the conjunction of his beginnings and the grand mission of *transition* even more explicitly and with the same sense of its all too likely failure:

> Crossing frontiers became an ideational goal, and this was the more desirable to me because, as a man from a European border, I had experienced the bursting of millenary boundaries from childhood onward, and was still living in the con-

sciousness of that aspiration. . . . *transition* had the ambition to demolish all frontiers, terrestrial as well as oceanic ones.[60]

Jolas's paternal grandmother had been jailed in the 1870s for speaking French after France lost Lorraine to the Germans in the Franco-Prussian War. His father was French; his mother spoke Rhenish German. He emigrated to America (where he also had family) when he was sixteen.[61] He grew up literally on a frontier, where he learned that languages always exist in politically divisive contexts and that political solutions—resulting in new treaties, new maps— are regularly followed by new wars. Facing the impending world war, Jolas speaks explicitly in his autobiography from his figuratively permanent, ideologically formative residence: "From my Lorraine borderland I knew that an epoch of chaos and disorder was about to begin."[62] He concludes publication of *transition* with an issue intended to defy communist and fascist totalitarianisms, sadly allowing in his autobiography that "the poet had not the right to remain entirely aloof."[63] But he cannot bring himself to use the word "political," openly banishing the term from his vocabulary: "ethical (I almost said political)," he writes in a biographical sketch in an earlier issue of the journal (*t* 6 [1927]: 179).

Joyce's "Work in Progress" stands preeminent among the linguistic experiments encouraged by Jolas—all of them, from Jolas's point of view, suggesting vitally important alternatives to nationalistic, narrowly political habits of mind, all of them offering avant-garde investigations concerning the intimate connections between words and the world. When Jolas writes, "I am still engaged in a search for this *language of night*" (*t* 27 [1938]: 245), when he tells his readers that "*Transition* is in search of the Euramerican language of the future" (9), he adamantly hopes that the discovery of a "de-rationalized grammar in which the word and syntax [follow] the organic laws of metamorphosis contained in the psyche" will join people at a level too deep for politics as it has been and is being practiced (244). His is a faith that we hear echoed in Philippe Sollers's description (in 1975) of Joyce's political consciousness:

> It is naively believed that Joyce had no political concern because he never said or wrote anything on the subject *in a dead language*. . . . Joyce's refusal to indulge in the slightest dead pronouncement is exactly *itself* the political act, an act which explodes at the heart of the rhetorical *polis* . . . : the end of nationalisms decided by Joyce at the time when national crises are at their most virulent.[64]

Sollers addresses an audience that did not come to the *Wake* through *transition*. Readers of that journal's installments of "Work in Progress," of the theoretical apparatus that bracketed numerous installments of Joyce's *Work*, and of the many pieces that examined other manifestations of culturally powerful "night-languages" would have been much more likely to take Joyce's and Jolas's refusal to engage in nationalist politics in its fully political context, whether or not they believed in the efficacy of that refusal.

To a politically thoughtful reader today, however, Jolas, Joyce, and *transition* can seem, by a terrible irony lying at the heart of modernism, to fall irrevocably into the embrace of fascist ideology. David Bennett, writing in *Contem-*

*porary Literature*, forcefully proposes the conjunction: "[F]ascism's aestheticiza-
tion of politics was the fulfillment in life praxis of the program [Jolas] defined
for poetry.... [F]ascism entailed the same erasure of difference and subjectivity
as *transition* sought to achieve with an 'esperanto of the subconscious.'"[65] For
Bennett, *transition* provides a particularly dangerous crossing of modernist
"insistence on the freedom of art from subordination to material and political
interests" with the avant-garde ambition "to undermine the institutional autonomy of art and reintegrate so-called aesthetic experience and values in the
praxis of everyday life."[66] The charge is closely related to that leveled by Norris
against modernism, although here it is precisely the avant-garde's tendency to
negate the space between the aesthetic and the political that constitutes its
threat. Bennett's cognate indictment merits attention as a representative gesture
toward twentieth-century history and art that simplifies the subjects on which
it passes damning judgment.

The pages of *transition* and the politics surrounding the journal's reception
were considerably more tangled than Bennett's analysis admits. In the last issue,
for example, readers could have found Kenneth Burke, concerned throughout
this decade over the unexamined "rhetoric of battle," advising in measured terms
that Jolas's linguistic innovations might make more of the unconscious "accessible to consciousness, hence assisting to greater rationality of conduct" (*t* 27
[1938]: 234).[67] But they could also have read an excerpt from *The Night-Side
of Life*, a study of German Romanticism by Albert Béguin that prescribed a
reintegration of the dream and waking states, a recovery of irrationalism in the
overly rational twentieth century, a return to the "partial somnambulism" characteristic of our "first ancestors" ( 206). Béguin's discourse on the politics of
dreams (the *Wake* came into the public eye framed by dozens of similar paeans
to night worlds) would have wakened fearful resonances for the substantial
number in Jolas's audience determined not to follow this urgent recommendation that all Europe aspire to a Germanic "super-consciousness" (205). One of
those horrified readers was doubtless Michael Gold, who responded in the
same issue to a questionnaire titled "Inquiry Into The Spirit And Language of
Night":

> The day mind seems to me the only important mind to understand today. Reason,
> objective truth alone can lead us out of this night-hell of a world of fascism and war.
>     Light, more light! is the need! The night-mind is closest to the dark, bloody
> fog of the Fascists; the sun-mind is communism! (236–37)

Gold's hoisting of the Communist banner would have confirmed others'
suspicions that Jolas presided over an agitprop journal based in France. Wyndham Lewis had most fully articulated this theory nine years earlier in a number
of his journal, *The Enemy*, devoted to unmasking the conspiracy among the
"new romantics," the "new nihilists," and Communists—all members of a
movement possessing a "political interest in Western Civilisation and the
problem of its political destruction."[68] But 1929, the year of Lewis's attack on
*transition*, saw a referendum on Jolas's "Revolution of the Word" in the Marxist
journal the *Modern Quarterly*, which utterly refused to admit Jolas as a fellow

traveler. "[T]he new order will be social and not individualistic," writes V. F. Calverton, one of the editors. "[R]evolution-in-the-wordists are moving in the wrong direction. . . . [T]hey are tending ever more and more to isolate the individual from society."[69] These ideological fault lines had existed since the beginnings of *transition*, when surrealists, variously allied with the Communists from the mid-1920s until 1935, wrote alongside Gottfried Benn, Carl Jung, and Pierre Drieu La Rochelle, each of whom would align himself with German or French Fascist parties in the 1930s.[70]

Jolas was himself soon to choose sides, enlisting with the United States Office of War Information in 1941 and returning to France with the Normandy invasion. But we should not condescendingly read his choice as a sign that the political naïf at last received his education. Jolas had recognized from the outset that renouncing politics meant trying to discover alternative ways of engaging with the world: "We who live in this chaotic age," he wrote in 1927, "are we not aware that living itself is an inferno? And having experienced it, can we not express it by seeking new outlets and new regions of probability?" (*t* 3 [1927]: 179). In 1938 he can still imagine a "new region" where words connect rather than divide:

> we shall sing in all the languages of the continents
> we shall discover les langues de l'atlantide [Atlantis]
> we shall find the first and last word.
>
> (*t* 27 [1938]: 224)

He can also, in this final issue, confront a darkness that is appalling even, or especially, to a celebrant of the potentials of the "nightmind":

> We stand before the Spirit of the Morgue
> And rain weeps over the vineyards of Alsace
> And midnight comes with a shudder[.]
>
> (58)

The night Jolas sees is both "metaphysical" and "materialist-economic."

In the shadowy pages immediately following those closing lines of his poem "Night of Grünewald," readers of *transition* 27 encountered Joyce's "Fragment from 'Work in Progress,'" where Butt and Taff—enemies, allies, opposites, twins—collaborate to assassinate the great man—"Emancipator," "Immensipater," "the sur of all Russers"—who oppresses them and insults their country (*FW*, 342.19, 342.26, 340.35).[71] But this gigantic embodiment of military force, a bellicose Russian general (who has been commander in dozens of wars by the end of Joyce's martial tale), won't stay shot for long; we need only wait a little while until "butagain budly shoots thon rising germinal" (*FW*, 354.34-35). For all of us accustomed to reading *Finnegans Wake* instead of "Work in Progress," this "rising germinal" brings us commodiously back to the text's endless expressions of unsuppressible life force. That metaphysical reading would already have been familiar to those following the introductions to Joyce's text in the pages of *transition*. But today we probably put less emphasis on the verb "shoots" and the grim sense of perpetual battle latent in "butagain." This "Fragment from 'Work in Progress,'" like any number of pieces in Jolas's journal, registers sorrow and disgust at the customary political arrangements that temporarily resolve conflicts by creating cause for new hostilities.

Joyce's excerpt concludes with an italicized, bracketed paragraph—final stage directions for an episode cast in dramatic form:

> [*The pump and pipe pingers are ideally reconstituted. The putther and bowls are peter-packed up. All the presents are determining as regards for the future the howabouts of their past absences which they might see on at hearing could they once smell of tastes from touch. To ought find a values for. The must overlistingness. When ex what is ungiven. As ad where. Stillhead. Blunk.*] (*FW*, 355.1–7)

Since Joyce's readers are required to count at the conclusion of this last installment of "Work in Progress," it is fortunate that, along with the General's renewed vitality, "the pump and pipe pingers are ideally reconstituted," though it's difficult to tell, in this darkness, to whom they belong. Joyce sets all of us to school, asking that we find equivalencies for zero and wondering, in the same breath, if there is anything at all that has value: "To ought find a values for." We have little to work with as we ponder the problem: "When ex what is ungiven. As ad where." "X" is not just a mystery, but a figurative representation—"as it were"—of nothing. When "ad" assumes its Latin meaning, we realize, in a truncated question, that we don't really know where we are: "As to where?" Sheer disorientation may explain the answers that end the episode, both of which are nevertheless correct: "Stillhead. Blunk." These terse solutions expand to include the Danish *stilhed*: "silence"; the stillness or death of a leader; unconsciousness; a "blank"; "blunt" (a word perhaps related to the Old Norse *doze*, tied as well to "blind" and "blend," or "mix," thus "render dark, confuse")—but all the choices leave us with nothing.

Taff was working desperately on a problem when the tale began: "hoisting of an emergency umberolum in byway of paraguastical solation to the rhyttel in his hedd" (*FW*, 338.7-8). The text finally offers an answer—"Stillhead. Blunk" —to the riddle in his head. (Joyce's nouns for "riddle" and "head" include "rifle," and the Welsh *rhyfel* for "war" and the Welsh *hedd* for "peace.") Like Jolas at moments in this last *transition*, Joyce and the reader can perhaps dream of alternative solutions, larger perspectives, answers other than "zero." But the equivalent value for naught most likely to occur to readers in 1938 was "two," as they realized that they lived in a century that would have to number its world wars.

# 2

# JAMES JOYCE

# ADULTEROUS BOOKS

*As the book goes out into a larger, a more varied audience these*
*influences become more and more complex. According to its wealth, its*
*poverty, its education, its ignorance, the public demands what satisfies*
*its own need—poetry, history, instruction, a story to make them forget*
*their own drab lives. The thing that the writer has to say becomes*
*increasingly cumbered.*

Virginia Woolf, "Anon"

Joyce's most flamboyant, entirely overt display of apparatus comes in what his
readers call the "Lessons" or the "Schoolroom" chapter of *Finnegans Wake* (II.2),
a chapter heavily encumbered with marginalia and footnotes. And these pages'
florid borders blossom further when we return the "Lessons" to *transition*, when
we place II.2 beside the first book devoted solely to "Work in Progress": *Our*
*Exagmination Round His Factification for Incamination of Work in Progress* (1929),
and when we search also for the origins of these glosses in the drafts of the
chapter. These additional framings perfectly suit Joyce's "Lessons," since II.2, in
conjunction with its focus on rambunctious children being schooled and eluding
their teachers' designs, concerns itself more generally with all readers—those
unrestrained, irrepressible generators of literal and metaphorical apparatus whose
interpretive and misinterpretive activity adds unpredictably to the dimensions of
every text over time. I turn to the details of II.2 only after looking at the issue of
*transition* in which the first annotated "Lessons" appeared, as well as at *Our Exag-*
*mination*, attending to the apparatus loosely attached to Joyce's text by other
hands. In addition to providing a sociopolitically relevant frame for "Work in
Progress," *transition* constitutes a crucially important theater for the elaborate,
elaborative production of *Finnegans Wake* and for many of the first exegeses of
Joyce's demanding book. The published *Wake* displays a more narrowly circumscribed, less fully annotated version of the "Lessons."

Before we consider the apparatus beyond Joyce's immediate control, however, a brief orientation to the nature of Joyce's schoolroom will prove helpful, since it is into that schoolroom that Joyce ultimately introduces all his readers, all his critics; it is there that his annotative impulses (and, later, our own) run free. Insofar as the *Wake* can be mapped with the inadequate instruments of "plot" and "character," the "Lessons" occur when the book's three children — the quarrelsome brothers Kev and Dolph and their younger sister Issy (also called Storiella for much of the chapter)—have come inside to do their homework after having played games outdoors at twilight. The children variously evade and pursue their assignments in a space that suggests sometimes a nursery, sometimes a study, sometimes a boisterous classroom. Joyce called II.2 "night studies" and gave an often-quoted description to Frank Budgen of the chapter's "technique": "a reproduction of a schoolboy's (and schoolgirl's) old classbook complete with marginalia by the twins, who change sides at half time, footnotes by the girl (who doesn't), a Euclid diagram, funny drawings etc" (JJ, *Letters*, 1:406). On the most basic level, the notes on these pages demonstrate Joyce's gesture toward imitative form. The annotated pages look something like a well-used schoolbook and figuratively reproduce students' unfocused minds, deflected by distractions in classroom and crowded study.

At a further remove from Joyce's simple explanation to Budgen, the marginalia and footnotes represent and initiate proscribed inquiries in a chapter built around unauthorized sexual investigation. From her space at the bottom of the page, the precociously sexual, inordinately sexualized Issy spins fantasies at once romantic, erotic, and alarming. Kev is "made vicewise" by his shameless, better-educated brother, Dolph, who transforms a geometry lesson into an outrageous class on their mother's genitals: "I'll make you to see figuratleavly the whome of your eternal geomater" (*FW*, 286.29, 296.30–297.1). These bold excursions into forbidden, irresistible territory — symbolic expressions of the psychosexual revolution staged by all children against their parents — are textually mirrored by the analogously illicit addition of extraneous material to the margins of II.2. At the chapter's close, the children proclaim their successful insurrection, consequent upon their prohibited explorations, when they force their way to the center of the page. After the ominous warning that "their feed begins" (*FW*, 308.15), they compose an obliquely threatening "Nightletter" to their feebleminded parents: "With our best youlldied greedings to Pep and Memmy and the old folkers below and beyant" (*FW*, 308.17-19) (Figure 1). These three rebellious "wranglers for wringwrowdy" children (*FW*, 266.21) cannot leave the family unshaken, the book unglossed. They join Joyce's readers who in the very act of reading necessarily appoint themselves critics and carry the book away from its author, and they join the annotating author himself— the instigator of his book's insubordination.

Given the affiliation of annotating students, critics, and author, it is appropriate that Joyce's earliest readers first found his glossed text in *transition*, the journal in which explicators regularly held class on the arcana of "Work in Progress." Two sections of II.2 were published in *transition* and subsequently in

| | | |
|---|---|---|
| *Xenophon.* | Delays are Dangerous. Vitavite! Gobble Anne: tea's set, see's eneugh! Mox soonly will be in a split second per the chancellory of his exticker. | |
| *Pantocracy.* | Aun | MAWMAW, LUK, YOUR BEEEFTAY'S FIZZIN OVER! |
| *Bimutualism.* | Do | |
| *Interchangeabil-ity. Naturality.* | Tri | |
| *Superfetation.* | Car | |
| *Stabimobilism.* | Cush[1] | |
| *Periodicity.* | Shay | |
| *Consummation.* | Shockt | |
| *Interpenetrative-ness. Predicam-* | Ockt | |
| *ent. Balance of* | Ni | |
| *the factual by the* | Geg[2] | |
| *theoric Boox and* | Their feed begins. | KAKAO-POETIC LIPPUDENIES OF THE UNGUMP-TIOUS. |
| *Coox, Amallaga-mated.* | | |

### NIGHTLETTER

With our best youlldied greedings to Pep
and Memmy and the old folkers below and
beyant, wishing them all very merry Incarnations in this land of the livvey and plenty
of preprosperousness through their coming
new yonks

from
jake, jack and little sousoucie
(the babes that mean too)

[1] Kish is for anticheirst, and the free of my hand to him!

[2] And gags for skool and crossbuns and whopes he'll enjoyimsolff over our drawings on the line!

308

**Figure 1.** The "Nightletter" from the children to their parents in *Finnegans Wake* (II.2, 308).

chapbooks before *Finnegans Wake* set the pieces down in their final order. Joyce
composed an unannotated segment of the chapter (*FW*, 282.5-304.4) in 1926
and published it in *transition* 11 (1928). Adding apparatus to II.2 did not occur
to him until sometime in 1934, and although the first section to receive glosses
in draft form (*FW*, 275.3-282.4) remained unpublished until *Finnegans Wake*,
Joyce's readers came upon an annotated portion of the chapter (*FW*, 260-275.2;
304-8) in *transition* 23 (1935).[1] So ardent is this issue's support of Joyce's proj-

ect, so completely does some of Joyce's marginalia match the style of Jolas's calls for a "Revolution of the Word," that the often uncertain boundaries between *transition* and Joyce's text grow particularly blurred in *transition* 23.[2] The glossed "Lessons" appear in their initial printing as part of a potentially endless series of commentaries on commentaries that stretches well beyond the limits of Joyce's contribution to the journal.

The title page to *transition* 23 reads "TRANSITION: An Intercontinental Workshop for Vertigralist Transmutation" (*t* 23 [1935]). Jolas's stilted subtitle bears a stylistic resemblance to the most pompous marginal notes of Joyce's "Lessons": "**The localisation of legend leading to the legalisation of latifundism**" (113); "**Gnosis of precreate determination. Agnosis of postcreated determinism**" (112); "**Panoptical purview of political progress and the future presentation of the past**" (121); "*Abnegation is Adaptation*" (126). After an introductory page, blank except for the portentously capitalized heading—"VERTIGRAL"—the issue opens with a note from the editor defining the "Paramyth" as the genre of the future: "I conceive it as a kind of epic wonder tale giving an organic synthesis of the individual and universal unconscious, the dream, the daydream, the mystic vision" (7). Jolas warns his readers that Paramythic literature "will probably express the irruption of the supernatural, the phantastic, the eternal into quotidian life" (7). His breathless, mantic announcement of the imminent new age (tempered only slightly by the wonderfully serene qualifier "probably") displays the aesthetic eschatology that accompanies the slow revelation of "Work in Progress."

Most of Joyce's episodes came before readers escorted by one or more brief manifestos. These proclamations often directly lauded "Work in Progress" for revealing a new world to true seekers; they always proved at least tangentially applicable to the latest sample from Joyce's enormous emprise. Joyce never openly joined the company under these banners, but he profited from the agitation around his words. (Recall, again, that Joyce's dissociation from *transition* was vehemently emphasized by critics writing well after his death; during the 1930s there existed considerably less distance between author and journal.) A scaffolding of insider's humor, promulgations of artistic revolution, and attacks against the "crumbling hierarchy of philologists and pedagogues" frames the presentation of "Work in Progress" (*t* 11 [1928]: 110). These miscellaneous declarations promise that Joyce's is an authentically bold, innovative work and not simply a random game with words. They confirm the audience's image of themselves as daring explorers of the new and promote the experimental status of *transition*.[3] Side by side with the annotated part of II.2 is a thirty-page patchwork selection of answers from living authors who have responded to Jolas's urgent "INQUIRY ABOUT THE MALADY OF LANGUAGE" (*t* 23 [1935]: 144). And he constructs a third of this issue with bits and pieces of prose and poetry that have caught his fancy as he rummaged around in the archives: Poe (from his "Marginalia"), Nietzsche, Blake, a Gnostic hymn, Saint Teresa of Avila, Emerson, Sir Walter Raleigh, and numerous others add their voices to the Jolas "Workshop" dedicated to spawning "the *language of the night*," which will be "the total expression of all the material that goes to make up the experiences of the daemonic-cosmic dynamis [*sic*] of the inner world in flux" (103). Jolas's recipe for a textual jumble applies equally to the "Lessons" segment and to the rest of *transition* 23. It would nicely suit the margins of II.2.

Immediately following Joyce's contribution to *transition* 23 are two overwrought essays that form perfect pendants to a chapter filled with raucous students and mock instruction. These tributes present us with problems that apply to much of the criticism in *transition*, as well as to the essays collected in *Our Exagmination*: What is the attitude of Joyce's avant-garde critics toward their undertaking or their subject? How are we to read their praise of Joyce, to take their interpretive tips? Who is laughing at whom? Léon-Paul Fargue depicts the artist as scientist for the vanguard, as satanic chemist: "Joyce . . . works . . . [words] over with his own instruments, makes new cultures which he reboils in that strange laboratory, that intimate hell, that he has lighted up for himself alone" (*t* 23 [1935]: 130). Armand Petitjean, assuring his readers in a footnote that "[i]t is of course understood that I am referring to the Joyce of *Work in Progress*, the only work that counts now in his eyes, and in our own, his greatest," presents a more visceral image of a grotesquely phallic author: "[H]e mobilizes man, he liquidates life itself: this is Joyce at work, his wanton head all irrigated with blood, his flesh full of sweat and savour. . . . He has . . . given us back the immense temptation of the world, on which we have been cast as on cream custard" (135n.1; 140-42).[4] This is the flavor—confident, playful, outrageous, and pretentious—of almost every piece written on Joyce in *transition*. Joyce's laughter at his critics may be matched at any moment by their laughter at him or at themselves.

That broadly diffused laughter reverberates around every aspect of *Our Exagmination Round His Factification for Incamination of Work in Progress*. This first cluster of keys to the *Wake* cannot appropriately be considered apart from *transition*. By the end of 1929, the year in which this collection of twelve essays and "Two Letters of Protest" was published, *transition* had brought its readers eleven separate guides to Joyce's work. Of these, all but two were collected in *Our Exagmination*; the authors of those uncollected pieces, William Carlos Williams and Thomas McGreevy, are nevertheless represented in the symposium. Only two authors, Victor Llona and Robert Sage, joined the volume as new explicators of "Work in Progress," and readers would already have encountered Sage, the journal's associate editor since 1928, in almost every issue. The tone of this curious guide to an already famously curious text, the volume's continual vacillation between exuberant parody and loyal promotion, comes directly from the pages of *transition*, where all authors share to some degree Joyce's simultaneous disapproval and celebration of critical practice.

On 30 July 1929, two months after *Our Exagmination* had appeared, Joyce described to Valery Larbaud his relationship with the twelve pathfinding essayists: "I did stand behind those twelve Marshals more or less directing them what lines of research to follow" (JJ, *Letters*, 1:283). Whether this is a boast or a confession is not clear. Joyce is equally ready to defend and to laugh indulgently at the supervised explication of "Work in Progress." He is alarmed that "up to the present though at least a hundred copies have been freely circulated

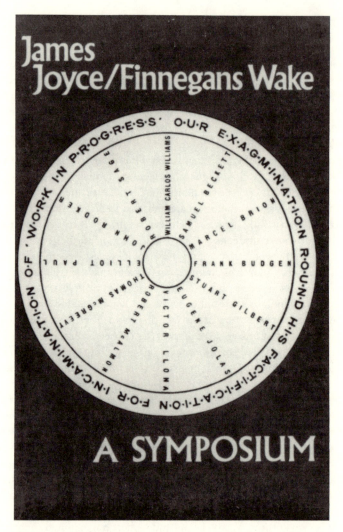

**Figure 2.** The design for the cover of the first guidebook
to *Finnegans Wake: Our Exagmination Round His
Factification for Incamination of Work in Progress* (1929).
This "grandfather's clock" emblem was repeated on the
title page and in advertising fliers for *Our Exagmination*.

to the press and press men not a single criticism has appeared" (JJ, *Letters*,
1:283). The world is not taking the *Exagmination* seriously: "My impression is
that the paper cover, the grandfather's clock on the title page and the word
Exagmination itself for instance incline reviewers to regard it as a joke, though
these were all my doing" (JJ, *Letters*, 1:283) (Figure 2). Larbaud had worked
with Joyce enough to realize that Joyce's admission of involvement would

hardly change the opinions of many who dismissed *Our Exagmination* as a hoax. Joyce absolutely obscures his attitude toward the book in a final plea for his sober intentions: "[S]ome fine morning not a hundred years from now some enterprising fellow will discover the etymological history of the orthodox word examination and begin to change his wavering mind on the subject of the book" (JJ, *Letters*, 1:283-84). But etymology only leads us further into uncertainty. "Examine," particularly if spelled "exagmine," calls up a number of Latin glosses on Joyce's design: the prefix *ex*: out; the verb *agere*: to lead; and two nouns—*ager*: field, place to which cattle are driven; and *agmen*: a group, a marching column. "Incamination" hopefully echoes the Italian *incamminare*: to put on the right road. Are the twelve critics actually "Marshals" (from an Old High German noun *marahscalc*: keeper of the horses), or do they only believe that they are able to guide their readers to a pasture of understanding? Perhaps Joyce is the genuine Marshal, driving his herd of commentators into an enclosure of his making or even urging them out of the pasture altogether, leading them astray.

After smiling at the work in *Our Exagmination*, Joyce invites Larbaud to write an article on Robert Bridges and James Joyce, "a curious meeting of extremes," for "that imaginary Reader let us call him, the Good Terrafirmaite" (JJ, *Letters*, 1:284).[5] Larbaud must have wondered at the tone of a request that he write for such an ordinary audience; nor would the conclusion of Joyce's letter have encouraged him to become an Exagminator: "I am now hopelessly with the goats and can only think and write capriciously. Depart from me ye bleaters, into everlasting sleep which was prepared for Academicians and their agues!" (JJ, *Letters*, 1:284).[6] It is not Larbaud whom Joyce playfully curses; it is the necessity for criticism. But Joyce is, of course, his own most committed critic. We have seen in Gorman's galleys a subject bent on controlling the portrait of his life. Scattered throughout that first *James Joyce* are footnotes, supplied by Joyce, that point us to motifs and structural guides that will ease our passage through the *Wake*.[7] Every reader of *Ulysses* has held more or less tightly to Joyce's carefully circulated schemata.[8]

If we follow the paths blazed by Joyce's letters, the seminars and readings held with his encouragement, and the essays produced by his associates, we come to appreciate how successful Joyce was in setting (for decades to come) the interpretive agenda for the *Wake* as well. His letters demonstrate, too, the depth of his concern that the greatest possible number of literary journals review his publications, that each important reader respond to his labors. He is aware that he must suffer the indignities of explication if he is to command an audience, though he is determined to remain poised above the exegetical commerce that he fosters.[9] In a revealing confession to Harriet Shaw Weaver, written at the end of 1922, shortly after he had given Larbaud a copy of the *Ulysses* schema, he dreams of collaborating with Larbaud on a French translation of selected portions of *Ulysses*. Together they will draw up "a mariner's chart where some regions are fully done, others sketched, others indicated and the whole representative." This would, he confesses, "allow me to send out to the world in those parts where [the commentator] uses critical exegesis certain suggestions as to the scheme and technique which I shall then have the pleasure of rehearing and rereading when they have gone the rounds," by which point each suggestion would have lived a life beyond Joyce's control, gathering to itself associations and applications that its author had never imagined, demonstrating its vitality (and the liveliness of a reading community) in every aspect of its altered sense (JJ, *Letters*, 1:199).

"Going the rounds" proves a resonant phrase for understanding the practices of Joyce and his critics, whose work regularly moves freely back and forth across the gap between author and commentators. The theorists and explicators who gather around "Work in Progress" as acolytes of the avant-garde praise Joyce with missionary zeal, but they do not neglect a parallel objective: the liberation of literary and philosophical discourse from traditional forms of address. Writing about language in *transition* 23, Petitjean calls for a "natural language" derived from an alliance between "the language of the philosophers" and "the language of the poets" (*t* 23 [1935]: 158-59). After reading the foregoing sample of his own prose, we could add that Petitjean welcomes hyperbole, the humorous, and the absurd in his program for the revitalized essay. He intends his defense of Joyce to illustrate a newly expressive manner of approaching art, in which the essay shares aspects of the creative work and the very concept of clarification is undercut by humor directed at the traditional critic's confident, objective stance. Everywhere in the pages of *transition* and *Our Exagmination*, the boundaries between theory and the art that embodies that theory blur, as do the boundaries between crusade and hoax.[10]

The Exagminators' tone is particularly difficult to gauge when they focus on the act of criticism itself. Victor Llona describes the disruptions that "Work in Progress" has wrought in the accepted sequence of art followed by explanation:

> To me, one of the most striking and illuminating things in connection with *Work in Progress* is that it has managed to reverse the consecrated order of things. We commentators simply could not be kept in leash—we had to have our say in a volume which will grace the stalls in advance of the text under consideration. (*OE*, 102)

Llona's image of unleashed critics barking at the stalls does little to promote the dignity or importance of their enterprise. The title of his essay should be read with the accent of a bewildered hayseed rather than an engagé reviewer: "I Don't Know What to Call It But It's Mighty Unlike Prose" (*OE*, 95). This unassuming opening reflects Llona's understandable fears of inadequacy; it assures us that nothing spectacular will follow. It sets him up as a clever comedian able to mimic the philistine audience that he must educate. But it also suggests that the critical business is less scientific, less directly productive, less elevated and demanding than we might suppose. Llona emphasizes this last suggestion in his essay, not only displaying admirable prescience, but also attempting to forestall laughter at his short piece by pointing to the humor ahead:

> Mr. Joyce will suscitate a host of commentators who may in some respects smooth the way for the vulgum pecus. These scholars, as is their wont, will fight and squabble over "obscure" passages, draw up glossaries and indulge in long-winded

dissertations as to the esoteric meaning of certain fragments. . . . I hope that Mr. Joyce will live long enough to enjoy the fun of which his literary forbear [Rabelais, who died before reading his critics] was so unfortunately deprived, for I suspect that the commentaries of future critics of his new work will not lack in amusing elements. (*OE*, 100–101)

Llona's impressive bravado almost makes him seem a fully knowledgeable partner in Joyce's games with his first twelve critics. But Llona did not know, as he broadcast his hopes for the author's future laughter, that Joyce was casting him as one of the twelve commentators who stumble through the *Wake* and make a signal appearance in II.2.

Joyce and his critics often appear to cooperate completely in their mocking distrust of presumptuous readers who aspire to answer all the riddles of "Work in Progress." Robert McAlmon wonders whether "that common man, if a simple and not too complex but healthily curious minded man might be more capable than the precious esthete or critic of responding to the evocative and suggestive quality of a literature" (*OE*, 115). Robert Sage laments the likely academic onslaught in the future:

> It is possible that some day, when the book has been completed and given a title, that it will be edited with columns of footnotes prepared by industrious pedants after years of research. I hope not, for one of the beauties of *Work in Progress* is its mystery and its inexhaustible promise of new revelations. (*OE*, 169)

*Our Exagmination* contains the arguments that could be used to render it superfluous; it sows the seeds for its own parody. And though Joyce will augment that parody in the *Wake*, he insists that it begin in this very volume.

Appended to *Our Exagmination* are "Two Letters of Protest" objecting to Joyce's linguistic experiments. One is signed "G. V. L. Slingsby"; the other, "Vladimir Dixon." The protests of Slingsby and Dixon, both offering comic, backhanded homage to Joyce's project, perform an essential service in this early defense of "Work in Progress." The letters anticipate and mock genuine objections; Slingsby's and Dixon's diverting examples present to Joyce's readers an appropriately irreverent, creative manner of encountering the *Wake*. We learn from Sylvia Beach's autobiography, *Shakespeare and Company* (1959), that she commissioned the first of these attacks on "Work in Progress" since "Joyce thought an unfavorable article should be included in the volume."[11] In 1932, as Jolas assembled a prominently featured "Homage to James Joyce" for *transition* 21, Joyce made a similar insistence that praise be balanced by objections. He minds particularly, he tells Harriet Weaver, that the issue is

> to be an attack on Goethe (whose centenary it is) and a homage to me: Not being able to stop this I made it a condition that a portrait of G. and a French caricature of me should be in it. . . . I also bargained that he should print passages from the three recent personal attacks on me by Lennon, O.G. [Oliver Gogarty] and "One who knows him." (JJ, *Letters*, 1:313)

Beyond simply desiring revenge against Lennon and Gogarty, drawing the venom from their pieces by placing them in the overwhelmingly friendly context of *transition*, beyond simply exhibiting to his admirers the hostility with which he and his work have been met, Joyce seeks a suitably unruly frame for his portrait — a frame that includes caricature and misreadings, that mirrors the discordant world into which his works wander.

Speaking the last words in *Our Exagmination*, Dixon and Slingsby perfectly play this necessary part of the opposition. So suited are their comic protests to the collection in which they appear that the reality of both protesting correspondents has been suspect almost since the publication of *Our Exagmination*. The parodist "G. V. L. Slingsby" was obviously pseudonymous.[12] Dixon's piece, written in *Wake*an prose, has long been mistakenly attributed to Joyce himself.[13] The literal confusion between the artist and his critics — a confusion so deep that for decades after an actual man named Vladimir Dixon adopted Joyce's image he was declared nothing more than a reflection — is simply a more radical expression of the confusion regarding the tone of attacks and defenses of "Work in Progress": both come from our search for Joyce's keys, his voice, for genuine rather than feigned or parodied authority in his texts' apparatus.

Slingsby's demurral was probably written by Mrs. Robert Woods Kennedy, who was clever enough to cast her objections to "Work in Progress" in the language of a willing but baffled middlebrow reader.[14] Kennedy wisely avoids the trap of being framed as an ignorant naysayer in the sophisticated company of the Exagminators. Instead she constructs the good-natured target "Slingsby," who ingenuously confesses inadequacy ("one can but struggle") and advises Joyce that the experiment has gone too far: "Whether or not a public can ever be trained to absorb this kind of thing seems to me extremely doubtful" (*OE*, 190). "Slingsby" hopes that "Mr. Joyce who is so profoundly respected and has been so ardently followed by the youth of his generation, is not turning on his current to make the animals jump instead of to shed further illumination on the paths of his real readers" (*OE*, 191). Refusing the challenge of a straightforward attack on Joyce, Kennedy further protects herself from ridicule by suggesting a couple of perceptive analogies that link Joyce's experiments with language to parallel innovations in contemporary music: "Work in Progress" is perhaps a "literary Sacre du Printemps"; Joyce may be the "Milhaud or Honegger of literature" (*OE*, 190, 191). Thus she offhandedly numbers herself among the substantial number of critics who early found the *Wake* a polytonal or deliberately cacophonous composition.

Dixon's "Litter to Mr. James Joyce" is the fourteenth and final contribution to the anthology. Dixon, "Leyde up in bad" with the flu, has been reduced to "reeding one half ter one other the numboars of 'transition' in witch are printed the severeall instorments of . . . 'Work in Progress'" (*OE*, 193). He writes "in gutter dispear," "disturd by [his] inhumility to onthorstand most of the impslocations constrained in [Joyce's] work" (*OE*, 193). Not only has his "in flew Enza" fractured his English, but it has forced him to wonder whether it is his fever or Joyce's art that has made "Work in Progress" so difficult: Is he "unable to combprehen that which is clear or is there really in [Joyce's] work some ass pecked which is Uncle Lear?" (*OE*, 194). Although *Our Exagmination* bills this confession of bewilderment as a "Protest" (*OE*, 187), Dixon's letter, in its accommodating suggestion that confusion might reside in a distracted reader rather than a misguided, maddening author, remains relatively uncommon among the many objections to Joyce's work raised during the 1920s and 1930s.

That Dixon was for so long identified with Joyce ironically marks the triumph of Dixon's "Litter"; it reveals something, too, about the nature of the *Wake* and of Joyce's authorship. *Finnegans Wake* is a book assembled from others' voices and with others' help. The history of its composition comprises numerous stories (some verifiable, some apocryphal but scarcely less germane) of associates and strangers consciously or unwittingly helping Joyce to piece his text together. He could talk about authorship as though it were a pursuit curiously removed from him: "Chance furnishes me what I need," he explained to Jacques Mercanton in the late 1930s: "I am like a man who stumbles along; my foot strikes something, I bend over, and it is exactly what I want."[15] In this endless harvest of life's randomly submitted details, distraction and accident complete rather than disrupt Joyce's design. For Joyce, the disheveled, multifarious world seems to contribute, almost without being screened, to the vast scheme of his fictions.

Seen from another angle, this expansive exercise of authorship creates the grand and disconcertingly solipsistic illusion that there is nothing external to Joyce's book, nothing that he has not already written, nothing that doesn't fit. Whatever we might designate "apparatus" belongs instead to the text itself—a fact that renders the reflexive pronoun "itself" misleadingly specific about that text's boundaries. Dixon's able mimicry must have pleased Joyce because it demonstrated that he was not alone: the language of "Work in Progress" existed beyond the borders of that work and had to some extent been duplicated by another writer. But in a fitting paradox, Dixon's words for a time became Joyce's—a transformation that demonstrates how readily the community surrounding Joyce collaborated with his disposition to subsume the world even as he delighted in evidence of that world's independence. As Joyce bends over to pick up something his foot has struck, he makes a text of the object and it becomes his work. An admirer's letter turns into his own; the twelve unwitting authors of *Our Exagmination* are already characters in the *Wake* before their essays appear in Beach's collection.

*Our Exagmination* entered "Work in Progress" sometime in May 1929, the same month that it went on sale at Shakespeare and Company.[16] Joyce realized that his commentators belonged in the schoolroom with Kev, Dolph, Issy, and assorted instructing voices. He recorded his addition on proofs for *Tales Told of Shem and Shaun* (printed in June 1929), a collection of three episodes, including the first part of II.2, previously published in *transition*: "Imagine the twelve deaferended dumbbawls of the whowl abovebeugled to the contonuation through rogeneration of the urutteration of the word in procress" (*JJA* 53:123) (Figure 3).[17] The first critics of "Work in Progress" fit neatly into a spot carefully prepared for them in Joyce's text, joining there the pedantic Twelve— obtuse interpreters who make their self-important way through the *Wake* as

Imagine the twelve deaferended dumbbawls of the whowl abovebeugled to the contonuation through rogeneration of the urutteration of the word in procress. It follows that, if the two antesedents be binyclitties and the three comeseek.venchers trundletrikes, then Big Wheeler restant upsittuponable, the N C H presents to us pictorial shine by pictorial shimmer so long as pictorial summer lets asheen, but parilegs

in eupreachd

and allanights bate him up jerrybly! Show that
the median intercting at royde angles the legs of
a given obtuse one biscuts both the arcs that are
bloundered behind. A Tullagrove pole to the
Height of County Fearmanagh has a septain
inaison and the graphplot for all the functions
in Lower County Monachan, whereat samething is
rivisible by nighttim, may be involted into the
zeroic couplet, palls pell inhis heventh glike
noughty times inchif you are not literally cooefficient how minney combinaisies and permutandies
can be played on the international surd hymn-
antelopz, hids cubid rute being extructed, taking
anan illitteretts, ififif at a tom. Answers, Ten,
twent, thirt, see, ex and three ones.
Binomeans to be comprendered. The axmones.
And their prostulates. For his neuralgabrown.
Equal to bears.
P.t.l.o.a.t.o.
So, bagdad, as I know and you know yourself
and the arab in the street knows better nor

icky totchty

SOANC
kaksi volts
Fkolne volts
yksi to the finish of halve's fractures.

(for teasers only).

F, if this cyclic order be outraciously enviolated, P brings us a rainborne pamtomomiom, equi-lavant to kaksitoista volts, yksitoista volts kymmenen volts yhdeksan volts kahdeksan volts seitseman volts volts nelja volts viisi

**Figure 3.** Joyce memorializes the publication of *Our Exagmination* by adding a reference to the title and its twelve authors in the margin of proofs for *Tales Told of Shem and Shaun*. He adds the marginal addition sometime in May 1929, the same month that *Our Exagmination* went on sale at Shakespeare and Company. The addition reads, "imagine the twelve deaferended dumbbawls of the whowl abovebeugled to the con-tonuation through rogeneration of the urutteration of the word in procress" (*JJA* 53:123).

characters "given to ratiocination by syncopation in the elucidation of complications" (*FW*, 109.4-5).[18] It is tempting to suppose that the Twelve owe their
habitual "-tion" constructions at least partly to the title of the journal that
became their forum: *transition*. They first appear as one of Joyce's sigla, an
empty circle, in a letter to Harriet Weaver written on 15 July 1926.[19] They are
already critics of Joyce's work: "I will do a few more pieces, perhaps . . . parts of
O discussing . . . *A Painful Case* and the ⊓-Δ ] household" (JJ, *Letters*, 1:242).
The "grandfather clock" on the cover of *Our Exagmination*, with a hollow
center and the critics' names marking the hours on its face, foretells their place
in the *Wake* and reduces their contributions to naught (Figure 2).[20]

These twelve explicators are the "deaferended dumbbawls of the whowl."
They are deaf and dumb, incapable either of hearing or of expressing themselves about the book before them, crying like babies, an assembly of different
dumbbells convinced that they see the "whole" clearly but in fact falling into the
hole (the "O," the zero of Joyce's mockery) while they attempt the impossible
task of elucidating a book that is fundamentally resistant to criticism. The
"aveugle" latent in "abovebeugled" suggests that these critics are blind to the
work they study. They are a noisy crew: "whowl" contains a "howl." The hidden
verb describes the brash, childish confidence of Joyce's early critics. Their
excesses are latent in the French beugler : "to low or bellow"; cows or
oxen—"bove"—lumber also in the midst of "abovebeugled," which describes a
critical function Joyce habitually exploited. A book such as *Our Exagmination*
trumpets the achievements of the author of "Work in Progress," giving the
novel advance publicity essential to its chances of success. The Twelve are "bel-
lowers" of Joyce's book to a skeptical public. Elliot Paul, for example, plays the
wholly committed salesman, assuring us that the *Wake* isn't as impenetrable as
we might suppose: "Whatever difficulties the individual words may present,
and they have been much exaggerated,—however baffling it may be to find the
elements of character and of plot extending forward and backward as well as
from left to right, the sentence structure and the syntax generally will offer no
obstacles" (*OE*, 136). These Twelve have joined a herd Joyce conjured with the
words "exagmine" and "beugler," a herd he planned to expand with another
book on the *Wake*. "To succeed O I am planning X," he writes to Harriet
Weaver on 28 May 1929 (a busy month for Joyce and his critics): "[T]hat is a
book of only 4 *long* essays by 4 contributors (as yet I have found only one). . . .
This for 1930, when I shall also, I hope, send out another fragment, this time
about ⊓, with another preface" (JJ, *Letters*, 1:281). He might have imagined
the volumes issued in a boxed set, "OX" branded on the spines.

Even before *Our Exagmination* found its place in "Work in Progress," the
scene for the lessons—children trying to untangle or reconfigure puzzles of the
adults' world—precisely captures Joyce's vision of his relationship with his
readers. In *transition* 11, where the first part of the "Lessons" chapter appeared,
there is already the challenge, announced to all students, to "find if you are not
cooefficient, how minney combinaisies and permutaudies can be played on the
international surd *thyndwrclxpz*. . . . Binomeans to be comprendered" (*t* 11
[1928]: 8).[21] Critics indulge like children in endless interpretive permutations

*a* Your exagmination round of his factification for incammination of warping process. Declaim! 204

Joyce's Work in Progress   188

tb the right! Rotacist ca canny! He caun ne'er be bothered but maun e'er be waked. If there is a future in every past that is present *Quis est qui non novit quinnigan* and *Qui quae quot at quinnigan's quake!* Stump! ●

— Arra irrara hirrara man, weren't they arriving in clansdestinies for the Oructions of *Ad Regias Agni Dapes*, fogabawlers all their centuries after the crack and the lean years scalpjaggers · and houthhunters, like the messicals of the great god a scarlet trainful, the Twoedged Petrard, totalling leggats and prelaps in their aggregate ages two and thirty plus undecimmed centries of them with insiders, extraomnes and tuttifrutties allcunct, from Rathgar, Rathanga, Rountown and Rush, from America Avenue and Asia Place and the Affrian Way and Europa Parade and besogar the wallies of Noo Soch Wilds and from Vico, Mespil Rock and Sorrento, for the lur of his weal and the fear of his oppidumic, to his salon de espera in the keel of his kraal like lodes of ores flocking fast to Mount Maximagnetic afeerd he was a gunner but affaird to stay away, Merrionites, Dumstdumb-drummers, Luccanicans, Ashtoumers, Batterysby Parkes and Krumlin Boyards, Phillipsburgs, Cabraists and Finglossies,· Ballymunites Raheniacs and the bettlers of Clontarf, for to contemplate in manifest and pay their firstrate duties before the both of him tweeve stone a side with their *Thieve le Roué* and their *Shvr yr Thrst!* and their *Uisgye ad Inferos!* and their *Usque ad Ebbraios!* at and in the licences boosiness primises of his delhightful bazar and reunited magazine hall, by the magazine wall,, Hosty's and Co, Exports, for his five hundredth and sixtysixth· bortday the grand old Magennis Mor, Parsee and Rahli taker of the tributes, there Rinseky Poppakork and Piowtor the Grape holding Dunker's durbar boot kings and indiarubber umpires and shawhs from paisley and muftis in muslim and sultana reiseines and Jordan almonders and a row of jam sahibs and a odd principeza in her pettedcoat and the queen of knight's sclubs and the claddagh ringleaders and the two salaames and the Halfa Ham and the Hanzas Khan with two fat Maharashers and the German selver geyser and he polished up protemptible tintanam-bulating to himsilf so silfrich, and there was J. B. Dunlop, the best tyrent of ourish times and a swanks of French wine stuarts · and Tudor keepsakes and the Cesarevitch for the current counter Leodegarius Sant Legerleger riding lapsaddlelonglegs up the oakses staircase on muleback like Amaxodias Isteroprotos, hindquarters to the fore and kick to the lift, and he handygrabbed on to his trulley natural anthem:

*Horsibus, keep your tailyup,* and as much as the halle of the vacant fhroneroom, Oldloafs Buttery, could safely accomadate of the houses of Orange and Betters, M.P. permeated by Druids D.P. Brehons, B.P. and Flawhoolags, and Agiapommenites, A.P. and Antepummelites, P.P. and Ulster Kong and Munster's Herald with Athclee Ensigning and Athlone Poursuivant and

*and parliburghers, imbandiment*

*b* His producers are they-not his consumers?

**Figure 4.** In April or May 1937, Joyce adds a second explicit reference to *Our Exagmination* on the galleys for "Work in Progress": "His producers are they not his consumers? Your exagmination round his factification for incammination of a warping process. Declaim!" (*JJA* 62:125).

on the father's incomprehensible, thundering pronouncements, crippled by the
fact that they are given an "international surd," a book crammed with various
tongues but not uttered in the language of ordinary men and women and therefore mute to its translators. "Surd" derives from the Greek *alogos* and means
"speechless, irrational." Joyce has conditioned his readers to hear Giambattista
Vico's *Scienza nuova* behind every thunderclap in the *Wake*. Fear of thunder,
according to Vico's historical outline, inspired in primitive mythmakers a "first
divine fable," which underlies all subsequent developments of civilization: "At
the end of this period of time after the flood, heaven must have thundered and
lightened, and from the thunder and lightning of its Jove each nation began to
take auspices."[22] The artist's awful Word comes first, bringing the world into
being; dazed critics follow later, dimly aware of that world's cause but ignorant
of its maker. The Twelve accept the challenge Joyce issues in *transition* 11,
though they do not heed his warning that they will never solve his riddle. Fifteen months later, when he welcomes them by name into the classroom of
"Work in Progress," he has no more faith in their eventual success. Commentators may hope to assist the "contonuation through regeneration of the urutteration of the word in procress," to mirror or perhaps merely to mimic the
father's original thunderous utterance ("contonuation" contains, and thereby
reduces, a little Latin thunder: *tono*), but their efforts will never amount to
much. Joyce's sentence begins with the skeptical invitation to "imagine the
twelve." Children and essayists make noise, not genuine thunder.

But their cacophony is at least evidence of a community beneath the
clouds. Joyce's letter to Larbaud discussing *Our Exagmination* is most concerned with the lack of response that often followed his utterances: "I hope you
got T[wo] T[ales] of S[hem] and S[haun]. . . . From your silence I fancy that
at least you find it difficult" (JJ, *Letters*, 1:284). Criticism, generally inadequate
to Joyce's expectations, is nevertheless a sign of readers, and it summons and
creates an audience. An active, interested community working around Joyce to
understand and explain his book helps ratify the validity of his fantastic vision.
Even misguided critics confer a measure of authority on the author.

By April or May 1937, when Joyce added a second explicit reference to *Our
Exagmination* in the *Wake* galley proofs, he had recognized this fact even more
fully, though he was perhaps less reconciled to his dependence on Exagminators: "His producers are they not his consumers? Your exagmination round his
factification for incammination of a warping process. Declaim!" (*JJA* 62:125)
(Figure 4).[23] The author is trapped in a reductive, circular economy in which he
is forced to deal with middlemen — his "producers," his explicators, his agents,
his criers. Because his creation is inaccessible to the general public, he must
watch as these same intermediaries become receivers, the sole customers for his
work. "Exagmine" contains another, darker gloss. "Agmin" means "host," in the
sense of an assembly of men. But if we hear the word's Christian overtones,
then "Ex agmin," or "out of the host," suggests that Joyce is consumed by those
he has brought forth — the author host and martyr to the small band of critics
he has gathered around him. The volume, here titled "Your" rather than "Our"
exagmination, has achieved a disquieting amount of independence from its

organizer. The "warping process" first occurred as Joyce reshaped languages to his ends. It is equally a "process" external to the *Wake*, under the awkward, haphazard control of the commentators. Joyce's wry acceptance of the comedy of misreading he has written for himself echoes in the terse command "Declaim!" The ensuing critical clamor becomes a part of what Joyce represents in the busy margins of his "Lessons" chapter.

Perhaps we ought to know better, but we come hopefully upon page 260 of *Finnegans Wake*, the first page of Joyce's "Lessons." Suddenly the book's daunting pages are broken into distinct components. Marginalia and accompanying footnotes framing a reduced central column of text promise long-awaited guidance and immediately relieve the eye. At last the page seems to cooperate with the rhythm of understanding Joyce's book enforces: brief periods of sense, of glimpsed associations, of momentarily lucid passages or uncovered puns surrounded by uncertainty. Here the text is already subdivided into pieces of manageable size. We are encouraged to focus our attention completely on each part. If that element refuses to become clear, we can begin our efforts afresh with the next. And those pieces themselves make traditional assurances of sense. Marginalia are there to orient the reader, to amplify and comment on the text; footnotes will clarify and explain our difficulties. Perhaps, then, it is our disappointed hopes that give this chapter the reputation for being, in Joyce's own words, "the most difficult" for readers (JJ, *Letters*, 1:406).[24] Seeking assistance, we find only different, puzzling voices.[25]

The first words from the four discrete territories on page 260 tell us much about Joyce's strategies throughout the chapter (Figure 5). We should pause over these beginnings and examine the way each works in concert with the others on the page: in the understandable urge to cover *Finnegans Wake* with its many subsequent elucidations, it is all too easy to overlook the texture of the book itself and miss its effect on the unaccompanied reader. Although Petitjean and Fargue added explanatory pieces to *transition* 23, the issue's annotated installment from "Work in Progress" offered its readers nothing more than its own enigmatic glosses.

The first two sentences of the central text drop us into a muddle of repetitive elements that simultaneously invite and resist grammatical organization: "As we there are where are we are we there from tomtittot to teetootomtotalitarian. Tea tea too oo" (*FW*, 260.1–3). Difficulties begin with "as," which looks like a conjunction that will locate the episode temporally. The sentence never clearly establishes itself with a main clause, however, and the consequence is an immediate suspension of time, of whatever event these words might describe. No plot can go forward in this hiatus. Instead, there follows a baffling string of nine simple words that are fundamentally ambiguous. They may be parsed (a comforting exercise frequently performed by critics) into three groups of three, each with a pronoun, a verb, and an adverb: "we there are"; "where are we"; "are we there." But the adverbs will not stop oscillating between a place asked about and a place pointed to, without ever specifically asking or pointing. This basic progression, no matter how often it is subdivided, returns on rereading to its

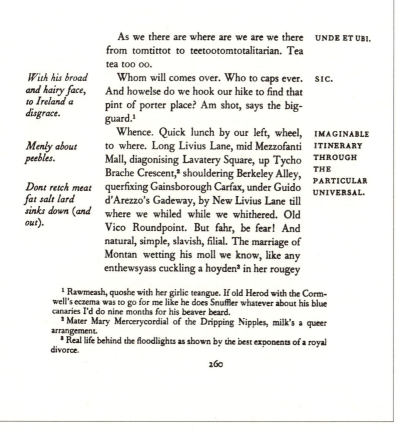

As we there are where are we are we there    UNDE ET UBI.
from tomtittot to teetootomtotalitarian. Tea
tea too oo.

*With his broad*    Whom will comes over. Who to caps ever.    SIC.
*and hairy face,*    And howelse do we hook our hike to find that
*to Ireland a*    pint of porter place? Am shot, says the big-
*disgrace.*    guard.[1]

     Whence. Quick lunch by our left, wheel,    IMAGINABLE
*Menly about*    to where. Long Livius Lane, mid Mezzofanti    ITINERARY
*peebles.*    Mall, diagonising Lavatery Square, up Tycho    THROUGH
     Brache Crescent,[2] shouldering Berkeley Alley,    THE
*Dont retch meat*    querfixing Gainsborough Carfax, under Guido    PARTICULAR
*fat salt lard*    d'Arezzo's Gadeway, by New Livius Lane till    UNIVERSAL.
*sinks down (and*    where we whiled while we whithered. Old
*out).*    Vico Roundpoint. But fahr, be fear! And
     natural, simple, slavish, filial. The marriage of
     Montan wetting his moll we know, like any
     enthewsyass cuckling a hoyden[3] in her rougey

> [1] Rawmeash, quoshe with her girlic teangue. If old Herod with the Corm-
> well's eczema was to go for me like he does Snuffler whatever about his blue
> canaries I'd do nine months for his beaver beard.
> [2] Mater Mary Mercerycordial of the Dripping Nipples, milk's a queer
> arrangement.
> [3] Real life behind the floodlights as shown by the best exponents of a royal
> divorce.

260

**Figure 5.** The opening page of book II, chapter 2 of *Finnegans Wake*, the "Lessons" chapter (*FW*, 260).

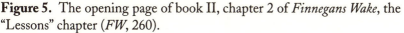

original, confusing, circular blur: three of the first four words are repeated in the next six ("we" and "are" twice). Location of the "we" or of the reader remains uncertain, an obscurity that the word "where" emphasizes at its pivotal position in the repetitive series. "From" quickly proves another feint at placing the subject and enlightening the reader. It is part of an idiomatic construction, and the cryptic nouns in that construction provide a radical contrast with the monosyllabic, elemental beginning, without giving any further clues to who the "we" is or where they are. The second sentence in this opening paragraph (at least the page is built with familiar textual shapes) picks up the first syllable of the last word in the preceding sentence ("tee"), provides a homophone ("Tea"), repeats that new word, gives us then "too," and finally, as though the sentence is running down, gives only the last two letters, "oo": "Tea tea too oo."

The first paragraph of II.2, if annotated by somebody other than Joyce's playful children, yields a folktale, "Tom Tit Tot"; a spinning toy called a "tee-totum"; a form of government, "totalitarian"; the song "Tea for Two"; the Danish word for "ten": (*ti*); perhaps, if we skip two syllables, the word "teetotal"; perhaps a suggestion, in the sound of the repeated "tea," of "titty"; a graphic representation of a woman's buttocks in the doubled "o"s, which may also be the sign for infinity, and which will be enlarged, with the same purport, on page 293 of this chapter.[26] Some of these associations, as well as others I haven't mentioned, will probably occur to readers as they puzzle over the opening paragraph. But the effect on the reader of Joyce's two sentences is absolutely unlike the momentarily reassuring sense produced by this list of latent meanings. And while a determined critic can muster into a single expressive body the curious assembly uncovered in this short passage, the active pieces refuse to limit their connections when they are again placed within the *Wake*.

Fritz Senn, in a description of the reader's activity that is especially apt for the "Lessons" episode, eloquently characterizes the operation that explains an excerpted passage while leaving the book mysterious:

> In practice the readers of the *Wake* slip into the roles of pedantic schoolmasters who emend the text's deficiencies of the most self-righting verbal artifact in existence. We mentally put things right, but of course no longer toward one correct solution. We are correctors, whether we dig up hidden allusions, or set up word lists, or simply paraphrase.[27]

More openly than any other chapter in *Finnegans Wake*, II.2 appears to countenance each reader's pedantic strain, to abet each potential schoolmaster. Dumbfounded by the first sentences, we may turn to the adjacent phrase in the right margin. Joseph Campbell and Henry Morton Robinson revealingly invent a character who produces these right-hand marginalia and christen him "the professor," suggesting that these "solemn" notes work as they are supposed to.[28] But the first three words next to the chapter's beginning are beside the point: "UNDE ET UBI" (*FW*, 260.R1).[29] They perform the most restricted function of marginalia, serving only to give the reader a cue about the subject of the text proper. Here the inadequacy of the pretentious tag, "whence and where," is augmented by the fact that it mirrors the confusion to its left: "there . . . where . . . there." The reader remains dislocated by this device that marks his or her position in the work.

The second paragraph of the "Lessons" brings with it the first contribution from the left-hand margin: "*With his broad and hairy face, to Ireland a disgrace*" (*FW*, 260.L1). This is the third typeface and the third distinct style on Joyce's dynamic page. We are invited to form a set of equations, all of which will be overthrown in time, linking small roman capitals and fruitless, self-important scholarship; standard roman body type and the central matter—whatever that may be—of the chapter; the least formal, italic face and an irreverent voice from the left (are political associations of left and right also applicable?). The left's flippant sneer is startling because through it a personality bursts suddenly onto the page. Although the vernacular style is an amusing relief from the austere material to the right, it holds even less assurance of providing useful information than its companion pieces in the opposite margin.

The relatively straightforward taunt on the left, however, does seem tenuously connected to the second paragraph, which switches from the "we" of the first to an unnamed individual: "Whom will comes over. Who to caps ever" (*FW*, 260.4). While the right-hand capitals are telling the printer and the audience that this inscrutable beginning is also grammatically or typographically incorrect—"SIC"—the equally unhelpful italics mock the subject (*FW*, 260.R2). As with the chapter's first paragraph, there are a number of applicable glosses that can make even this decidedly anticerebral jeer part of a seamless presentation of Vico's war between the Father and the sons. Readers of *Portrait* might see Stephen's hairy father still staring from this late page. The phrase about Ireland's disgrace evokes historical episodes of struggle against oppression.[30] Nor do I wish to ignore these echoes: their creation is largely what kept Joyce at work on the *Wake* for seventeen years; I named some of them at the end of the preceding chapter. My aim is not to recover a pristine, unannotated *Wake*, but to show, in some detail, how the book's own annotated page functions without the additional layers of subsequent notes. I am concerned in this exegesis to determine how the book's glosses work and fail to work rather than how Joyce's notes combine with those superimposed by succeeding critics, even though the effects of those combinations of glosses are also, as we have already seen, an important part of Joyce's subject. Paradoxically, critics' further commentary creates a palimpsest that in some senses profoundly simplifies by obscuring the comparatively clean, deeply fissured pages of II.2.

The reader's next adjustment to a different, discretely placed voice comes with the first footnote, tied by the number [1] to the end of the second paragraph: "Rawmeash, quoshe with her girlic teangue. If old Herod with the Cormwell's eczema was to go for me like he does Snuffler whatever about his blue canaries I'd do nine months for his beaver beard" (*FW*, 260.F1). That [1] challenges us, even more specifically than the placement of the marginalia, to bring wildly disparate but textually connected elements together in spite of the gulf of style and sense that separates them. The footnote is closest in tone to the material in the left margin: colloquial, saucy, unimpressed by its obligation to remain subservient to the text it annotates. Having taken us from the text above and then frustrated our desire for clarification, these sentences at the bottom of the page—equally though differently elusive—proceed to refocus our attention altogether. Like the marginalia, they interrupt the reader's attempt at a linear progress through the chapter's paragraphs. They are particularly distracting since they are the most linguistically complex of the four openings to II.2. They are also powerfully infused with a markedly individual voice largely absent from the three other introductory passages on page 260 and are therefore intriguing to a degree that text and marginalia are not. However chastened Joyce's audience has been by the rigorously impersonal, formal aspects of the *Wake*, however strenuously educated not to expect a realistic novel, it will naturally gravitate toward the slightest suggestion of the incipient creation of character. Although the phrases themselves make only intermittent sense, the first-person, confessional quality of the initial footnote arouses a hope that this part of the page might present an individual's portrait—a portrait that would, in turn, tie at least some of the chapter's scattered pieces into a manageable bundle.

In his letter to Budgen about II.2, Joyce reports that the footnotes are "by the girl" (JJ, *Letters*, 1:406). His cue encourages us to attribute at least part of this first note to an unnamed "girl." (Of course, since the publication of this hint in the *Letters* in 1957, Joyce's letter has itself become a gloss that creates expectations of a feminine point of view at the bottom of the page.) But a girl's is not the only voice that we hear in this first note. A narrator has appeared from somewhere to tell us that the peculiar expletive "Rawmeash" has a source: "quoshe with her girlic teangue." The mysterious "girlic" declaration continues, evoking a sexually charged world where "Herod" might "go for" the speaker (Salome?), who would "do nine months for his beaver beard." An assembly of meanings congregates around this sentence, urging the critic to devise coherent alternative stories, characters, and themes more congenial to sustained interpretation. Like the marginalia, only more intricately, the note acts both centrifugally and centripetally. Its inferior location beneath the text dictates its traditional operation: it should direct us back into the center of the page after administering a brief lesson designed to clarify or deepen the significance of that center. And the energetic reader does return, if possible, from note to text, having worked at building a more or less viable bridge of sense between the two. The note's composite substance, however, propels us away from the *Wake*, out into a world bordered only by the limits of language and our ability or inclination to make connections between Joyce's words and material that is comparatively extrinsic to the book. Then, when Salome returns from this larger world, attracted to "old Herod" and perhaps auditioning for the part of her with the "girlic teangue," it is not easy to dismiss her as out of place, since she fits her role as if specifically summoned by the *Wake*. The three margins of this page function primarily not to restrain or direct our reading but to increase the commerce between the relatively few printed words chosen by Joyce and their constantly compounding links with one another and the reader's particular knowledge. On the literal level of the text, the pages of II.2 represent the reader's fragmented journey through the *Wake*. The annotations demand that we pull similar and disparate matter together, that we discover and create the integrity of each assorted page.

In the same letter to Budgen in which he remarks on the difficulty of II.2 and describes his technique, Joyce explains that he has simply made a copy of an "old classbook," its margins filled with students' comments, aimless observations, and classroom notes.[31] That model classbook would possibly have carried its own explanatory material, though it would doubtless have acquired further additions as it was used in the classroom. From the outset, Joyce's children conspicuously trespass on three sides of the adults' textual space. But a careful investigation of II.2's annotations soon reveals the inadequacies of Joyce's explanatory model. Of the numberless tangents his glosses bring into the chapter, only a few suggest a student's inconstant attention. Nevertheless, there is an important representational aspect to the form and the multiple linguistic strata of his "Lessons," and we should take Joyce's hint about "technique" seriously enough to discover how and where it is applicable. The glosses do periodically delineate characteristics of the children—those figures who come momentarily into focus throughout II.2 before fading again almost immediately into the changing verbal ground.

In addition to offering a representation of a heavily emended classroom text or notebook, the crowded pages of II.2 metaphorically approximate the games children play and the infinite ways their minds wander throughout their instruction. This delightful disarray of early lessons has never really changed, Joyce tells Budgen: "It was like that in Ur of the Chaldees too, I daresay" (*JJ, Letters*, 1:406).[32] It was like that in *A Portrait of the Artist as a Young Man*, too. Moynihan, murmuring into Stephen's ear, provides notes to the science lecture in the fifth chapter. If they were printed in II.2, they would be set in italic type. The old Jesuit professor speaks of "a ball having the form of the ellipsoid," and Moynihan takes up the topic: "What price ellipsoidal balls! Chase me, ladies, I'm in the cavalry!"[33] When the lecturer turns to "a compound called platinoid lately discovered by F. W. Martino," Moynihan brings Saint Martin, patron of innkeepers and reformed drunkards, into the class: "Good old Fresh Water Martin!"[34] Joyce's schoolrooms are always territories crisscrossed by disruptive energies that can often be traced to the students' awakening obsession with their own bodies and the sexual mysteries of their origins.[35] Pupils will learn what they desire to learn; their classes will be startlingly germane and more, though differently, affecting than adults ever realize, regardless of their teachers' tamer agendas.

In the rough-and-tumble classroom of the *Wake*, the students' impertinence becomes a visually significant element of the page. When the superior text sets up a slightly mangled version of the heading for essays required in Jesuit schools—"Ad Majorem Dei Gloriam" ("At maturing daily gloryaims!" [*FW*, 282.6])—Issy responds in a laughing footnote with her version of the concluding prayer, "Laus Deo Semper": "Lawdy Dawdy Simpers" (*FW*, 282.F2). Her laughter is equally irreverent as she transforms the pompous introduction of the supreme kabbalistic God—"Ainsoph, this upright one"—into a "Groupname for grapejuice" (*FW*, 261.F3). All religions and their ceremonies (specifically the taking of Communion) become children's play. The notes easily overthrow adults' assertions of grandeur or self-importance.

While the center waxes lyrical, for example, as it slips into the romantic language of legend—"Wherefore Petra sware unto Ulma: By the morals' frost! And Ulma sware unto Petra: On my veiny life!" (*FW*, 264.12-14)—Dolph scoffs, his two expletives displayed one on top of the other, each emphatically punctuated by a period for maximum effect:

*Bags.*
*Balls.* (*FW*, 264.L1)

Or, on the opposite page, the center has been conducting a geographical tour of sorts, reviewing the location of various landmarks, as Dolph's mind ranges to the places named "Dublin" in the United States: "*Here's our dozen cousins from the starves on tripes*" (*FW*, 265.L2). The subjects of geography and eating are equally present to the distracted Dolph. His unsolicited additions, in particular, characterize him as a lively but inattentive student. When the central text refers to "B.C." and "A.D.," a musical staff with those four notes—a silently composed meditation for the eye—appears in the left margin (*FW*, 272.L2).

Many of Dolph's puns must be seen before being heard and make most sense as graphic games in a notebook: "*Dear Brotus, land me arrears*" (*FW*, 278.L3); "*Hearasay in paradox lust*" (*FW*, 263.L4); "EUCHRE RISK, MERCI BUCKUP" (*FW*, 304.R1). The misspelling of "hesitancy" elicits a long multilingual mockery of a spelling list, quickly degenerating into word games that we must see to follow.[36] The Italian phrase "come si compita?" (how do you spell?) and the Latin for "hesitancy" (*cunctatio*) begin Dolph's list: "COME SI COMPITA CUNCTITITITILATIO?" (*FW*, 305.R1). The Latin syllable *cunc* next takes a rambunctious physical turn: "CONKERY CUNK." Dolph's play depends on repetition with a difference. The curious spelling of "thigh" provokes a one-word jingle that requires careful display:

    THIGH—
    THIGHT—
    TICKELLY—
    THIGH

This column of syllables exhibits the phonetic mysteries of "th" and "gh" while hinting at tights and tickled thighs.[37] The continuing list suggests conundrums that appeal first to visual consideration. The note loses much of its ebullient appeal if we imagine Dolph simply speaking rather than writing the phrases that follow:

    [THIGH,] LIG—
    GERILAG,
    TITTERITOT,
    LEG IN A TEE,
    LUG IN A
    LAW, TWO
    AT A TIE,
    THREE ON A
    THRICKY
    TILL OHIO
    OHIO
      IOIOMISS.

The narrowness of the margin works well to break this note into short units, each looking similar, some almost interchangeable. Many of the elements are nearly homophonic. The slim column rings changes on "thigh" and "leg"; the properties of "t" and "th" fascinate, as does the hint of palindromes latent in "thigh-thight" and "Ohio." The longer we stare at Dolph's collection of letters, the more the whole runs together. We might be peering over this student's shoulder at the endlessly evolving diversions he writes to amuse himself.

And even as Joyce moves far beyond reproduction of what children at their playful work might actually have written in a book, he can still maintain the fiction that his annotations are rooted in these children's minds. Issy's letter, a long footnote that sounds in part as if it were addressed to a teacher, perfectly illustrates this more complex operation of Joyce's glosses.[38] The footnote, three times the size of the passage to which it is attached, appropriately signals its distracting powers by bringing to a standstill the text to which it is supposedly subservient (Figure 6). With the interruption that turns our attention to the appended note—"A halt for hearsake[1]"—the annotation, in spite of its reduced type size and lesser position, has proved insubordinate. The central passage functions momentarily like a marginal gloss, arresting its progress to introduce what looked like ancillary material.

This sudden upsetting of the page is fitting, given the note's breathless, insistent beginning: "Come, smooth of my slate, to the beat of my blosh!" (*FW*, 279.F1). The preoccupied student—weary of attending to the overbearing voices that have dominated the chapter, bored by the subjects she is required to study, rebellious at always being restricted to a few inches at the bottom of the page—begins her disturbance with an invocation to her receptive slate. As she ignores her schoolwork, choosing to fill her slate's smooth surface with her own thoughts instead of dutifully taking properly directed notes, she pushes anyone else's concerns out of her mind—a displacement represented literally by the overwhelming dimensions of her gloss. Issy's preoccupations immediately surface in the second half of her first sentence. "The beat of my blosh," while suggesting that strokes from a brush might fill her slate, also evokes the girl's "beet" blush, which colors her smooth cheeks when she flirtatiously addresses a man or when she recalls what she has learned in life's school. This warm writing bears ample testimony to Issy's aroused, overwhelming interest. Her note reveals a mind engaged by thoughts of seduction ("seduction" is etymologically diverting; "seduce" comes from *seducere*: to lead away, "distract" from *distrahere*: to draw away or apart). Her suggestive meanderings, leading the reader's eye and attention astray, disclose how completely sex suffuses lessons, how fully a body can blush through text.

Issy immediately starts to fill her slate by proclaiming life almost unbearably tiresome in the absence of sex: "With all these gelded ewes jilting about and the thrills and ills of laylock blossoms three's so much more plants than chants for cecilies that I was thinking fairly killing times of putting an end to myself and my malody" (*FW*, 279.F1). Her complaint, expressive without making literal sense, identifies a number of obstacles to the course of love. The oddly sterile and androgynous "gelded ewes" betray the cause of romance by "jilting about"; the blossoming lilacs demand an inordinate amount of time—time that might be better spent cultivating relations with the opposite sex. Or perhaps, although the syntax groups "blossoms" and "ewes" as equally bothersome interferences, and although there are "more plants" than chances for love, the flowers already signify what is uppermost in Issy's mind. "Miss Laycock," Roland McHugh informs us, is a synonym for "cunt." And when we first see Cecily Cardew, in *The Importance of Being Earnest*, she is watering and the face in the treebark feigns afear. This is rainstones ringing. Strangely cult for this ceasing of the yore. But Erigureen is ever. Pot price pon patrilinear plop, if the osseletion of the onkring gives omen nome? Since alls war that end war let sports be leisure and bring and buy fair. Ah ah athclete, blest your bally bathfeet! Towntoquest, fortorest, the hour that hies is hurley. A halt for hearsake.[1]

MODES COA-LESCING PROLIFER-ATE HOMO-GENUINE HOMOGEN-EITY.

[1] Come, smooth of my slate, to the beat of my blosh! With all these gelded ewes jilting about and the thrills and ills of laylock blossoms three's so much more plants than chants for cecilies that I was thinking fairly killing times of putting an end to myself and my malody, when I remembered all your pupil-teacher's erringnesses in perfection class. You sh'undn't write you can't if you w'udn't pass for undevelopmented. This is the propper way to say that, Sr. If it's me chews to swallow all you saidn't you can eat my words for it as sure as there's a key in my kiss. Quick erit faciofacey. When we will conjugate to-gether toloseher tomaster tomiss while morrow fans amare hour, verbe de vie and verve to vie, with love ay loved have I on my back spine and does for ever. Your are me severe? Then rue. My intended, Jr, who I'm throne away on, (here he inst, my lifstack, a newfolly likon) when I slip through my pettigo I'll get my decree and take seidens when I'm not ploughed first by some Rolando the Lasso, and flaunt on the flimsyfilmsies for to grig my collage juniorees who, though they flush fuchsia, are they octette and viginity in my shade but always my figurants. They may be yea of my year but they're nary nay of my day. Wait till spring has sprung in spickness and prigs beg in to pry they'll be plentyprime of housepets to pimp and pamper my. Impending mar-riage. Nature tells everybody about but I learned all the runes of the gamest game ever from my old nourse Asa. A most adventuring trot is her and she vicking well knowed them all heartswise and fourwords. How Olive d'Oyly and Winnie Carr, bejupers, they reized the dressing of a salandmon and how a peeper coster and a salt sailor med a mustied poet atwaimen. It most have bean Mad Mullans planted him. Bina de Bisse and Trestrine von Terrefin. Sago sound, rite go round, kill kackle, kook kettle and (remember all should I forget to) bolt the thor. Auden. Wasn't it just divining that dog of a dag in Skokholme as I sat astrid uppum their Drewitt's altar, as cooledas as cul-cumbre, slapping my straights till the sloping ruins, postillion, postallion, a swinge a swank, with you offering me clouts of illscents and them horners stagstruck on the leasward! Don't be of red, you blanching mench! This isabella I'm on knows the ruelles of the rut and she don't fear andy mandy. So sing loud, sweet cheeriot, like anegreon in heaven! The good fother with the twingling in his eye will always have cakes in his pocket to bethroat us with for our allmichael good. Amum. Amum. And Amum again. For tough troth is stronger than fortuitous fiction and it's the surplice money, oh my young friend and ah me sweet creature, what buys the bed while wits borrows the clothes.

279

**Figure 6.** Issy's longest footnote from book II, chapter 2 of *Finnegans Wake* (279). Joyce refers to it as a "Letter" in a holograph draft (*JJA* 52:227).

flowers expressly to avoid the less becoming occupation of student: "I know perfectly well that I look quite plain after my German lesson."[39] Readers must decide for themselves whether Cecily belongs in this passage. She shares with Issy her concern for flowers and her own beauty at the expense of her lessons. That Wilde, too, might be hidden at the foot of the page suits the associative illogic of the entire note, itself a result of Issy's daydreamy nature.

Issy was never forced to perform her romantic threat of "putting an end" to herself because, no matter how repressive her lessons, no matter how censorious her teachers, the classroom was always saturated with sexuality: "I remembered," she explains to her unidentified addressee, "all your pupil-teacher's erringnesses in perfection class" (*FW*, 279.F1). Even in the hygienic "perfection class" teachers somehow trip into the risqué; pupils wander happily toward the taboo.[40] Grammar involves intimate exercises: "When we will conjugate together toloseher tomaster tomiss" (*FW*, 279.F1). "Together" breaks down into an infinitive and an object pronoun suggesting pursuit of woman. The series of romantic inflections, a brief love story, spurs Issy on to an excited declaration of her allegiance to love, which she slips neatly between the lines of her bookish tasks. She performs her own operations on the phrases that interest her, making provocative sense by repeating words with slight variation: "verbe de vie and verve to vie, with love ay loved have I on my back spine and does for ever" (*FW*, 279.F1).[41] Her pronouncement, like much in this long note, might have begun with a tag from a teacher ("verve de vie," for example) that could be easily elaborated in the student's restless mind and then set down in the margin of her schoolbook. As Issy's ardor transforms her dry lessons — even books themselves can function as sensual props — the young girl's pliant "back spine" merges with those of her texts.

Everything in Issy's classroom is similarly invested with desire by her heated imagination. She anticipates a racy graduation: "[W]hen I slip through my pettigo I'll get my decree and take seidens when I'm not ploughed first by some Rolando the Lasso" (*FW*, 179.F1). The German *Seiden* (silk) and the English phrase for becoming a King's or Queen's Counsel—"to take silk" — scarcely mask the seductive impact of Issy's costume. In University College slang, to be "ploughed" is to fail one's courses. Issy uses the verb in a more corporeal sense, and she obviously yearns for some Rolando's "ploughing" more than she fears it, as evidenced by her hopeful beginning—"*when* I'm not ploughed"— instead of the expected "if." In what sounds like titillating revisions of jokes for younger children, Issy tells us how food shamelessly misbehaves: "How Olive d'Oyly and Winnie Carr, bejupers, they reized the dressing of a salandmon and how a peeper coster and a salt sailor med a mustied poet atwaimen" (*FW*, 279.F1). Toward the end of her note, she creates a detailed, violently sexual scene, involving a foreboding altar and a virile companion who shouts out to a group of fearful onlookers that he has found an accomplished sexual partner:

> Wasn't it just divining that dog of a dag [Danish for "day"] in Skokholme as I sat astrid uppum their Drewitt's altar, as cooledas as culcumbre, slapping my straights

till the sloping ruins, postillion, postallion, a swinge a swank, with you offering
me clouts of illscents and them horners stagstruck on the leasward! Don't be of
red, you blanching mench! This isabella I'm on knows the ruelles of the rut and
she don't fear andy mandy. (*FW*, 279.F1)[42]

The young virgin in her fantasy is a supremely confident mistress of the alleys
(French, *ruelles*), a girl with a "pretty head" (Irish, *cúil-deas*) who has received
genuinely useful instruction from a wise old woman outside the classroom:
"Nature tells everybody about but I learned all the runes of the gamest game
ever from my old nourse Asa. A most adventuring trot is her and she vicking
well knowed them all heartswise and fourwords" (*FW*, 279.F1). We have
strayed far from the empty slate and the unendurable boredom with which this
note began.

Any extended discussion of a specific, named portion of II.2 (Issy's letter)
or any presentation of a composite portrait made from carefully chosen selections (Dolph's marginalia) misleads the reader because the unbroken thread of
explanation belies the piecemeal quality of every page. The traditional fictional
components of character, setting, and action do operate throughout the book,
but only intermittently and inconsistently.[43] It is precisely their intermittence
that prompts the uneasy reader to construct temporarily applicable narrative
scenarios—"Issy writes a note to her teacher"—and prepares her or him to
abandon each scenario as it quickly proves inadequate. These repeated provisional fabrications find their textual analogue in the marginalia of II.2. Each
gloss potentially offers a purchase on a part of the chapter, even as it becomes
itself a piece demanding another interpretive approach. These glosses are never
transparent lenses; they are discrete filters through which the suddenly distant
adjacent material appears, if at all, in a peculiarly colored light. They demonstrate how quickly Joyce's volatile frames solicit the reader's undivided attention. Like critics' clarifying schemata, like readers' mentally composed, perpetually contingent parallel narratives, each marginal fragment or footnote turns,
on examination, into a new center of an endlessly reproportioned text.

In fact, we cannot meaningfully apply Joyce's facile explanation that the
apparatus is "by" Kev, Dolph, and Issy, even to a single page. With Dolph and
Issy no predictable style, no recognizable voice endures long enough to give
either child a truly distinguishing, consistent identity. The two often strike
interchangeable poses. Dolph's opening volley against "his broad and hairy
face" could be his sister's; any number of Issy's footnotes might be slipped into
Dolph's space without seeming incongruous. Although each has what might be
called a "tone" or "manner" loosely attached to his or her textual space, and
although both possess a definite, distinct cluster of particular significance
within the frame of the *Wake*, it is not possible to draw firm boundaries between
Issy's and Dolph's material. The divided areas on the pages of the "Lessons," in
other words, do not act as reliable cues for the reader. The page actually asserts
its own laws, forcing Dolph and Kev to exchange typefaces halfway through the
chapter (*FW*, 293)—although to agree with Joyce that the twins change sides,
we must grant that the shifting stylistic signals of II.2 are to be trusted more
than the chapter's typography.

Nor do the pieces collected at a single site necessarily evoke a unified impression. The character named Issy can begin a group of notes like a mother baby-talking to her child—"Now a muss wash the little face"—and then sound like a lexicographer in the note immediately following. "Brandnewburgher," her second note tells us, is "[a] viking vernacular expression still used in the Summerhill district" (*FW*, 265.F1, 2). But within this note itself, the ensuing "definition" forces us to relinquish the momentary fancy that we are reading a dictionary. The explanatory opening collapses under the absurd description of a "Brandnewburgher" that follows: "a jerryhatted man of forty who puts two fingers into his boiling soupplate and licks them in turn to find out if there is enough mushroom catsup in the mutton broth" (*FW*, 265.F2). This might indeed come from a young girl imagining a funny picture; and, following Joyce's cue to Budgen, critics of II.2 almost invariably work to make the glosses fit the children.[44] Since these annotations do not illuminate the central text, at least they might reveal something about each of the distracted pupils. But the girl laughing at the "jerryhatted man" vanishes with the third note on this sample page: "H' dk' fs' h'p'y" (*FW*, 265.F3). Roland McHugh's substitutions of "handkerchief" and "halfpenny" do little to help fit these elided words to Issy. And if she sounded motherly at the outset of this page, her penultimate gloss places her in very early childhood: "Googlaa pluplu" (*FW*, 265.F4). The industrious critic can compose an integrated portrait of Issy if he or she is allowed to rummage through the heap of material Joyce has assigned to his elusive girl. To read the entire body of her footnotes, however, is to realize how much must be excised before she might be presented as a distinct fictional figure from whom these annotations spring.[45] Not only do Joyce's notes often fail to clarify other pieces of his chapter; much of the time they do not even unlock themselves but stand apart, detached from the adjacent text and from their ostensible authors.

This lack of reliable connection between notes and character or annotated text marks those notes ascribed to Dolph and Issy. Kev's side of the page further complicates the nature of the glosses in the "Lessons" chapter. Issy and Dolph sometimes sound like infants, young children, or adolescents. Kev, at least in the margin, never does. A boy does not describe a journey as an "IMAGINABLE ITINERARY THROUGH THE PARTICULAR UNIVERSAL" (*FW*, 260.R3). He does not explain the conflict between himself and his brother in these ornate terms: "INGENIOUS LABOURTENACITY AS BETWEEN INGENUOUS AND LIBERTINE" (*FW*, 286.R2). Nothing about these marginalia suggests that they are the work of a child.[46] In an effort to keep Kev and Dolph fixed as young, enfranchised representatives of the patriarchy who can "participate in the central narrative" and annotate that narrative from which Issy is excluded, Shari Benstock suggests an elaborate and I think unworkable temporal scheme in which

> [t]he marginal notes in the left- and right-hand columns are supplied by Shaun [Kev] and Shem [Dolph] and are not contemporaneous with the action of the chapter. The marginal asides display a later perspective, as though written when the boys were older, when they appear as the prototypes of twins under the names

of Shaun and Shem. Issy's commentary seems simultaneous with the action, although its perspective displays a knowledge and maturity beyond her years.[47]

Every detail of this scenario—the chapter's "action," the older, more mature boys' return to their schoolbooks, the simultaneity of Issy's apparatus—relies for its plausibility on a narrative stability that the *Wake* wholly lacks. Benstock's summary relies, too, on overlooking important qualities that keep Kev's notes absolutely different from those of his brother and sister. Unlike a number of Issy's and Dolph's notes (and I use possessive proper nouns only for clarity of reference, recognizing as I do that these notes scarcely "belong" to anyone), Kev's comments consistently distance us from what we might take to be a pupil's thoughts. They leave us instead with a shell of cliché and circumlocution. Generally tied to the text opposite by relatively discernible strings, they do little to encourage subtle understanding. They comment earnestly from too great a distance to penetrate the tangled thicket of the text itself. To those searching for thematic orientation in the "Lessons," Kev's sweeping pronouncements prove useful. They give structural keys—"PROBA-POSSIBLE PROLEGOMENA TO IDEAREAL HISTORY" (*FW*, 262.R1); "INCIPIT INTERMISSIO" (*FW*, 278.R1); "*Illustration*" (*FW*, 301.L1)—and often present Viconian glosses that elevate the children's struggles to mythic status: "PRE-HAUSTERIC MAN AND HIS PURSUIT OF PANHYSTERIC WOMAN" (*FW*, 266.R1); "EARLY NOTIONS OF ACQUIRED RIGHTS AND THE INFLUENCE OF COLLECTIVE TRADITION UPON THE INDIVIDUAL" (*FW*, 268.R1). Kev's annotations are the only component of II.2 that actually sounds something like scholarly apparatus throughout the chapter. With these notes Joyce offers an equally unsatisfactory alternative to non sequiturs—his version of an academic gloss.

If we turn from the fractured but finished *Wake* to Joyce's drafts for II.2, we uncover the compositional origins of the brokenness of the "Lessons." It was not until some time in 1934, as Joyce worked on shaping notes made during the intervening years into material he could add to II.2, that he decided on the schoolbook "technique."[48] Revising a troublesome draft, he began instead to cannibalize that draft, taking pieces from it and turning them into marginalia and footnotes for the section (*FW*, 275.3-282.4). Many of Issy's and Dolph's glosses were not added to a chapter already composed; these notes, every bit as snarled as the opposing text, came from within. Only Kev's textual scaffolding, in keeping with its distance from the complex prose to which it is attached, could not be built from earlier drafts. Joyce, by constructing his notes from the text he was revising, ironically made the sense of his "Lessons" more elusive, more in need of and resistant to clarifying additions.

Watching this perversely mystifying practice of annotation in progress, we see the draft pages dissolve into discrete marginal elements. Joyce's first annotated page (*JJA* 52:197; *FW*, 275) (Figure 7) takes a number of its notes from a single locus in an earlier draft, a meditation on looking back through history:

> Pendent this time there [he who] will be either crowned or hanged scans the errors of history from the parrotbook of Dates. If the santimeter of Hairyoddities Noah's misbelieving missus was . . . velivole back all the ways from Wallhollow

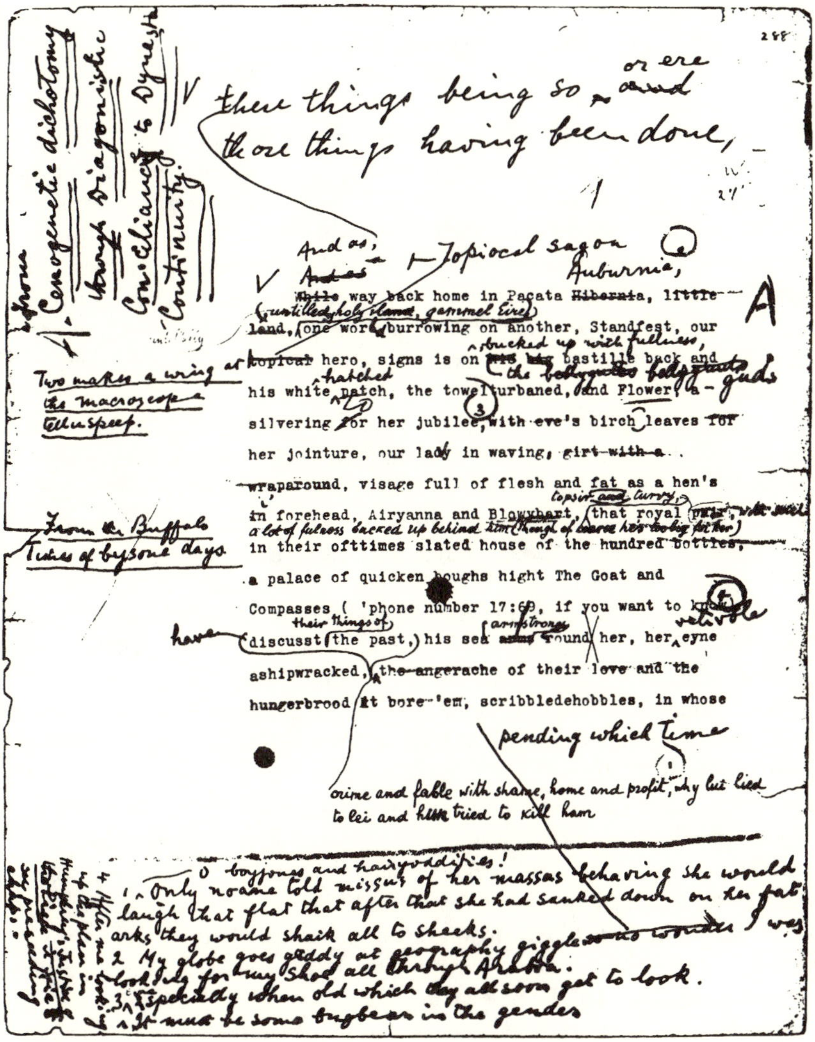

**Figure 7.** Joyce's draft of the first annotated page for the "Lessons." It is at this point in his composition of book II, chapter 2 (sometime in 1934 [*JJA* 52:147 §4.5]) that Joyce decides to arrange material from an earlier draft around the margins of the page, thereby creating the chapter's earliest marginalia and footnotes (*JJA* 52:197; cf. *FW*, 275).

and through telluspeep of whatsowhatness, just boyjones upon those pages she would laugh that flat that after that she had sanked down on her fat arks they would shake all to sheeks. (*JJA* 52:170-71)[49]

Dolph claims the first phrase from this quarry: "*Quick quake quokes the parrotbook of dates*" (*FW*, 275.L4). Issy takes a generous portion of the rest: "O boyjones and hairyoddities! Only noane told missus of her massas behaving she would laugh that flat that after that she had sanked down on her fat arks they would shaik all to sheeks" (*FW*, 275.F5).[50] "Telluspeep" pops up in Dolph's second note on the same page. This might all be grouped under the classroom heading of "History," but the text did not generate its accompanying material, and that material has been in some senses more intimately connected to other marginal points (though we cannot know which ones by reading the finished version of the chapter) than it ever will be to any portion of the central text. As we see the folding over of one part of the draft on another—the pieces of an earlier compositional stage now divided between two characters and split between two parts of the page—we realize that Joyce's apparatus represents a solution to a structural problem, not the belated addition of a reader's guide.

Joyce's manuscripts, typescripts, and revised proofs—filled at every new stage with additions scrawled in the margins—offer an even more telling image than the classbook for understanding the rationale behind the notes to the "Lessons." As Joyce explained to Harriet Weaver early in the process of composition, much of "Work in Progress" was composed in short segments whose ultimate order only gradually became clear: "I work as much as I can because these are not fragments but active elements and when they are more and a little older they will begin to fuse of themselves" (JJ, *Letters*, 1:205). Even as Joyce grows increasingly certain of the overall design, his customary compositional ingredient is the self-contained unit, what David Hayman calls the "node," which he then surrounds with more or less directly related units at each stage of revision.[51] He creates with tesserae rather than long sweeps of a brush. The marginal embroidery to the "Lessons" looks like glosses, but its first function was to allow Joyce to use a significant amount of draft material in a more suitable form. In a sense, II.2 openly displays the process, concealed elsewhere in the book, by which Joyce built *Finnegans Wake*.

This form came to him as he was casting about in 1932 to 1934 for a way to bring Issy more fully into the chapter. Dolph does receive a significant portion of the recast section, but the passage to which the notes are first added and the annotated sections which Joyce then composed revolve around Issy.[52] The separately published, annotated portion of II.2, *Storiella as She Is Syung*, is predominantly Issy's piece.[53] That Issy and the glosses appear more or less simultaneously in the construction of II.2 provides a richly suggestive manifestation of a complicated, deeply sexualized bond between Joyce and his text; the conjunction suggests, too, the part apparatus plays in the representation of that bond.

Once his books became public, once they were open to others' puzzled readings, outraged criticism, enthusiastic praise, or utter indifference, Joyce found himself both protective and distrustful of his work. Skeptical of his readers' capacities for understanding, profoundly aware of his books' hospitality to an endless variety of interpretations, he vacillates between impulses to defend and to abandon texts that he regularly figures as his spouse or his offspring. Particularly as *Ulysses* and "Work in Progress" make their way piece by piece into print, we see him—most directly in his letters, but with equal thoroughness in the novels themselves—ruefully considering those points where the author's authority over his words fades in the reader's erring eye. His reading public becomes an unscrupulous "other man" waiting impatiently for the attentions of his spouse or, in an even darker scenario, the affections of his daughter. This illicit courtship would certainly fail if the wandering book itself were not so ready to commit the ultimate betrayal—unwilling to declare its loyalty to its loving progenitor, prone to damaging misrepresentations, easily swayed by every critic's propositions, apt to follow any new reader anywhere. Ironically, although annotations represent a bid for authoritative interpretation, for control of the book to which they are secured, a text with marginalia and footnotes has literally been adulterated—stolen, in a sense, from its author—its visually homogeneous central text altered by the addition of discrete, typographically distinct groups of words attached by number or position to that center. Annotation stands as an emblem of and an incitement to the reader's haphazard, busily evolving affair with the book.

Knowing that adulteration is unavoidable and even perversely alluring, knowing too that competition over a desired object increases our sense of that object's worth, Joyce the annotator initiates the corruption of his text at the very moment when he holds the coveted, desirous, sexually precocious and confused Issy fully in his gaze. We should recall here Joyce's lifelong fascination with infidelity.[54] Nora found her friendship with the Triestine journalist Roberto Prezioso encouraged by her husband to the point that Prezioso tried to become her lover. Gabriel stumbles upon Michael Furey when he supposes himself alone with Gretta. Richard Rowan has his wife describe in detail Robert Hand's advances and then grants her "complete liberty" to pursue Robert further. Leopold Bloom displays Molly's "slightly soiled" photograph before Stephen, thinking "the slight soiling was only an added charm like the case of linen slightly soiled."[55] David Hayman has written at some length on Joyce's "emotional commitment, dating at least from 1909, to the theme of cuckoldry," a theme that "evolved into a concern for the problem of incest" during the years Joyce spent composing the *Wake*.[56] As he traces the development of the young Issy, who perpetually invites and eludes her pursuers and who embroiders the pages of II.2, Hayman turns directly to Joyce's life and to the triangle consisting of James, Nora, and Lucia, marking "Issy/Is/Isolde as the young daughter who, in fairly orthodox Freudian fashion, displaced her mother in [Joyce's] erotic imagination."[57] He further asserts that "the curious shape taken by Issy's personality can be traced in astonishingly large measure to Lucia Joyce's incipient schizophrenia."[58] Shari Benstock, while resisting this linking of Lucia and Issy, finds abundant evidence of sexual trauma emerging from the plural, partial utterances of Joyce's girl: "[I]ncestuous sexual violence emerges through Issy's pockmarked memories."[59] Sexual abuse leaves its brutal mark in "the pathological splits of her multiple personalities, signified textually as 'torn letters.'"[60]

Both critics present compelling psychosexual readings of Issy, and both suggest, with different emphases, that sinister familial or social forces work at the roots of her misshapen, unnaturally divided character. Both look for explanations either (in Hayman's case) to Joyce's relationship with his daughter, who was losing her sanity from mid-1932 through mid-1935 as Joyce struggled with great difficulty on the "Lessons," or (in Benstock's study) to the ways in which our culture leaves "[w]ives, sisters, and daughters . . . especially vulnerable under patriarchal law, their physical safety and sanity at risk."[61] Joyce plays a deeply divided part in the family romance that lies somewhere behind this glossed chapter—a part reflected in his creation of the inscrutable Issy: charmer and victim of her brothers and her teacher, begetter of apparatus, disrupter of lessons, diverter of the reader, adulteress of the book.

Although these readings are essential for understanding the pieces of the "Lessons" that we gather around Issy, and although explorations of a perversely sexualized culture and the sexual energies circulating within all families are central to Joyce's chapter, I hesitate to close my discussion of Joyce's glosses by educing a sense of resolution, of coherence derived from an appeal to a single character as the key to the apparatus. Even when we ascribe to that character a broken, multiple psyche—and it is entirely appropriate to discover analogical bonds between Issy's plural selves, Lucia's psychological distress, and Joyce's annotated text—the wholeness suggested by a proper noun belies the disorder of the chapter. Benstock, for example, focusing in her astute studies of II.2 almost entirely on Issy, simplifies those portions of the chapter that lie beyond her concern and designates the footnotes a uniquely germane addition: "It is Issy who establishes relations, hints at origins, provides references, inverts hierarchies (taking over the narrative by establishing her own), and takes the academic into the real, lived, experienced world."[62] But it is precisely Joyce's point that interpretive authority resides at no single location in the "Lessons." Every reader and every reading will assign relevance and irrelevance differently; Joyce gives us no consistently privileged set of glosses.

Lawrence Lipking, another shrewd analyst of II.2, perfectly illustrates how a critical agenda quite different from Benstock's will produce a differently configured chapter. Lipking finds Kev's scholastic marginalia "[c]onsistently relevant" though limited in scope.[63] Dolph, by contrast, "is a writer—perhaps *the* writer. His puns and parodies, like Joyce's own, unlock the shackles of language."[64] And Issy, dramatically different from the girl seen by Hayman and Benstock, "is a pushover for romance. While she does not respect the text, therefore, she confirms its authority."[65] Each of these assertions, flawed insofar as it relies on consistency from the chapter's "children," will seem sometimes accurate, sometimes wrong, often simply extraneous to our analysis of a given gloss. Pondering Issy, brooding on Lucia, mulling over drafts, Joyce found his form for II.2; but with its apparatus in place, the chapter scatters authority everywhere across each page.[66]

We do the greatest justice to the dynamic nature of Joyce's form when we consider the glosses not so much as the product or province of a character or characters, but as a textual manifestation of Joyce's long-standing sense of the triangular relationship between his texts, his various critics, and his conflicting authorial desires to shelter and to disseminate the words he puts into print.

Joyce presents this unending contest for and with his fickle creations most vividly in a gloss he provides Gorman for the biography. Explaining the origins of a song he composed in 1921, "Molly Bloomagain," Joyce records in a letter of corrections for Gorman a now famous "dream" (included as a footnote in Gorman's *James Joyce*) in which Molly Bloom steps from *Ulysses* to dismiss her author. This remarkable fantasy should be exhibited in full because it so clearly uncovers the contests of interpretation at the heart of the uneasy ménage à trois comprising Joyce, his audience, and his work:

> He saw Molly Bloom on a hillock under a sky full of moonlit clouds rushing overhead. She had just picked up from the grass a child's black coffin and flung it after the figure of a man passing down a side road by the field she was in. It struck his shoulders, and she said, "I've done with you." The man was Bloom seen from behind. There was a shout of laughter from some American journalists in the road opposite, led by Ezra Pound. Joyce was very indignant and vaulted over a gate into the field and strode up to her and delivered the one speech of his life. It was very long, eloquent and full of passion, explaining all the last episode of *Ulysses* to her. She wore a black opera cloak, or *sortie de bal*, had become slightly grey and looked like *la Duse*. She smiled when Joyce ended on an astronomical climax, and then, bending, picked up a tiny snuffbox, in the form of a little black coffin, and tossed it towards him, saying, "And I have done with you, too, Mr. Joyce." Joyce had a snuffbox like the one she tossed to him when he was at Clongowes Wood College. It was given to him by his godfather, Phillip McCann, together with a larger one to fill it from. (Gorman, 283n.1)[67]

The dream carries us quickly, with a dream's elided logic, from a marital struggle, in which the beleaguered husband proves incapable of defending his masculinity and loses possession of his headstrong wife, to an artistic contest, in which Joyce tries unsuccessfully to insist on the significance of his work. Joyce wages this battle for his dignity with the artist-critic's weapon of explanation. He does not directly rebuke Molly for her rejection of Bloom but instead strikes back by talking about *Ulysses*. His strategy indicates the symbolic equivalence of the relationship between husband and wife and that between author and book. His explication stands in relation to the scene between Molly and Bloom as gloss does to text: attempted mastery turns quickly into an occasion for the text's further rebellion. If only his heroine understood the meaning of her book and her place in Joyce's work, the dream suggests, if only she would heed the additional explication de texte with which Joyce now earnestly, hopefully furnishes her, she would obediently assent to her husband's will and her author's plot. She has impudently misread "Penelope," has put on finery and found dignity beyond her author's intention, and now stands unchastened, unconstrained by the book that gave her birth, scornful of the critical apparatus belatedly marshaled by her author.[68] Pound and the laughing journalists — those readers reluctant to follow Joyce faithfully in his literary experiments — make Joyce's clarification more urgent. These unsympathetic men, though their presence ironically remains desirable since they signal and contribute to the text's importance, witness the author's eroding authority and will undoubtedly publish accounts of his failure to keep his woman and his book in line.[69]

Joyce's masculinity, like Bloom's in *Ulysses*, is everywhere at issue in the dream. That his passionate exegesis of his novel ends with a climax of which the author is extremely proud only makes Molly's nonchalant rejoinder more painful. The child's coffin will remind Bloom of his dead son and subsequent impotence; its alternative shape, "a tiny snuffbox," transforms Joyce again into a nervous, uncertain boy at Clongowes. John Joyce, who as Simon Dedalus exacerbates Stephen's physical timidity, fills a Freudian niche in the dream as Joyce described it to Gorman, though Gorman excised Joyce's father before publication. In his letter, Joyce cannot describe his vaulting of the gate without adding a parenthetical confession: "(I have never vaulted gates but my father used to vault all the 4 or 5 bar gates he could find whenever he visited me at Clongowes much to the joy of any boys who chanced to be near)."

Joyce offers Gorman the dream as the origin for a ballad about "the buxom Molly Bloom."[70] The maudlin, bawdy, self-pitying song makes explicit the sexual aspects latent in the dream. The balladeer sings of a handsome, powerful Molly who has proved faithless: "Now every male she meets with has a finger in her pie." In the last verse, Joyce dwells heavily on the irony of his betrayal:

My left eye is wake and his neighbour full of water, man,
I cannot see the lass I limned for Ireland's gamest daughter, man,
When I hear her lovers tumbling in their thousands for to court her, man,
If I were sure I'd not be seen I'd sit down and cry.

(Gorman, 282)

His own limned lass leaves the almost blind poet ashamed and alone, pleading: "[I]f I cling like a child to the clouds that are your petticoats, / O Molly, handsome Molly, sure you won't let me die?" (Gorman, 283). Like the dream, the song concludes with an infantilized author.[71] Also like the dream, the song pivots on the spectacle of a character turning against her creator—a rebellion, dream and song imply, that will result in exuberantly practiced sexual freedom for the promiscuous, disloyal woman and unbridled critical freedom for the receptive, unpredictably assertive, feminized text.

We have seen the same revolution figured at the conclusion of the "Lessons," when "the babes that mean too"—the children who have their own agendas—move from the margins to the page's center (Figure 1). Once the glossing begins, once the border of the page is broken, the contest over priority and precedence increases without promise of resolution or cessation. "Text" and "commentary" point ineffectually to untenable demarcations: Joyce marshals his exagminators into pens, but they too construct frames that he at once desires, in part designs, no less deplores, around the hapless subject of their inquiry. Fully aware of these consequences, aware too that *transition* already functions as an unstable, expanding frame for every episode of his "Work in Progress," Joyce builds into his book an element, the gloss, that sets the chapter and its readers free. Restriction begets vagrancy. The book slips beyond control the moment its obtrusive author vaults the fence.

# 3

# VIRGINIA WOOLF
# THE BOOK UNBOUND

*"Really it is not I who am writing this crazy book," he said in his*
*whimsical way one evening. "It is you, and you, and you, and that man*
*over there, and that girl at the next table."*

James Joyce, describing the composition of
*Finnegans Wake* to Eugene Jolas

As we turn to Virginia Woolf and her work during the last decade of her life, we might begin by considering her on an April day in 1937. She sits in a room with three earnest young men—Julian Bell, Kingsley Martin, and Stephen Spender—as they conduct "[a] long close political argument." Sometimes all speak together: "[W]e discussed hand grenades, bombs, tanks, as if we were military gents in the war again." But Woolf remains generally silent, hearing the points for and against pacifism, listening while the men debate the merits of joining the fight in Spain: "I sat there splitting off my own position from theirs, testing what they said, convincing myself of my own integrity & justice." And as she weighs their words against her conviction that the entire conversation is importantly, destructively misguided, she feels compelled to resume work on her current project: "I felt flame up in me 3 Gs." (VW, *Diary*, 5:79–80). In *Three Guineas*, as in almost everything she wrote during this decade, Woolf will ponder the dynamics affecting this argument and dozens like it, wondering how to avoid the familiarly unproductive taking of sides, the fruitless marshaling of rhetorical forces to predestined, brutal ends, the exchanges in which all become "military gents in the war again." That last terrible adverb, "again"— carrying freight similar to that in *Finnegans Wake*, when "butagain budly shoots thon rising germinal"—marks the pattern Woolf hopes to mar.

The scene comprising Woolf and the three men who represent both the generation of English writers succeeding her own and, potentially, the soldiers of the next war gives us a fitting image for characterizing Woolf's labor during the 1930s. Dissatisfied with the prevailing political discussion, committed to participating in a conversation that is differently engaged with the issues of this tendentious decade, Woolf searches for ways to assert her authority to speak, to write, that will establish the importance of her contributions to the argument without implicitly endorsing the terms and tactics of the debate being carried on everywhere around her.[1] She finds her nephew particularly difficult to reach, deafened as he is by martial rhetoric that Woolf can only half dismiss with a rueful smile: Julian is "[o]bstinately set on going to Spain—wont argue; tight; hard fisted—has amusing phrases 'joining for duration of the quarrel'" (VW, *Diary*, 5:79 – 80).

Within three months Julian will have been killed in Spain; within another three months Woolf will be talking to Philip Hart, the doctor who was with him when he died. Hart insists that England would "save thousands of lives" by helping to arm the Loyalists. She goes upstairs after Hart leaves, finds Leonard "enraged" that England continues to withhold weapons from Spain, and pauses again (having attended before to impassioned assertions leading into the same lethal cul-de-sac) to "split off" her position: "[W]e shall sit on the fence: & the fighting will go on—But I am not a politician: obviously. can only rethink politics very slowly into my own tongue" (VW, *Diary*, 5:114). But once she has convinced herself of the validity of her position, once she has rethought the impasses that madden Hart and Leonard (and that maddened the other three men) and has translated their positions and those of their opponents into her different terms, how will she teach others, particularly those habituated to the commonplace phrases that constitute political discourse, to understand her unfamiliar tongue? Will anyone prove capable of distinguishing between "indifference" as she comes to define it in *Three Guineas* and a morally irresponsible "sitting on the fence"? And when she has declared, "[A]s a woman, I have no country. As a woman I want no country" (*TG*, 109), to whom will she address her explanations? Who will discover the integrity and justice of her alternative position?

On 12 October 1937, the day before Hart's visit, Woolf had written "the last page of 3 Gs.," remarking in her journal that she "must now add the bibliography & notes" (VW, *Diary*, 5:112). These two days belong together—the days on which she begins constructing the elaborate apparatus to *Three Guineas* and realizes afresh her thoughtful estrangement from the ordinary urgencies of politics—since Woolf's notes for her extended essay stand at the center of her most deliberate, detailed, complex public meditation on her power as a writer in the political arena and on the deadly absurdity of that arena itself. In these notes, and in similarly significant if less fully developed glosses that she composes in the late 1920s and the 1930s, Woolf simultaneously disseminates the enormous body of evidence she has gathered to make her case against the patriarchy and turns the gloss against itself, exploring and dismantling one of the quintessential forms by which texts traditionally lay claim to authority in the culture she anatomizes. Like Joyce, she exploits the paradoxical nature of the gloss: the way in which an author's addition to the margin incites every reader's insubordination at the very moment that it registers the author's powerful, always unsatisfied appetite for control over the wayward text. She and Joyce both recognize, too, how apparatus can summon an audience and divert that audience's attention. In Woolf's work, as in Joyce's, though for different reasons and in dramatically different form, those diversions come largely from the sheer variety of material that a text can incorporate in its glosses. Having troubled her texts with superscripted numbers or violated a narrative frame with argumentative essays, Woolf finds herself pouring into her books a vast assortment of clippings, questions, abbreviated essays, facetiously conceived and carefully planned ideas, suggestions for reform and for rebellion, samplings from other books and from conversations, quotations from centuries past and from the day's newspaper. She also knows with Joyce (and, as we shall see, with Pound) that the text's margins, potential loci for an author's comparatively direct addresses to the reader, easily become spaces in which to consider the absence of readers, the lack of conversational turmoil around the silent book.

Enumerating the characteristics that distinguish gloss from central text in Woolf's work proves no easier, no more fruitful a task than it does with Joyce's. I anchor my discussion in the footnotes, explanatory essays, and endnotes that Woolf attaches to *A Room of One's Own, The Pargiters,* and *Three Guineas.* But because she is always possessed by the impulse to alternate exposition and illustration or to interrupt a sentence with a tangentially connected thought, because she habitually constructs embroidered, many-stranded texts, I could conceivably range from beginning to end of her career finding examples of plural utterance, of interlineated composition. The parenthesis or the dash might, for example, be considered a typographical sign for the intruding gloss that follows: a note lodged in midsentence rather than in the page's margin. I restrict myself, however, in order particularly to explore how Woolf employs apparatus that she knows will strike her audience as generically familiar and therefore open to discernible innovation. Because the categories of novel, essay, footnote, and endnote are likely to evoke certain expectations from her readers, and because Woolf subjects to radical scrutiny those readers and the culture she and they share, her formal revisions of these categories should figure centrally in any discussions of her polemical writings. Her journals from the 1930s, overflowing with explorations of the connections between genre and content, between the design of her texts and the ideas she hopes to impress on her audience, invite us to weave these separable strands closely together.[2]

The 1930s themselves figure importantly in the determination of my chapter's scope, since Woolf's impulse to frame her books with commentary occurs primarily during this decade. It would be a mistake to maintain an absolute divide between Woolf's works of the 1920s and the 1930s, characterizing that divide as the difference between fancy and politics, subject and object, rainbow and granite.[3] But the balance in her texts does shift from portraits of interior worlds to presentations of impenetrable surfaces, from sentences that evoke the meditative whorls of thought to equally complex though differently cadenced prose that leads the reader through detailed analysis and arguments unfolding so subtly that their radical import only gradually becomes apparent. Beginning with the handful of notes to *A Room of One's Own* (1929) and the pointed examination of scholarly method in that essay, Woolf in her subsequent texts introduces her readers directly to complications that are present but less pivotal in her major works of the 1920s. With a newly heightened degree of attention to the world beyond the self, Woolf compels us to consider the mire of contemporary politics; history in all its confusion; the troubling, unstable body of material called "facts," deployed by all sides with equally unwarranted certainty; and readers—almost as vexing in their presence as in their absence—equally ready to praise, condemn, or ignore the artist who ventures to stand before them with an argument to make.[4]

After *The Waves* (1931), and until *Roger Fry* (1940) and *Between the Acts* (1941), she adds critical apparatus to each of her most important projects. *Three Guineas* concludes with its substantial collection of "Notes and References." Behind *The Years* and *Three Guineas* lies *The Pargiters*, Woolf's unfinished draft of a family chronicle with an interspersed series of expository essays—extended glosses aimed at demonstrating how actual political and social forces shape the lives of the novel's fictional characters.[5] Following an examination of the notes to *A Room of One's Own*, I focus in this chapter on Woolf's efforts in *The Pargiters* and *Three Guineas* to discover a form that accommodates history, fiction, political analysis, and a substantial variety of facts and figures while simultaneously allowing her to examine what each of these categories means for herself and her readers. Taking calculated steps in *A Room of One's Own*, Woolf strays farther and farther in *The Pargiters* and *Three Guineas* from the path defined by her preceding novels and by nineteenth- and twentieth-century strictures against mixing art and politics. In her unsanctioned wanderings, Woolf vacillates between seeking to speak with an authority that comes naturally only to insiders and cherishing her status as someone who does not belong in a savage, inequitable society. Her annotations answer both of these ends as they remap the borders tradition prescribes for novel and essay.[6]

The first footnotes to *A Room of One's Own* make their appearance at the moment when Woolf's essay introduces the subject of women's history. Up to this point Woolf, dispersed among an ostentatiously fictitious gathering of possible personae—"call me Mary Beton, Mary Seton, Mary Carmichael or by any name you please" (*ROO*, 5)—has mused on literary matters and sketched selected scenes set in the fabricated university town of Oxbridge. After a meager dinner at "Fernham," an exemplarily impoverished women's college, the narrator now finds herself a guest in the sitting room of Mary Seton, who apologetically begins a truncated historical narrative: "Well, said Mary Seton, about the year 1860—Oh, but you know the story, she said, bored, I suppose, by the recital" (*ROO*, 20). The fluid "I," narrating but scarcely visible, slips farther into the background, simply listening to another who seems no less reluctant to assume the role of speaker. The rhythm of the following sentences emphasizes what Mary Seton's offhand introduction implies—that this is an outline, not an analysis of events: "And she told me—rooms were hired. Committees met. Envelopes were addressed. Circulars were drawn up. Meetings were held; letters were read out; so-and-so has promised so much; on the contrary, Mr.——won't give a penny. The *Saturday Review* has been very rude" (*ROO*, 20). This perfunctory presentation, obscuring agency behind a screen of passive verbs, simultaneously gives the history of the women's movement as a body of knowledge so familiar that recital of details would be superfluous—a strategy likely to embarrass inadequately informed readers—and suggests that women's history cannot be readily assimilated by prevailing models of historical narrative.[7]

Mary Seton also betrays uneasiness at speaking from a position customarily occupied by a male historian. She cannot easily assume the authority that would enable her to sketch an account beginning with one date, 1860, and progressing regularly through other landmark years to arrive neatly at the present day. Within ten pages Woolf will have begun an equivocal celebration of this inability, urging her readers to perceive the failings of traditional histories that consist almost entirely of those events amenable to a narrowly conceived practice of cataloguing the doings of great men, governments, monarchs, and their wars.[8] With increasing confidence and success over the next ten years, she will redemptively employ her doubts about speaking in the register her culture recognizes as historical writing. Advertising that she is unfit to overwhelm her opponents by commanding scores of recognized facts or presenting political issues and their historical antecedents in familiar forms, she will reinforce her arguments concerning women's exclusion from a wide range of conversations about the past and the present, all the while proving in her notes that she is quite capable of combing through sources, of reading histories, of making political assessments. But the full exploitation of her disenfranchisement still lies some years and a great deal of effort in the future. This tentative Mary Seton would fare miserably from the point of view of the men caught up in the "long close political argument" of that April day in 1937. Julian Bell and the others would find her vague, unfocused, unsure of her facts and her position. And she is not yet strong enough to turn silently within, discovering there her own vindication, her own thoughts of what she will write in response to that passionate, futile discussion. We would be mistaken to hear nothing but unqualified celebration of this lack of authority at this moment in *Room*. Here, in her first extended polemical composition, speaking in the uncertain voice of Mary Seton, Woolf acknowledges her own hesitation and her anxious sense that her listeners are probably bored and skeptical.

The notes accompanying Mary Seton's "story" (the noun makes no promises of comprehensiveness or depth) are generated in part by those fears with which they contend. The mention of a specific figure, "thirty thousand pounds," brings with it a corroborating quotation at the bottom of the page: "'We are told that we ought to ask for £30,000 at least. . . . It is not a large sum. . . . But considering how few people really wish women to be educated, it is a good deal'—Lady Stephen, *Life of Miss Emily Davies*" (*ROO*, 20.1).[9] This citation offers more than simple factual support of the text; Emily Davies's anger makes an effective rhetorical contribution to the argument. For a moment we hear a powerful voice from the nineteenth century, a voice lost in the modern summary. Woolf's footnote temporarily frees one of the long line of women imprisoned in men's accounts of the past and, ironically, silenced too whenever a woman glances apologetically over her own troubled history, agreeing with her male auditors that there is nothing much to uncover in women's lives: the sums of money are so small, the stakes are comparatively so low, the creative or protesting gestures so tiny, so difficult to discern.

Both the patriarchal and the self-defeating narratives scarcely make a place for the disempowered—women who are "all but absent from history," though "one often catches a glimpse of them in the lives of the great, whisking away into the background, concealing . . . a wink, a laugh, perhaps a tear" (*ROO*, 45, 47). This brief gloss, containing the names of an author and her subject, demonstrating that here at least is one woman worthy of a *Life*, counters the anonymity to which women have been condemned by tradition. It adds more voices to a text that, from its opening pages, deliberately submits an argument belonging to no single speaker, no ruthlessly logical, utterly confident "I": "I need not say that what I am about to describe has no existence. . . . 'I' is only a convenient term for somebody who has no real being" (*ROO*, 4). We will never fix on the speaker of *A Room of One's Own* a single identity, and yet a small but significant procession of specific individuals, including a few named women, will troop across the bottom of the essay's pages.

The marginal space for this procession does mean that it will likely be given comparatively scant attention by readers of the printed text. These two women, sequestered in a footnote, achieve only a partial and fleeting rehabilitation. Neither Emily Davies nor her biographer, Lady Stephen, even appeared in Woolf's speeches to the women of Newnham and Girton in October 1928 as she delivered the talks that would become *A Room of One's Own*.[10] They belong to a supplementary portion of the text; they are at once noticeable and easily dismissed, their status always in question. The story of women's battles for equality (the passage that evokes this first note) proves differently demure and tacitly explains why Davies remains confined to a note. Mary Seton throws us into the middle of a scattered series of efforts:

> How can we raise a fund to pay for offices? Shall we hold a bazaar? Can't we find a pretty girl to sit in the front row? Let us look up what John Stuart Mill said on the subject. Can any one persuade the editor of the —— to print a letter? Can we get Lady —— to sign it? Lady —— is out of town. (*ROO*, 20)

This breathless set of questions re-creates the atmosphere in which so many women's struggles have been conducted and displays with pitiless clarity the makeshift, demeaning, often self-destructive stratagems forced on desperate combatants. It demonstrates the terrible effects of society's demand that, even in rebellion, its women remain decorous and presentable, that they seduce rather than argue with their opponents, appeal to male authorities, hold yet another ladies' bazaar that will raise another pittance for the cause. Literally beneath these accommodating displays, appropriately printed in smaller type, runs the forceful quotation directly exposing the injustice that motivates the bazaar and the attempts to find an office and a place to publish editorials. It is presented without framing commentary, unclaimed by any of the speakers of *Room*: the footnote's space dissociates the outraged Emily Davies from the speaker and the listening "I." We will see some of the most vitriolic portions of *Three Guineas* similarly delivered sotto voce, from the relatively unobtrusive corner afforded by annotations.[11] There, at the bottom of a page, at the end of a book, the anger burns brightest—anger that destroys a woman's social standing, her reputation for reasonableness, her claims to a place at the table presided over by wealthy, powerful men.

Mary Seton concludes her survey by acknowledging the poverty of her surroundings at "Fernham" College: "'The amenities,' she said, quoting from some book or other, 'will have to wait'" (*ROO*, 21). The second footnote in *A Room of One's Own* follows this casual reference to "some book." It is impossible to say whether Mary Seton privately recalls the book, whether she deliberately suppresses the author and title as she has seemed to dismiss so much else in this self-deprecating report on women's education. The naive, narrating "I" cares little about the detail. But Woolf gives us the exact quotation and names its source: "Every penny which could be scraped together was set aside for building, and the amenities had to be postponed.—R. Strachey, *The Cause*" (*ROO*, 21.2). The note adds almost nothing tangible to the argument of *A Room of One's Own*. Its silent, inconsequential, perhaps even unnecessary revision of Mary Seton's memory may seem harmlessly pedantic—we might imagine this sort of mild correction from a tiresome professor bent on accuracy—but Woolf's note, if it is read as a cooperative rather than an oppositional addition to the text, does not diminish her character's point. Rachel Strachey endows Mary Seton with some substance: a shadowy figure quotes a living author. The quotation also suggests how books such as *The Cause* contribute to women's sense of identity in times of personal and social change. Strachey's simplest descriptions of hardship become part of the story women tell themselves and one another. Woolf relies on *The Cause* often in *Three Guineas*; her own political essays add to this collection of works that redefine a woman's place and her potential. These first two unadorned quotations at the foot of the page evoke the community that stands behind and beside Woolf as she makes her appearance among women engaged in social criticism and reform.

Woolf's notes signal her awareness, deepening over the course of the next decade, that she writes always as part of a community of writers, and that every sentence of hers is framed in innumerable ways by the culture from which it springs, into which it is placed. To a degree, she fills her novels of the 1920s with scraps from that culture, but in those works she tends to conceal the evidence of her gathering. Even *Orlando*, replete with historical material, subsumes its sources in the arranging narrator's style. *A Room of One's Own*, by contrast, begins to reveal a patchwork surface divided into samples of distinct voices from the past and the present. The unstable narrative persona, meeting often with restrictions that prevent her from adding to her archival store, wanders around college grounds, in libraries, through histories, collecting what information she can from diverse sources without claiming that she can provide a synthesis or a unifying conclusion. There is no place in *Room* for the confident acrobatic "biographer" of *Orlando*. The notes to *Room* openly record Woolf's recognition that a writer cannot fully assimilate either past or present-day culture, that each idea or quotation represents only a selection from a vast body of pertinent evidence. And the locked doors and high fences surrounding the patriarchy's repositories of information contribute to the fragmented quality of this woman's book. *A Room of One's Own* stands by design as a collection of pieces from a world larger than the individual psyche; its notes record instances of Woolf's forays into that varied, contentious world.

The remaining footnotes in Woolf's *Room* constitute her abbreviated experiments with a protean form. She cites her sources for reactionary quotations (*ROO*, 56.2; 116.2); misogyny spills over into the catch basin underneath the page (*ROO*, 78.2, 3). The annotations also leave space for excerpts from her reading that add weight to her argument. Boswell quotes Johnson on women's intelligence; Frazer tells us that the ancient Germans turned to female oracles; F. L. Lucas ponders the "inexplicable fact" that women's power onstage vastly exceeds their power in the street (*ROO*, 30.1, 2; 45.1). Each of these subordinate contributions corroborates the surmise made by Woolf's narrator in the body of the essay while proving to Woolf and to her audience that *A Room of One's Own* is rooted in the civilization it scrutinizes.

But even as she claims her right to the status that annotation bestows on the annotated text, Woolf undercuts the premises on which the form of the footnote traditionally relies. *Three Guineas* will explore this paradoxical attitude toward authority more completely; its notes will often address their own ambiguous standing. In *A Room of One's Own*, the notes themselves remain relatively straightforward, but the essay contains an interrogation of the means by which an author, methodically collecting data from accepted sources, constructs a solid platform from which to speak. Employing a pattern that will also govern the alternating sections of *The Pargiters*, Woolf balances the scenes in her first chapter of *A Room of One's Own* with a chapter devoted to research and attempted explanation. She describes a morning's investigative work in the library: "The inevitable sequel to lunching and dining at Oxbridge seemed, unfortunately, to be a visit to the British Museum. One must strain off what was personal and accidental in all these impressions and so reach the pure fluid, the essential oil of truth" (*ROO*, 25). The narrator, hopefully commencing her search for essences, proves a perfect foil for Woolf, who makes a wry examination of the troop of experts and chroniclers responsible for maintaining Western society's record of itself.

What begins as a purposeful search for answers—"where, I asked myself, picking up a notebook and a pencil, is truth?" (*ROO*, 26)—soon turns into an illustrative tale of the academy's shortcomings and society's narrow definition of "truth." Seated near Woolf's narrator in the British Museum is a student, "trained in research at Oxbridge," who extracts from his reading "pure nuggets of the essential ore every ten minutes or so," carefully classifying his hoard in "the neatest abstracts, headed often with an A or a B or a C" (*ROO*, 28, 30).[12]

The narrator, not schooled in the mechanical process of distillation, finds that reading only multiplies her confusion: "[T]he question far from being shepherded to its pen flies like a frightened flock hither and thither, helter-skelter, pursued by a whole pack of hounds" (*ROO*, 28). The record of her frustrating labor reflects this haphazard chase: "[M]y own notebook rioted with the wildest scribble of contradictory jottings" (*ROO*, 30). Her unsettling morning in the British Museum produces unfocused musings where it was supposed to yield a few simple explanations.

The narrator's notes finally offer a literal illustration of an alternative to the Oxbridge undergraduate's clipped outlines: "I had unconsciously, in my listlessness, in my desperation, been drawing a picture where I should, like my neighbour, have been writing a conclusion" (*ROO*, 31). Her picture expresses an insight that her neighbor will never achieve: the world is bigger than an outline of its parts. But we should not miss the genuine apology in her confession. Centuries of rigorously directed scholarship compel her to propose a defense that will never convince the men who have concluded so much about the female sex: "[I]t is in our idleness, in our dreams, that the submerged truth sometimes comes to the top" (*ROO*, 31–32). Here is a researcher more at home in *The Waves* than in the British Museum.

Woolf's portrait of a woman uncertainly beginning research clarifies the tensions present everywhere in her publicly oriented work. Addressing an audience that expects political arguments to be prosecuted with logic and supported by historical scaffolding, she summons Dr. Johnson, Mussolini, Napoleon, Samuel Butler, and dozens of others onto her page. She promises to serve us only facts. She includes footnotes that point accurately to her sources and enhance her text with figures. But she is equally aware of the fatuity of wise men's pronouncements on women, of the vastness of the world beyond the bounds of logic, and of the damning truth that "facts" about women are rarely facts at all—that they have "been written in the red light of emotion and not in the white light of truth" (*ROO*, 33). She recognizes how a book presented with the formal attributes of a scholarly text—footnotes, bibliography, index, acknowledgments, organized points leading to a consistent conclusion—easily achieves a spurious significance. Thus she discards all pretense to accepted method at the end of her morning in the library. She forgoes, with some reluctance, the conventional credibility such painstaking work brings and falls naturally into what only appears to be a more congenial manner of inquiry: "I strolled off to find a place for luncheon. . . . Some previous luncher had left the lunch edition of the evening paper on a chair. . . . I began idly reading the headlines" (*ROO*, 33).

Her irregular study, although successful on its own terms, leaves her somewhat frustrated. Her potentially fruitful idleness exacts its different toll: "It was disappointing not to have brought back in the evening some important statement, some authentic fact" (*ROO*, 43). Woolf smiles here at her narrator's naive desire for certainty; but her journal records a similar fear that *A Room of One's Own* lacks the weight of reason, the ballast of fact that will convince her critical audience: "I am afraid it will not be taken seriously. Mrs Woolf is so accomplished a writer that all she says makes easy reading . . . this very feminine logic . . . a book to be put in the hands of girls" (VW, *Diary*, 3:262). None of Woolf's earlier books had forced her so fully into a world with which she is determined to argue while deploring her adversaries' methods of argument.

Having imagined her critics' likely condescension toward *A Room of One's Own*, Woolf steadies herself with the knowledge that she is already descending into the hermetic world of "The Moths" (later *The Waves*): "& I have that to refer to, if I am damped by the other" (VW, *Diary*, 3:262). Within two years, however, she has returned energetically to the public arena. On 20 January 1931, eighteen days before she marks the completion of *The Waves*, Woolf briefly notes that she has conceived her next project. Four years earlier she had traced the intensely private beginnings of *The Waves* to a meditative pair of journal entries in which she assessed her "profound gloom, depression, boredom, whatever it is," and hoped that she might convey something of "the mystical side of this solitude" (VW, *Diary*, 3:113). Now, at the beginning of 1931, her "Novel-Essay," *The Pargiters*, originates in her preparations for the speech about her professional life that she delivered to the meeting of the Society for Women's Service, an association of working women for which Philippa Strachey was secretary (*P*, 5).[13] From the outset, Woolf thinks of her new undertaking as a companion piece to *A Room of One's Own*. It is connected to its precursor by its focus on the status of women in English society and by its ties to a public forum:

> I have this moment, while having my bath, conceived an entire new book—a sequel to a Room of Ones Own—about the sexual life of women: to be called Professions for Women perhaps—Lord how exciting! This sprang out of my paper to be read on Wednesday to Pippa's society. (VW, *Diary*, 4:6)

This new venture affords a respite from the psychological depths of *The Waves*: "Too much excited, alas, to get on with The Waves," she writes, two days after she had appeared before the Society for Women's Service. "One goes on making up The Open Door, or whatever it is to be called. The didactive demonstrative style conflicts with the dramatic: I find it hard to get back inside Bernard again" (VW, *Diary*, 4:6).

Getting "back inside" Bernard's final soliloquy means turning away from the worldly concerns of her lecture and from the audience she has just addressed. It means ignoring this recently assembled public, literally present and appreciative, to accept Bernard's austere pronouncements: "I need no words. Nothing neat. . . . None of those resonances and lovely echoes that break and chime from nerve to nerve in our breasts making wild music, false phrases. I have done with phrases. How much better is silence. . . . Let me sit here for ever with bare things" (*Waves*, 295). Bernard's renunciation of language for the unmediated object, his vision of "the world seen without a self," stands as a radical expression of Woolf's exploration throughout the 1920s of the mysteries of identity (*Waves*, 287).[14] She has followed one of her characters into that indescribable core of being where the self cannot even construct its own linguistic reflection.[15] But this moment in *The Waves* quickly reveals its limitations. "Things" may come simply to Bernard when he explicitly purifies himself, when he consciously stops thinking about or with words. (We can only hear of his preparation; the success of his effort must remain fleeting and untold.) He works deliberately to divorce himself from his thoughts, which invariably take linguistic shapes, and from the limited "I"—a circumscribed, individual "elderly man, rather heavy, grey above the ears" (*Waves*, 292). And yet he soon stumbles against the irreducible limitations of his specific situation: "I must haul myself up, and find the particular coat that belongs to me; must push my arms into the sleeves" (*Waves*, 296). Although he may temporarily escape these binding clothes, he must always assume the garment of individuality, the coat of words that comes between his skin and the naked world. Woolf composes Bernard's adieu to books while she chafes to begin her "didactive demonstrative" essay on the status of British women. She bids farewell to language that leads, in the most subtle form of meditation, to a dissolution of the ego and a surrender of words themselves.

But in spite of important differences, *The Waves* and the didactic works by which it is framed, *A Room of One's Own* and *The Pargiters*, all interrogate the ego's tyranny. What changes throughout the 1930s is the openness with which Woolf recognizes and exposes the sociopolitical effects of that tyranny and the rigor with which she attempts to eradicate the marks of the ego from her own work. "I came to the stage 2 years ago," she writes in her memoir of Julian Bell (1937), "of hating 'personality'; desiring anonymity."[16] Of course, we have already seen her unsettling the dominion of the "I" in *Room*. By 1935, however, she does more than speak in multiple voices. She rebels against the author's most basic manner of self-assertion: her own signature. She was unable in 1935, she says, to "sympathise with [Julian Bell's] wishing to be published. I thought it wrong from my new standpoint—a piece of the egomaniac, egocentric mania of the time. (For that reason I would not sign my Janet article)."[17]

Woolf's refusal to claim authorship in a decade when those around her are ever more adamantly asserting what they believe (recall the arguing young men with which this chapter opened) exposes a central paradox of her work on *The Pargiters* and *Three Guineas*. Renunciation of the "I" in the experimental fiction and poetry of our century is not particularly unusual. We need look no farther for an example than to this chapter's epigraph, where Joyce tells Eugene Jolas that "Work in Progress" represents a collaboratively achieved assembly of voices.[18] But to relinquish the assertive self while conducting the most rigorous possible political inquiry, to abandon the "I" as one proposes a renovation of one's culture, and to make the ego's abdication central to that renovation— these gestures would probably seem contradictory, even self-defeating to the majority of Woolf's readers, since argument and social analysis are rhetorical occasions that in our culture are generally assumed to require the first person. In her efforts to alter the shape of the argumentative essay itself, Woolf returns constantly in her diary entries of the 1930s to her desire for inclusion of material that she has collected but not recast as her own. And apparatus of some sort naturally occurs to her as part of the solution to a technical problem with extensive political ramifications: how to construct a book that can accommodate, address, and change the world beyond her words. In the essays of *The Pargiters* and the notes to *Three Guineas*, she finds a form that will simultaneously command and disperse authority, that will convey polemical history and social analysis while letting the author's voice be only one among many.

Never has Woolf cast a wider net at the outset of composition. "I have entirely remodelled my 'Essay,'" she writes on 2 November 1932:

> Its to be an Essay-Novel, called the Pargiters—& its to take in everything, sex, education, life &c; & come, with the most powerful & agile leaps, like a chamois across precipices from 1880 to here & now. . . . Everything is running of its own accord into the stream, as with Orlando. (VW, *Diary*, 4:129)

A few weeks later she comments again on the affiliation between *Orlando* and her new, all-encompassing chronicle: "In truth The Pargiters is first cousin to Orlando, though the cousin in the flesh: Orlando taught me the trick of it" (VW, *Diary*, 4:133). Woolf's biography taught her the "trick" of including vast amounts of historical material within the province of a single book. But she gives the even more extensive historical selections of *The Pargiters* greater weight, embodying them in their circumstantial "flesh" by preserving a number of quotations in their own words and by a more careful, more restrained presentation of historical events. She enumerates her sources and illustrates assertions that would have been cavalierly tossed off in *Orlando*. Although *Orlando* and *The Pargiters* are ideologically affiliated, the enormous structural differences between the two books signal Woolf's searching, revisionary consideration of the form her work must take in this different decade.[19]

When Woolf extends the boundaries of her "Essay-Novel" to "everything" and likens her narrative to a chamois leaping across precipices, she expresses her intention to write a book whose landscape has not been brought absolutely under the author's control. She formerly moved in a fictional world of her own design; she braces herself now for an alarming exploration of rugged territory that she had no part in making. Her name for this perilous terrain is "fact":

> What has happened of course is that after abstaining from the novel of fact all these years—since 1919—& N[ight]. & D[ay]. indeed, I find myself infinitely delighting in facts for a change, & in possession of quantities beyond counting: though I feel now & then the tug to vision, but resist it. This is the true line, I am sure, after The Waves—The Pargiters—this is what leads naturally on to the next stage—the essay-novel. (VW, *Diary*, 4:129)

Her buoyant tone indicates the thrill of her new project, but the rough surface beyond the shaping power of "vision" will not always be so easily negotiated. We have already watched Bernard slip from his contemplative pinnacle into mundanity: "Lord, how unutterably disgusting life is! What dirty tricks it plays us, one moment free; the next, this. Here we are among the breadcrumbs and the stained napkins again. . . . Disorder, sordidity and corruption surround us" (*Waves*, 292). His fall at the end of *The Waves* aptly introduces the emphasis Woolf places for the rest of her career on contingencies, on the material surroundings that frame even the most exalted spirit, on all that refuses to be shaped by the ego: on facts.

Woolf's deliberate wanderings beyond the self-created boundaries of her fiction expose her to new dangers during the long, rambling process of constructing *The Pargiters*.[20] The structural consequence of her decisions to allow the flood of external reality into her book and to leave this sampling from the larger world comparatively untransformed by her imagination, untranslated into her voice, quickly becomes clear to her as she works on her draft. *The Pargiters*, aiming "at immense breadth & immense intensity . . . should include satire, comedy, poetry, narrative, & what form is to hold them all together? Should I bring in a play, letters, poems?" (VW, *Diary*, 4:152). A year and a half after she has decided on "leaving out the interchapters—compacting them in the text," she still maintains that her wide-ranging work has taught her to gather disparate pieces together by assembling a generically composite book: "The lesson of Here & Now"—the work's title remains as restless as its shape—"is that one can use all kinds of 'forms' in one book. Therefore the next might be poem, reality, comedy, play: narrative; psychology, all in one" (VW, *Diary*, 4:146, 238). In *A Room of One's Own*, Woolf's day at the British Museum left her with a notebook filled with jottings, sketches, quotations, and disconnected ideas. The sequel to *Room* duplicates the fruitful and frightening illogic of that notebook on a larger scale. Woolf grows increasingly aware of the burden of compassing her unwieldy text. Eight months after she has begun writing, she ruefully reassures herself: "[Y]es: the proportion is right; though I at the top . . . suffer an intensity of anguish ineffable . . . holding the thing—all the things—the innumerable things—together" (VW, *Diary*, 4:162). The repeated phrases themselves expand, forcing the sentence into its appropriately awkward shape.

Her untidy innovation stands most openly on display in the essays that frame *The Pargiters*. In fact, so extensive, so various are these essays that run beside the fictional episodes describing the Pargiters' lives, and so regularly do those fictional episodes openly anticipate or repeat points made in the essays, that, as was the case with the material surrounding and included in Joyce's work, the distinction between frame and framed text grows difficult to sustain. Fiction and gloss alternate in roughly equal proportion, and these categories do not remain segregated. Woolf often immediately follows a point with an illustrative scene; she obviously manipulates her characters with an eye toward their status as examples. The entire draft bespeaks her overriding concern with her audience, and her willingness to weave that concern into the fabric of the work itself.

Even though Woolf begins drafting her "Novel-Essay" some twenty months after she addressed the Society for Women's Service, she preserves the comforting premise that she lectures to a friendly gathering of working women. This fiction breaks the novel's frame. Characters cannot completely fill the space on every page; *The Pargiters* is not their book. They compete for center stage with the author, whose primary task has shifted from constructing a self-sufficient fiction to assuring herself that her audience fully understands the points her characters dramatize. Woolf is capable of treating her imaginary creations with open disregard for the minutiae of their lives.[21] "In considering the life of the Pargiters," she writes in her second essay,

> it is well from time to time to ask ourselves, What convictions lay beneath them? If we shut our eyes to the detail—how Crosby came in with the tea cake; how Eleanor took off her gloves and blew into her fingers; and so on—we shall find certain principles underlying that particular scene and controlling it, so that it [is] not a succession of unrelated events. (*P*, 30)[22]

Capturing Mrs. Ramsay's essence had meant, for Lily Briscoe, being so close to her subject that "had you found a crumpled glove in the corner of a sofa, you would have known it, from its twisted finger, hers indisputably."[23] Now Eleanor's way with her glove evokes no reverent attention from Woolf. But the author's cool distance from the habits and trappings of the characters in this later book is offset by the relationship she establishes with her imagined audience—a relationship characterized by an extraordinary degree of intimacy. Interrupting the daily lives of her hypothetical family in order that she may sharpen our historical understanding, Woolf assumes the unprecedented role of guide through her fiction. She even professes to grant us the privilege of looking over her shoulder at a work in progress: "I am going to read you chapters from an unpublished novel which I am in process of writing, called 'The Pargiters'" (*P*, 9). That Woolf, who composed in absolute secrecy, employs as a narrative device the fiction that she quotes publicly from an unfinished draft demonstrates how profoundly her ambitions for this new work differ from those she held for any of her preceding novels.

In addition to welcoming her audience into *The Pargiters*, Woolf's interchapters also make room for other books. The number of specific sources cited has increased considerably since *A Room of One's Own*. These references both diminish and heighten the significance of her fictional offering. Individual Pargiters never attain the stature of Clarissa Dalloway or Mrs. Ramsay, and yet Woolf's commentary insists that her exemplary figures from "one of those typical English families" possess a substantiality that characters in any mere novel lack (*P*, 9). This family rests securely on a foundation constructed not by an author meditating in isolation but by an expansive collection of society's observers. The word "fact" returns, connoting the alien nature of her supporting texts, just as it stands in Woolf's journal for the history that her new book incorporates. It guarantees that these other writers are strangers. Their words exist independently from Woolf's composition; their observations cannot be colored by Woolf's subjectivity:

> This novel, "The Pargiters," moreover is not a novel of vision, but a novel of fact. It is based upon some scores—I might boldly say thousands—of old memoirs. There is scarcely a statement in it that cannot be [*traced to some biography, or*] verified, if anybody should wish so to misuse their time. I hope that I am not making an empty boast if I say that there is not a statement in it that cannot be verified. (*P*, 9)

*The Pargiters* contains no innocent, half-apologetic narrator making a first trip to the library. Supporting each assertion of this text are Woolf's scrapbooks, filled, as Brenda Silver has shown in some detail, with a rich harvest from an astonishingly wide field of printed sources.[24] In *The Pargiters*, and even more openly in *Three Guineas*, Woolf emphatically broadcasts the extent of her research, the hours spent in libraries and over newspapers, the care with which she has pursued her exfoliating topic.

At the same time, however, the bold tone of her assertion, the audacious invitation to "verify" whatever we wish, only partly conceals the anxiety, evidenced too in *A Room of One's Own*, with which Woolf enters the lists of polemical writing that is based on historical research. Although she maintains at the outset of *The Pargiters* that "it would be far easier to write history" than fiction, claiming that the fictional "method of telling the truth seems to me so elementary, and so clumsy," she balances this claim later in the book with the apposite sketch of a young woman who lacks the confidence to immerse herself in facts as her father defines them: "For a week or so, Kitty [*herself*] had [*dreamt*] cherished a dream of becoming a learned woman, an historian herself. But then she remembered her fathers irony—[*how no woman*] [*about having*] about [*the*] 'sharing the inability of your sex to grasp historical truth'" (*P*, 9, 103).

Dr. Malone's discouraging voice echoes throughout each of Woolf's books that directly address historical matters. He dampens his daughter's spirits from the draft of *The Pargiters* to the completed *Years*. We hear his like-minded colleagues often in *A Room of One's Own*. He reappears in a dozen forms in the text and notes to *Three Guineas*. Giles and Old Oliver retain a full measure of his skepticism about women's powers of understanding, though no man or woman in *Between the Acts* manages to practice comfortably the tidy historical meditation that sustains Kitty's father. All who will examine *The Pargiters* for points at which the text may be verified or disproved speak through Dr. Malone. He and Woolf will never agree on what constitutes historical study. His endlessly detailed project—a "monumental work" recording the "careers of every man who had ever been at Katharines in the course of five hundred years"—turns his attention away from the broad expanses of the world and of the past (*P*, 93). He progresses in circles of decreasing circumference toward an utterly limited goal, lamenting the fact that his daughter will not join him in "deciphering, transcribing; & helping him in those minute researches which were the delight of his life," though he disparages her ability to comprehend minutiae (*P*, 93). His strictly accurate work unfolds as neatly as the busy undergraduate's in *A Room of One's Own*. His province is the quiet study, not the pinnacles of differently defined and deployed fact on which Woolf risks everything.

And his completed history, were we ever to settle into its formidable shallows, would doubtless carry a scrupulously arranged series of notes across the bottom of each page—dry records of his industry. Woolf, too, retains numerous tokens of her research; she wants the attention of Dr. Malone even as she scorns his constricted approach to his subject. But the overall effect of her apparatus is to expand rather than defend the borders of her books. The interruptions, corrections, asides, and additions with which she augments *The Pargiters* and its related sequels testify to Woolf's headlong pursuit of unfamiliar material. Her historical surveys hurl her into a wide domain. *The Pargiters* grows beyond control (and the notes to *Three Guineas* turn frequently into short essays) because Woolf's record of her explorations cannot be confined to the small type and terse style decreed by historians, whose first concern is the symmetry of their systems. The "torrent of fact" that fills *The Pargiters* almost immediately after Woolf commences writing sweeps aside all thoughts of mastering her subject. She can scarcely hold her draft in check: "Such a wealth of things seen present themselves that I cant choose even—hence 60,000 words all about one paragraph. What I must do is to keep control" (VW, *Diary*, 4:133). But the danger proves delightful. Dr. Malone's stifled daughter, Katherine Hilbery, dreams of living a carefree life on the Yorkshire moors; Virginia Woolf dances with her subject into outrageous territory: "Anyhow, what care I for my goose feather bed?" she writes after she has reminded herself of the need for control. "I'm off to join the raggle taggle gipsies oh!" (VW, *Diary*, 4:133). Facts have spirited her away, leaving her no chance to object that she is not properly prepared, that she has responsibilities at home, that her friends and family will try to recall her from her wild companions.

At first, life with the gypsies seems blissfully free. Words come to the author so effortlessly that her only difficulty is constructing a form quickly enough to contain them, and those words encompass more than she ever dreamed possible: "[M]y thoughts turn with excitement to The Pargiters, for I long to feel my sails blow out, & to be careering with Elvira, Maggie & the rest over the whole of human life" (VW, *Diary*, 4:134). But she soon worries that "it was only that spurious passion" of didacticism that made her "rattle away before Christmas" (VW, *Diary*, 4:145). She tries to reassure herself that her studied denial of lyricism and inner life is not misguided: "Looming up behind the P.s I can just see the shape of pure poetry beckoning me. But the P.s is a delightful solid possession to be enjoyed tomorrow. How bad I shall find it" (VW, *Diary*, 4:145). Woolf's protracted and extraordinarily difficult labor over the "one book" that comprises *The Years* and *Three Guineas* derives largely from her determined confrontation with the world's "wealth of things," all pressing insistently on her psychic boundaries and on the form of her fiction. And it is not until *Three Guineas*, in the notes and in the deliberately broken form of the text, that Woolf discovers what is for her a satisfactory structural solution to the problems posed by the world's interruptions of the visionary's reveries.[25] The essay exemplifies the open book that she began to write when she turned from Bernard to an audience of working women, from the meditative "I" to facts: the disheveled, unredeemed band waiting outside her door.

It is a book that Woolf can write only when she has fully dismantled the division suggested by the subtitle with which she marks the hybrid nature of *The Pargiters—A Novel-Essay* (P, 5)—only when she has gained the confidence, the conviction necessary to confront directly the dishonesties surrounding what her culture accepts as evidence or proof of authority. The dichotomy between fact and fiction around which Woolf had conceived of her different labor during the 1930s, already unsettled in *A Room of One's Own*, fully collapses under her continuing scrutiny during her years of work on *The Pargiters* and the novel and the essay that are its siblings.[26] As her startling transfiguration of facts into gypsies suggests, the very category called *fact*—that most dependable guide to conclusions, that most reliable source of understanding, that foundation on which we might together agree to build a more humane society—ultimately proves no less elusive of capture than did character: the "fin passing far out" that lured her on in her earlier fiction (VW, *Diary*, 3:113). In the text and notes of *Three Guineas* we see particular truths and Truth itself evade all attempts at control. And we see Woolf rejoicing, with less ambivalence than at any other point in her career, at the formal and political consequences of this confusion, this instability, this unruliness. Facts, tired of being servants to Dr. Malone and soldiers for the patriarchy, slip away to the fields and woods—becoming vagrants declaring allegiance to nobody, no state, no program. Woolf catches some of them in her book, placing them most often in her "Notes and References," but even there they will not stay still.

One of Woolf's first titles for *Three Guineas* was "The Open Door." Others—"A Knock on the Door," "Answers to Correspondents," and "Letter to an Englishman"—similarly imply active engagement with the surrounding world. Her journal reflects her desire that this book be cast as a response, the motivation for its writing clearly displayed, instead of being presented merely as a product of its author's imagination or yet another self-assured political answer from another confident analyst surveying the world in 1938. She might "pretend its all the articles editors have asked me to write during the past few years—on all sorts of subjects. Shd. women smoke. Short skirts. War—&c. This wd give me the right to wander: also put me in the position of the one asked. And excuse the method: while giving continuity. And there might be a preface saying this" (VW, *Diary*, 4:361). Or perhaps she should resist her impulse to wander too far by conjuring up a single correspondent, an "Englishman . . . because after all separate letters break continuity" (VW, *Diary*, 5:18). Both ideas partially shield Woolf from claiming sole responsibility for her forceful political views. More important, however, these explanatory fictions locate the rationale for the book's form in its audience rather than its author. An editor demands articles; a man asks for a letter: *Three Guineas* is the answer. The fiction of correspondence with which Woolf gathers the pieces of *Three Guineas* together is analogous to the framing device of the lecture that contains *A Room of One's Own* and *The Pargiters*. In each case Woolf evades the constrictions associated with printed texts, preferring to offer an actual or ostensible transcript of a public or private event.[27] She also discovers, in all three texts, structural devices by which she may assert her opinion that the single voice, the ego alone, cannot effectively address a culture's problems and that any such attempt is finally not merely fruitless but immoral, an echo of the dictator's unmodulated, unopposed decree.

But though she casts *Three Guineas* in a form that offers greater potential for intimacy than does a speech, Woolf instantly dispels any illusions that this letter will reach its recipient easily: "Three years is a long time to leave a letter unanswered, and your letter has been lying without an answer even longer than that" (*TG*, 3). Her first, quietly absurd sentence (especially comical when we consider Woolf's copious correspondence) leads us to wonder if her response will even find its recipient still interested in an answer. Drawing "a sketch of the person to whom the letter is addressed" promises at least some degree of proximity, since "without someone warm and breathing on the other side of the page, letters are worthless" (*TG*, 3). Ironically, the recipient's more vivid presence establishes only the first of many apparently insurmountable obstacles to communication: the differences between men's and women's education leave the sexes worlds apart, even when they come from the same "educated class"; "speak with the same accent; use knives and forks in the same way; expect maids to cook dinner and wash up after dinner; and can talk during dinner without much difficulty about politics and people; war and peace; barbarism and civilization" (*TG*, 4). Refusing repose in this civilized, circumscribed room where all problems are reduced to the same small conversational scale, Woolf also revises the optimistic figure that described her ambition for *The Pargiters*—a chamois skillfully negotiating the crevasses that open suddenly beneath her feet. Five years later, between her and her distant addressee lies "a precipice, a gulf so deeply cut . . . that for three years and more I have been sitting on my side of it wondering whether it is any use to try to speak across it" (*TG*, 4). In *A Room of One's Own* and *The Pargiters*, Woolf ostensibly speaks only to women, though both books betray her awareness that her actual audience includes both sexes.[28] When she predicates *Three Guineas* on the contradictory fiction—that she writes a letter directly to an Englishman—she loses her voice.[29]

Since Woolf feels incapable of crossing this divide alone, she welcomes assistance from another woman: "Let us then ask someone else—it is Mary Kingsley—to speak for us" (*TG*, 4). Following Kingsley's outraged comparison of her education with her brother's comes the first reference to the endnotes for *Three Guineas*. Woolf's culturally produced silence brings her to an impasse that paradoxically generates a crucial component of her book's structure. Even before the subject exerts its own strenuous demands on the book's shape, the absence of consensus between author and audience calls for Woolf to deploy a variety of communicative strategies within a single frame. After only a page and a half, this "letter" has included a few sentences that sound as though they were actually taken from a letter, a rudimentary biographical sketch, the beginnings of an argument conducted in an essayist's style, and a quotation with note number. The superscript [1] demonstrates Woolf's sensitivity to her audience. The note is a quiet gesture that will perhaps calm the prosperous, sensible middle-aged man who will almost certainly be dismayed by the anger Kingsley's revelation introduces.[30] It suggests that this hybrid epistolary piece will incorporate the results of research and will acknowledge others' contributions, however revolutionary they may be, in a reassuringly traditional manner. Like the selected quotations in *A Room of One's Own*, this contribution from Mary Kingsley immediately proclaims that Woolf does not speak alone. Like the notes to *Room*, Woolf's reference inspires confidence in her diligence, her attention to detail.

But if the number brings the text closer to tradition, the text of the note does the opposite. The structural differences between *Three Guineas* and *A Room of One's Own* emerge dramatically when we turn to this first note—a 500-word essay on women and education. The handful of glosses to *Room* remains subordinate to the text; Kingsley's *Life* initiates a discussion that leads us down a meandering path through other women's related testimony. As we finish this anthology of opinions, which expands to fill more than one page, we are likely to glance at the substantial number of pages remaining in *Three Guineas*—a glance that forces us to acknowledge the extent of Woolf's blandly titled "Notes and References." The heading usually describes an easily surveyed part of a book, primarily significant as a record of the steps by which an author prepared herself to offer her own opinions in her own words. Instead, we discover what amounts to an unexpected final chapter, a complex assembly so extensive that it calls for separate study even as it defies the possibility of sequential reading.[31] When any apparatus grows beyond a certain point (the limit changes with every reader and each reading), it requires us to treat it as something other than mere "notes and references"— to read it in sections longer than the individual notes and to offer possible explanations for its length. Many readers will explore the last part of *Three Guineas* not when the superscripted numbers mandate but when they reach a place in the text where interruption becomes convenient or desirable: at the end of a chapter, at the conclusion of a line of argument, or when they have finished the rest of the book. They may simply continue reading notes at once, leaving the letter to an Englishman in abeyance until they tire of jumping from one fragment to the next.

Woolf carefully calculated her apparatus's effects on her reader. Five days after the publication of *Three Guineas*, she wrote to Ethel Smyth that the endnotes were appended but not subordinate:

> Notes. Yes that was a question; bottom of the page or end. I decided for end, thinking people might read them, the most meaty part of the book, separately. Gibbon wished to do this, but gave way to friends. Pippa Strachey writes that she's glad they are at the end. I had a mass more and still have. Yes—very hard work that was. (VW, *Letters*, 6:235)

Woolf's letter declares that the book's final section contains the substance of her labor, the underpinnings of her case against the patriarchy, the keys to her ideas about women's history. "It was such a grind, collecting and compressing the notes," she writes to Shena, Lady Simon, a few days later, "slipping in facts and keeping up enough of a dance to lead the reader on so that I couldn't keep my eye on the general aspect, and was much in the dark as to the whole" (VW, *Letters*, 6:239). An entry in her journal, written just after Leonard had read a draft of *Three Guineas*, further implies how heavily she relied on the notes to carry her argument: "I didnt get so much praise from L. as I hoped. He had to swallow the notes at a gulp though" (VW, *Letters*, 5:133). Woolf insists that her argument stands on the notes, though she realizes that we will probably first direct our attention to the more obvious appeals she makes for our notice and assent in the body of her text—the intermittent fiction that we are reading a letter, the rhetorical flourishes, the brief dramatic interludes, the frequent shifts in voice.

Woolf's pivotal notes, immediately violating our expectations, teach us that much in England's past and present has never been measured or recorded and that the apparatus can be a more speculative literary form than most annotators would have us believe. After locating the source for her quotation from Mary Kingsley, Woolf admits that she cannot continue precise citation: "It is difficult to get exact figures of the sums spent on the education of educated men's daughters. About £20 or £30 presumably covered the entire cost of Mary Kingsley's education (*b*. 1862; *d*. 1900)" (*TG*, 145.1). The parenthetical inclusion of birth and death dates, while underlining the brevity of Kingsley's life, juxtaposes accuracy and imprecision. Woolf's notes repeatedly make this shift from numbers to hypotheses. Where there should be certainty, there are questions and guesses about women's lives and their history. Their portraits exist only in the most tentative colors. But even when facts prove scarce, this initial note swells with women's accounts of obstacles and evidence of men's discrimination. After citing Kingsley's *Life*, Woolf stitches six related references into her discussion, which, in the first of two highly compressed paragraphs, holds together the connected issues of untutored women feeling "the lack of education very keenly" and "the efforts of such uneducated women to conceal their ignorance"; the corresponding association by "educated men" of femininity and simplemindedness; and women's complicity in concealing their meager hoard of learning (*TG*, 145.1).

In this first note's shorter but equally suggestive second paragraph, Woolf considers why "the educated man's daughter in the nineteenth century was even more ignorant of life than of books" (*TG*, 146.1). Keeping middle-class women "confined to a very narrow circle" provided men with sufficient social space for the sexual proof of their manhood, but did not contaminate their carefully protected future wives or allow virtuous women more than a hint of men's destructive pursuit of virility. Discerning victims from the class of supposedly sheltered females understood their part in this sexual charade, a fact Woolf proves by allowing Mary, Countess of Lovelace, to discuss the supposition "that most men were not 'virtuous'" (*TG*, 146.1). "'Virtue' and virility," Woolf concludes in a succinct, provocative formulation, were thus incompatible.

Her compendious note proves, at the beginning of this section of the book, that Woolf has ranged far beyond the restrictions imposed on her forerunners. She will periodically inform us that she lacks proper training for her endeavor; she will use her culturally produced deficiency to buttress her arguments concerning her exile from English culture, and yet this first gloss, with the long procession of notes following, bestows an undeniable authority on Woolf. She has fruitfully engaged in research that would have been largely impossible for or forbidden to her predecessors. She has presented her argument in a form traditionally employed by men: assertions supported by quotations rather than solely by her own passionate rhetoric. She has embodied, in this method of argument through others' voices, her scorn for the solitary ego. Woolf's notes defeat the "I" that, in *A Room of One's Own*, is "honest and logical; as hard as a nut, and polished for centuries by good teaching and good feeding": the masculine "I" that protests "against the equality of the other sex by asserting his own superiority" (*ROO*, 104, 105). Her last gesture in her opening note continues to multiply the citations in this single gloss, directing us to "a well-known passage" in Thackeray where the author discusses how his art suffers under the opposing requirements of virtue and virility.[32]

A note of this length and subtlety, far from establishing certain ground on which we may proceed, makes the landscape of *Three Guineas* even less predictable than it was when we turned from the interrupted letter to the back of the book. Woolf designed the notes to *Three Guineas*, in combination with her text, to complicate her argument. The numbers scattered liberally throughout *Three Guineas* mark fissures in an already discontinuous text. Reading through Woolf's notes with an eye toward their place in the plan of *Three Guineas*, we realize how thin, how much less heterogeneous the book would be without this generous space for additions. Where else, for example, would Woolf place the portrait of a woman who has learned to kill: Sergeant Amalia Bonilla, Republican soldier in the Spanish Civil War (*TG*, 177–78.15)? Woolf quietly presents the description of "the amazon" from a horrified but admiring man's account. She leaves a complex, unresolved emotional aura surrounding this powerful woman who has developed "the fighting instinct" against which *Three Guineas* is written, this fighter for the cause that took her nephew's life. Woolf deplores the war, but she celebrates Sergeant Bonilla's victory over the fiction, so comforting to men as they prosecute their ruinous campaigns, that nature allows brutality only in men, preserving apart the gentler sex. Violence can flower wherever it is nourished; gender offers no unbreachable sanctuary from war. Less ambivalent but just as moving is Octavia Hill's image of the role allotted to pioneers for women's rights:

> "You and I know that it matters little if we have to be the out-of-sight piers driven deep into the marsh, on which the visible ones are carried, that support the bridge. We do not mind if, hereafter, people forget that there are any low down at all; if some have to be used up in trying experiments, before the best way of building the bridge is discovered." (*TG*, 165.35)

This brief biographical resurrection, like the immediately following tribute to the maid's role in "English upper-class life from the earliest times until the year 1914" (*TG*, 165.36), and like the dozens of similar tributes to struggling predecessors, complements and enriches the annotated text while making its own parallel arguments.[33] Woolf finishes her note to maids, for example, with a cutting glance at the limitations of her father's monumental project: "It is much to be regretted that no lives of maids, from which a more fully documented account could be constructed, are to be found in the *Dictionary of National Biography*" (*TG*, 166.36).

The "Notes and References" provide a space for much more direct attacks, whose presence in the text itself would either have shattered the "beautiful clear reasonable ironical prose" (VW, *Diary*, 4:298) in which she cast *Three Guineas*, or have distracted or shocked her readers enough that they would have abandoned the book altogether.[34] Woolf's longest note constitutes a stunning assault on Pauline Christianity. She begins in a tone of measured condescension (familiar in its terms to her and to all the women in her audience): "From internal evidence it seems clear that he was a poet and a prophet, but lacked logical power, and was without . . . psychological training." She shifts easily into sarcasm: "If St. Paul had said openly that he liked the look of women's long hair many of us would have agreed with him, and thought the better of him for saying so." She then breaks into an outraged assessment of Paul's effect on civilization: "[H]e was of the virile or dominant type, so familiar at present in Germany, for whose gratification a subject race or sex is essential. . . . The grip of [chastity's] white if skeleton fingers can be found upon whatever page of history we open from St. Paul to Gertrude Bell" (*TG*, 166 – 68.38).

Other examples, scarcely less vitriolic, demonstrate that Woolf viewed her notes as the appropriate site for her case against Christianity. Unwritten laws, Woolf tells us, "were not laid down by 'God,' who is now very generally held to be a conception of patriarchal origin, valid only for certain races, at certain stages and times" (*TG*, 184-85.42). The Bible has been "dismembered weekly," "doled out on Sundays from the mouths of priests in snatches," its beauty marred by the dispensing church (*TG*, 180.29). The *Report of the Archbishop's Commission on the Ministry of Women* finds that devout women, unlike their male counterparts, are able to listen to sermons without dwelling on the sexuality of the priest: "[T]he natural is more easily made subordinate to the supernatural, the carnal to the spiritual than is the case with men." Following the commission's logic to its absurd conclusion, Woolf declares that "Christian women are more spiritually minded than Christian men — a remarkable, but no doubt adequate reason for excluding them from the priesthood" (*TG*, 161.10).

These accusations take their place in a dazzling annotative assortment. The last section of *Three Guineas* initiates a hundred new beginnings, a dozen different essays. Her notes include a proposal for an equitable, productive system of reviewing books (*TG*, 175–76.10); a meditation on "the various manifestoes and questionnaires issued broadcast during the years 1936–7" (*TG*, 172.1); an account of women's instruction in the arts at the Royal Academy (*TG*, 183–84.39); a facetious suggestion for solving "the hostess's dilemma" of conflict between the sexes ("[i]f those who prefer the society of their own sex at table would signify the fact, the men, say, by wearing a red, the women by wearing a white rosette, while those who prefer the sexes mixed wore parti-coloured buttonholes of red and white blended . . ." [*TG*, 159.4]); a cold-eyed examination of the "playboys and playgirls of the educated class who adopt the working-class cause without sacrificing middle-class capital, or sharing working-class experience" (*TG*, 177.13); an exposure of the insidious "power of the Press to burke discussion of any undesirable subject" by simply remaining silent (*TG*, 162.16); definitions of the phrases "educated man's daughter" (*TG*, 146.2) and "ring-the-bell-and-run-away-man" (*TG*, 176.11); and a qualified condemnation of the public lecture (*TG*, 155.30). My abbreviated list — a selection and an encapsulation — does violence to Woolf's apparatus. If we read the "Notes and References" straight through, we realize that any single note could be omitted without changing the form of the whole, and that the form of the whole absolutely resists summary or outline. The rationale for the notes' order comes from outside, from the text to which they are in turn an attachment, an appendage. The structure of each note is regularly at least as allusive and elliptical, as difficult to comprehend, as that of the chapters of Woolf's essay. The collection of Woolf's glosses has a shape that cannot be fully perceived or diagrammed: that shape is the totality of the apparatus in its irreducible jumble.

Woolf waits until the conclusion of her last chapter of *Three Guineas* to reveal most openly the reasons for her book's studied disorder. To do so at the outset would perhaps relieve us of a measure of confusion, but we would miss much of her point if we avoided the constant struggle to follow her bewildering path through the essay. She represents the political incarnation of certainty in a terrifying image that imposes itself "upon the foreground": a man who is "the quintessence of virility. . . . He is called in German and Italian Führer or Duce; in our own language Tyrant or Dictator" (*TG*, 142). Men and women alike possess the frightening potential to mirror this figure, to lose all sense of the variety characteristic of the world's people, the multiplicity of their attitudes, the complexity of every individual. This Dictator's refusal to perceive difference has left him firmly bound and blinded: "His eyes are glazed; his eyes glare. His body, which is braced in an unnatural position, is tightly cased in a uniform" (*TG*, 142). Woolf tells the recipient of her letter that she and he must always summon the face on the other side of the page as each writes to the other, lest "you in the immensity of your public abstractions forget the private figure, or . . . we in the intensity of our private emotions forget the public world. Both houses will be ruined, the public and the private, the material and the spiritual, for they are inseparably connected" (*TG*, 142–43).

On the level of the text, tyranny manifests itself as any monologic form, any collection of sentences sealed firmly against alternative points of view, any stylistically monotonous work. It is not easy to resist this unity when it appears in guises more beguiling than that of the deadly man in uniform. But whenever Woolf slips into hopeful reverie, dreaming of perfect accord between men and women or an equally homogeneous text, she moves herself and her listeners closer to identification with the enemy—the single voice:

> Even here, even now your letter tempts us to shut our ears to these little facts, these trivial details, to listen not to the bark of the guns and the bray of the gramophones but to the voices of the poets, answering each other, assuring us of a unity that rubs out divisions as if they were chalk marks only; to discuss with you the capacity of the human spirit to overflow boundaries and make unity out of multiplicity. (*TG*, 143)

Her style almost persuades us to follow, particularly since *Three Guineas* by design leaves us starved for hopeful rhetoric cast in uninterrupted phrases. But Woolf reluctantly calls herself back from her vision:

> But that would be to dream—to dream the recurring dream that has haunted the human mind since the beginning of time; the dream of peace, the dream of

freedom. But, with the sound of the guns in our ears you have not asked us to dream. . . . Let us then leave it to the poets to tell us what the dream is; and fix our eyes upon the photograph again: the fact. (*TG*, 143)

Although Woolf frequently expressed similar skepticism in her novels of the 1920s about the ability of individuals to overcome their fundamental isolation, she has never before turned so explicitly away from aesthetic forms of perception—those forms that pronounce economic and political chaos subordinate to the shaping power of the imagination. Even more extraordinary is her unmistakable linking of the tyrant, absolutely contained in his close-fitting uniform, and the perfectly framed, strictly ordered work of art.

It is therefore essential to Woolf's argument that she preserve in the final form of *Three Guineas* the unresolved questions and contradictory conclusions raised by her prolonged scrutiny of her country's past and present. The complexities of her "Notes and References" derive naturally from the variety of material she has gathered and from her refusal to force on it an ideological or a narrative coherence that it does not possess. And yet, however enthusiastically she embraces her theoretical decision to eschew aesthetic order, on a practical level the ramifications of her decision make it virtually impossible to sustain communication with her audience. Central to the rhythm of *Three Guineas* is Woolf's frustrated longing for a point of agreement, of shared perception: a point on which she and those she desires to engage in conversation might begin to talk. Throughout *Three Guineas* Woolf moves from one potential occasion for agreement, one possibly shared position, to another, deliberately leaving her naive persona always disappointed: "But is there no absolute point of view?" she asks after the first few pages of attempted dialogue. "Can we not find somewhere written up in letters of fire or gold. 'This is right. This wrong'?—a moral judgment which we must all, whatever our differences, accept?" (*TG*, 9–10). Beginning an inquiry on this lofty theoretical level, however, produces discord: "[T]he more lives we read, the more speeches we listen to, the more opinions we consult, the greater the confusion becomes" (*TG*, 10).

Perhaps an opposite approach, one based on irreducible, irrefutable data, will generate consensus beyond debate. In her starkest prose Woolf displays a verbal picture of a photograph chosen from Spain's record of its civil war, one of several "pictures of actual facts" (*TG*, 10).[35] For a moment, she feels confident that she knows, with pseudoscientific precision, exactly what occurs in the mind of her fellow viewer:

> Those photographs are not an argument; they are simply a crude statement of fact addressed to the eye. But the eye is connected with the brain; the brain with the nervous system. That system sends its messages in a flash through every past memory and present feeling. When we look at those photographs some fusion takes place within us . . . our sensations are the same. . . . And the same words rise to our lips. (*TG*, 11)

The passage at once parodies any hope of absolute comprehension of another's reaction, suggests (only half in jest) how each of us might struggle to find our way out of our subjective maze, and indicates the enormous obstacles confronting analysis of more complex responses. Both viewers, in spite of their differences, share the sensations of "horror and disgust," but the imperative of political action demands further response. Once each offers his or her "practical suggestions" that might prevent this destruction or explain its cause, we return to the disconcerting variety of opinion that impelled Woolf's reductive experiment with the photograph.

The complexities of what initially seems a simple appeal to the photographic incarnation of fact grow more evident when we leaf through any early edition of *Three Guineas*, noting the five photographs that Woolf includes as complements to her argument—an instance of apparatus that has been excised from our less elaborately produced modern editions (Figures 8–12).[36] By 16 February 1932, already delighting in plans for her incendiary text, "for which I have collected enough powder to blow up St Pauls," she knows that "[i]t is to have 4 pictures" (VW, *Diary*, 4:77). Assembled by Woolf, the sardonic anthropologist, these pictures of proud men absurdly encumbered with the regalia of the military, the Crown, the academy, the court, and the church receive no direct analysis as subjects in Woolf's text. Signifying in every symbolical detail the "many inner and secret chambers that [women] cannot enter" (*TG*, 22), these snapshots remain open to bemused speculation but closed to any woman's exegesis. Although Woolf makes general references to a figurative, "crudely coloured photograph . . . of your world as it appears to us" (*TG*, 18), each of the five images is framed by her silence about its details. The fundamental impenetrability of her trophies from the world of men eloquently expresses the distance Woolf's voice would have to travel before it might be heard by these patriarchs in uniform. Woolf makes her disingenuous assertion early in *Three Guineas* that "[p]hotographs, of course, are not arguments . . . they are simply statements of fact addressed to the eye" (*TG*, 10) in order that she may doubly undercut that assertion. She demonstrates how easily images, set in a polemical context, become part of that polemic (consider the self-satisfied, imbecilic grin of the officer in Figure 8; note the literal horse's ass to the right of the four men in Figure 9; shudder at the adamantine, aged bishop in Figure 12). She shows as well how gnomic are these "statements" of indecipherable fact.

The only photographs that she describes and studies in detail are ones we never see: the week's record of carnage from the Spanish Civil War. In the sole footnote to *Three Guineas*, she adds that her description is "written in the winter of 1936–37," thereby allowing us, if we wish, to search through English newspapers for the pictures of "actual fact" absent from this book. Were we to discover the photographs from which Woolf makes her portraits, however, we would not find the same details; each of us would read the images according to our idiosyncratic, largely unarticulated grammars. We could not even agree on a single interpretation of a shattered house, emptied of virtually every signifying artifact, or of the barest corpse, stripped to its awful minimum of cultural trappings. Of course Woolf studied the eccentricities of individual perception long before writing *Three Guineas*. But now, as the 1930s slouch toward "death; ruin; perhaps the end finally of all order," these aborted chances for communication carry the direst political consequences (VW, *Diary*, 5:177). Photographs,

**Figure 8.** Figure 1 from *Three Guineas*.

present and absent, speak eloquently of missed occasions for exchange; only if
Woolf forced them to signify an artificially delimited point would their message
be darker, more sinister.

A student of the public record during this decade, a reader of newspapers,
a collector of photographs, an assembler of scrapbooks could hardly avoid
becoming increasingly skeptical of even the most apparently disinterested
reporting of events, the most neutral selection of subjects for the camera's
ostensibly unbiased eye. Already in *A Room of One's Own* Woolf had paused,
early in her search for answers, to consider the fact that for the most part men
with essentially similar interests financed, edited, and wrote for English newspapers (*ROO*, 33–34). By 1937 she has assayed conflicting, often obviously
censored, and otherwise biased reports of the massive depression in her own
country and in the world beyond Britain's borders. She has tried to glimpse
truth behind the veils of justification thrown up by Hitler and Stalin as each
purges his party and begins the murderous task of ridding his country of real
and imagined enemies. She has heard Italy broadcast its campaign in Ethiopia,
complete with mustard gas and bombing of civilians, as "protection" for its citizens living in Eritrea and Somalia and "revenge" for a defeat of its colonialist
army in 1896.[37] She has followed from a baffling distance the first terrible year

**Figure 9.** Figure 2 from *Three Guineas*.

**Figure 10.** Figure 3 from *Three Guineas*.

**Figure 11.** Figure 4 from *Three Guineas*.

and a half of the Spanish civil war, including, in the spring of 1937, the contradictory reports surrounding the bombing of Guérnica.

These are, of course, only a few of the largest, most famous wildernesses of the 1930s, where facts prove practically impossible to grasp. Each day's papers contain their own thickets — advertisements, brief articles, editorials, letters to the editor — where Woolf finds even the most basic information tangled in the snarls of frequently undeclared agendas that invariably advance the interests of those in power. Particularly in its apparatus, *Three Guineas* displays her unpleasant discoveries, demonstrating why one must "read at least three different papers, compare at least three different versions of the same fact" (*TG*, 95), and why, even then, much will remain unascertainable. Such jaded reading habits further confuse the division between fact and fiction that has preoccupied Woolf ever since she began working with material belonging to the public record:

> [T]he literature of fact and the literature of opinion . . . are not pure fact or pure opinion, but adulterated fact and adulterated opinion. . . . In other words you have to strip each statement of its money motive, of its power motive, of its vanity motive, let alone of all the other motives which, as an educated man's daughter, are familiar to you, before you make up your mind. (*TG*, 96)

Woolf's atypical apparatus relentlessly refuses to grant us the security of repose in a false purity of style or of data. Although she does work on the simplest level to earn the confidence of the fact checkers, the Professor Malones who will chase after sources, she will not allow that confidence itself to escape

**Figure 12.** Figure 5 from *Three Guineas.*

critique. For every note that remains demurely confined to citing a quoted text, there are a handful that serve to explode the reassuring stability of the readily quantifiable. Woolf takes particular delight in demonstrating how the most basic numerical facts, when followed farther than almanacs allow, lead us down circuitous, surprising, sometimes disturbing and hilarious paths. Suppose, for example, that we bothered to survey something other than salaries: "The number of animals killed in England for sport during the past century must be beyond computation. 1,212 head of game is given as the average for a day's shooting at Chatsworth in 1909 (*Men, Women and Things*, by the Duke of Portland, p. 251)" (*TG*, 146.3). The single figure, grotesquely exceeding expectations, conjures up a country where violence on an extraordinary scale is routine and pervasive. The title of the duke's memoir, in conjunction with the absence of women from sporting history, leads Woolf to venture afield at the conclusion of her note: "It is highly probable that there was held to be some connection between sport and unchastity in women in the nineteenth century" (*TG*, 146.3).

Elsewhere Woolf cites numbers that will startle her audience into speculation or force them to face striking examples of inequity. Responding to the facile suggestion, made by a former headmaster of Eton, that women should attack the problem of education "by some original genius on quite different lines," Woolf comments dryly that "[i]t scarcely needs genius or originality to see that 'the lines,' in the first place, must be cheaper." She juxtaposes a casual gift of £2,000 from a single benefactor to one of Eton's scholarship funds with another figure: "The entire sum spent at Cheltenham College for Girls in 1854 upon salaries and visiting teachers was £1,300; 'and the accounts in December showed a deficit of £400'" (*TG*, 154–55.29). Or she compares a man's pursuit of the "stars and ribbons" that are "his chief means of advertising intellect" with a woman's interest in "powder and paint," with which she advertises "her chief professional asset: beauty." Quoting from a source that sets the cost for a knighthood at £75,000, Woolf notes that "[t]he sum paid for a Knighthood in 1901 would seem to provide a very tolerable dress allowance" (*TG*, 150–51.17).

Each of these additions to Woolf's text strengthens her arguments concerning inequality at the same time that it confronts us with another interruption, a new set of numbers, a novel angle from which to survey a shifting subject. Most important, Woolf's apparatus exposes the dangers latent in all annotation. Annotators, seeking concision and authority, often reduce their material to measurable quantities and neatly contained detail. Scholars are apt to lose themselves in the production of lists, catalogues, and meticulous descriptions, failing to keep sight of the larger significance of their subject. In her notes Woolf occasionally, illustratively joins the company of trivializing apparatus makers, becoming an earnest, pedantic researcher with a scheme that will guarantee proof. To ascertain the relative economic power of the sexes, "[a] beginning might be made . . . by chalking on a large-scale map of England property owned by men, red; by women, blue. Then the number of sheep and cattle consumed by each sex must be compared; the hogsheads of wine and beer; the barrels of tobacco; after which we must examine carefully their physical exercises; domestic employments; facilities for sexual intercourse, etc." (*TG*, 149.15). In the same spirit, she adopts her own parodic implement of sociometric research—"any ironmonger will provide us with a foot-rule"—offering, in the process, dramatic proof that, compared with men's colleges, women's colleges are "unbelievably and shamefully poor" (*TG*, 30):

> The men's scholarship list at Cambridge printed in *The Times* of December 20th, 1937, measures roughly thirty-one inches; the women's scholarship list at Cambridge measures roughly five inches. There are, however, seventeen colleges for men and the list here measured includes only eleven. The thirty-one inches must therefore be increased. There are only two colleges for women; both are here measured. (*TG*, 154.27)

By the end of this painstaking report, the various forms of the verb "measure," repeated so often and applied so literally, become absurdly inadequate to the subject. The annotator, bent on precision and preoccupied with the act of measuring, works at a remove from the annotated subject—from the woman, for example, who cannot afford an education.

Woolf's most direct statement of the dangers inherent in the gloss as it is traditionally employed comes in a note attacking the division of labor along sexual lines, whereby women "undertake the care of the household and the family," leaving men free for pure speculation. Her association of certain forms of annotation and political evil is startling:

> [T]here can be no doubt that we owe to this segregation the immense elaboration of modern instruments and methods of war; the astonishing complexities of theology; the vast deposit of notes at the bottom of Greek, Latin and even English texts; the innumerable carvings, chasings and unnecessary ornamentations of our common furniture and crockery; the myriad distinctions of *Debrett* and *Burke*; and all those meaningless but highly ingenious turnings and twistings into which the intellect ties itself when rid of "the cares of the household and the family." The emphasis which both priests and dictators place upon the necessity for two worlds is enough to prove that it is essential to their domination. (*TG*, 180–81.31)

Woolf's fascist, it appears, not only stands at unblinking attention. He also slips surreptitiously into universities; his endless activity has formed England's social hierarchy and produced its fabric of theology. In addition to refining military apparatus, he has designed sugar bowls, dining-room tables, and drawing-room chairs. And he has worked tirelessly in silent libraries and cloistered studies, composing note after note, forcing his way, line by tiny line, up from the bottom of the page. His annotations, unlike those to *Three Guineas*, stay scrupulously focused on the subject to which they are attached. They expand the size of the text without widening its scope. They follow editorial logic instead of leading us off on tangents. Woolf's notes reflect her contrary desire to stray beyond every conceivable framework constructed in her book.

When Woolf wrote about women and fiction in 1929, she encouraged her audience to find "a room with a lock on the door" and to cultivate silence and darkness in order to encourage "[s]ome collaboration . . . in the mind between the woman and the man before the act of creation can be accomplished" (*ROO*, 109, 108). Seven years later, she insists with even greater vehemence that men and women (or the masculine and feminine qualities in a single mind) cannot create alone. But she no longer sends her readers searching for an asylum where they may encounter their opposite. At the end of 1936, just before she begins composing *Three Guineas*, Woolf publishes in the *Daily Worker* "Why Art To-Day Follows Politics." She argues there that "the practice of art, far from making the artist out of touch with his kind, rather increases his sensibility."[38] The scene of artistic conception she draws in this essay bears no resemblance to the hushed room of 1929, where "there must be freedom and there must be peace. Not a wheel must grate, not a light glimmer. The curtains must be close drawn" (*ROO*, 108). Woolf's revised studio is "far from being a cloistered spot where [the artist] can contemplate his model or his apple in peace. It is besieged by voices, all disturbing, some for one reason, some for another."[39] And although she cannot welcome this siege as an ideal prelude to creation, she urges the artist "to take part in politics; he must form himself into societies like the Artists' International Association."[40]

Woolf never completely abandons her vision of the artist at work in a sanctuary. In May 1940, speaking before the Workers' Educational Association in Brighton (she later titled this talk "The Leaning Tower"), she returns to her mystical image of unconscious discovery realized in perfect silence: the writer's "under-mind works at top speed while his upper-mind drowses. Then, after a pause the veil lifts; and there is the thing—the thing he wants to write about—simplified, composed."[41] The tower in which this luxurious meditation once occurred, however, leans daily at a greater angle as the walls crumble. Again, Woolf cannot help longing for peace, and yet her essay applauds the frightening social changes that have forced her to emphasize wandering far afield rather than finding a room of one's own. Those rooms, after all, mostly belong to the men—fascists, busy theologians, annotators, inventors of weapons and genealogical trees—whose war now threatens the world. Woolf concludes her address by proudly urging her audience of workers to "become critics because in future we are not going to leave writing to be done for us by a small class of well-to-do young men who have only a pinch, a thimbleful of experience to give us. We are going to add our own experience, to make our own contribution."[42]

Women belong with workers in this irreverent, creative company, though Woolf deliberately keeps her artistic development and the advances of her sex out of her speech, scrupulously resisting an easy equation of class and gender in the history of oppression. Political changes in the late 1920s and the 1930s obviously affected Woolf herself, but she prefers to focus our attention on the circle of younger writers who came to maturity in the decade preceding the Second World War. She can extend only an ambivalent welcome to the new aesthetic aims for an uncertain world, recognizing, as she does, that she cannot return to her earlier work. She knows from her struggles during the 1930s with what difficulty she constructs books in these cacophonous surroundings. But her spirits lift as she exhorts her liberated audience to "trespass at once" on any territory ruled out of bounds.[43] In *A Room of One's Own* she had dutifully returned from the turf to the path on the grounds of Oxbridge, obeying an officious beadle's anxious gestures. Now she refuses to admit any policing of her domain: "Literature is no one's private ground; literature is common ground. It is not cut up into nations; there are no wars there. Let us trespass freely and fearlessly and find our own way for ourselves."[44]

Woolf's glosses bear comparison with Joyce's apparatus in the *Wake* insofar as the glosses for the "Lessons" represent children and readers beyond the author's control. Joyce welcomes as artistically generative moments all failures to command meaning, though he exerts an unparalleled amount of energy constructing his highly artificial arena in which anything goes. Throughout the 1930s Woolf tries to avoid designs that call attention to themselves; she eschews flamboyant displays of artistry. Her pursuit and promotion of open-ended forms express her related conviction that political, aesthetic, or personal domination of a subject satisfies a destructive instead of a creative impulse. Appropriate forms should feel to the reader as though they are unfolding on that reader's terms—unfolding as they might if she or he were turning the pages of a scrapbook. *The Pargiters* and *Three Guineas* are to seem "Works in

Progress." Both Woolf and Joyce also comb assiduously through their culture for pieces that will fit into their work, though Woolf, unlike Joyce, does not break and recombine her fragmentary selections at the level of the word. She wants her sources to be immediately visible; she wants to give over a substantial measure of her work to the voices of others, without first forcing those voices to speak in her language. She wants us to inquire with her into England's past and present, not to marvel at the ingenious creation of a perpetual-motion device.

The impulse to trespass is closely tied to a desire to leave the book behind in others' hands. Woolf, having wandered away with the gypsies, refuses to assert dominion over what the world might consider her own literary property. At the end of *Three Guineas*, Woolf vanishes just as surely as she did at the beginning of *A Room of One's Own*. She apologizes "for writing at all," disavowing any impulse to express herself: "The blame for that however rests upon you, for this letter would never have been written had you not asked for an answer to your own" (*TG*, 144). It would be easy to dismiss Woolf's disappearance as a failure of nerve, an unwillingness to take responsibility for her work; but to do so, we would have to ignore her consistent, repeated struggles against the claims of self-sufficiency made by the unfettered "I." Nor should we overlook the fact that *Three Guineas* has a second ending—one that eloquently demonstrates what she gains by her escape from self-designed aesthetic rooms, her trespasses on unfamiliar realms beyond her governance. In Woolf's final glosss, Coleridge espouses a society that leaves the individual free; Whitman exposes oppression's effect on the entire community: "as if it were not indispensable to my own rights that others possess the same." And George Sand, "a half-forgotten novelist" for whom Woolf has cleared a place on the stage, offers an uncompromising corrective to the self's sense of separation: "Toutes les existences sont solidaires les unes des autres, et tout être humain qui présenterait la sienne isolément, sans la rattacher à celle de ses semblables, n'offrirait qu'une énigme à débrouiller" [All lives are interdependent, and any human who would hold up his own life in isolation, without binding that life together with one of his fellows, would present us with nothing but an enigma to untangle] (*TG*, 188.49). The solitude that so often encloses Woolf's fictional characters has taken on a disturbing political significance in this altered decade. She has not changed her estimation of that solitude's depth—her sense of isolation grows more heartfelt and unalleviated with each year of her life—but she feels compelled to break its hold on the forms of her books. Sand cautions us that people gather meaning, that their lives have consequence, only insofar as they participate in "la vie générale" (*TG*, 188.49). *Three Guineas*, its closing words written by another author in another language, asserts its importance at every point where its author makes a space on her page for voices and gleanings from the world beyond the ego's intimate range.

Joyce equivocally greets the adulteration of his "Lessons" by footnotes and marginalia. Woolf, politically committed to inviting others into her books, also proves ambivalent as she retreats to the peripheries of her texts. Her annotations collect signatures from the numerous shadowy members of the "Outsiders' Society" (*TG*, 106); her "Notes and References" point to a community, an echoing chamber of voices other than her own. But the form she has selected forces Woolf to ponder her dissolution, an act that fills her with both terror and elation. She is frequently silent in that chamber crowded with presences from her reading. She wonders if anyone else hears the voices she has summoned and if she might easily slip from the vociferous circle altogether. Her journal and the history of English literature that she left unfinished at her death provide important last glosses to the ramifications of the experimental project that begins with *A Room of One's Own*. Lying behind her public venture is a closely related pair of private anxieties. As she renounces the egoism implicit in her single voice, her powerful, unmistakable style, her impulse toward synthesis, she relinquishes control over a vehicle for asserting and defining her self. And in her final years she incessantly broods that she risks her identity, opening the frames of her books and turning toward the public, only to see that public desert her entirely.

Woolf's fears that she, her books, and her audience may cease to be—the entire fragile triad sinking under personal and cultural pressures hostile to coherence on any level—haunt Joyce and Pound as well. These three writers, born within three years of one another in the 1880s, confront in their fifties different but comparable versions of vanishing, and all signal and pursue that confrontation in part through the glosses that frame their newly uncertain labors. For each author finds new cause for doubts during the 1930s—doubts that Woolf articulates with particularly painful lucidity and intensity after the publication of *Three Guineas*. And although the concerns of Joyce and Pound are of course in large part differently motivated and take different inflections, pausing over selected musings from Woolf's last years offers thematic links with our examination of Joyce's apparatus and of his doubts about the reception of his "Work in Progress." Reading Woolf also proves a surprisingly apt preparation for facing Pound's writings of the 1930s. Woolf and Pound, who could hardly speak in more dissimilar voices, from more distant points of view, for more different purposes, are finally more skeptical than Joyce that anything they have loved or cultivated will survive the second fall of European culture. Both bring us more immediately, more vividly to the blankness, the zero, that lurks as a shadow in Joyce's *Wake*.

Woolf worried about her readers from the moment of her first publication, but her diary entries from the 1930s disclose in the starkest possible terms how acutely she covets an audience.[45] A writer who has lost her readers loses her words; they vanish without effect, leaving no record of their passing. And Woolf, deprived of language, cannot assemble her personality. In May 1933, momentarily flushed with the excitement of *The Pargiters*, she embraces her essential profession: "I thought, driving through Richmond last night, something very profound about the synthesis of my being: how only writing composes it: how nothing makes a whole unless I am writing" (VW, *Diary*, 4:161). Her construction of herself through language grows more arduous as the decade, filled with the deaths of family and friends—the most intimate audience of all—ends in war, with all Europe mired in "a perfunctory slaughter, like taking a jar in one hand, a hammer in the other. . . . And all the blood has been let out of common life" (VW, *Diary*, 5:235). In these maddened times Woolf cannot follow her words into the world. "Complete silence surrounds that book," she writes on 2 August 1940 after the publication of *Roger Fry*. "It might have sailed into the blue & been lost. 'One of our books did not return' as the BBC puts it" (VW, *Diary*, 5:308). The broadcaster's masking of death with a quiet euphemism perfectly conveys what alarms Woolf even more than reviewers' hostility: a preoccupied populace that simply ignores her biography because her writing offers them nothing substantial. Waiting to hear that the French government has fallen, thinking of the suicide that she and Leonard would choose were the Germans to invade England, Woolf revealingly laments a loss that has already occurred:

> Another reflection: I dont want to go to bed at midday: this refers to the garage.[46] What we dread (its no exaggeration) is the news that the French Govt. have left Paris. A kind of growl behind the cuckoo & t'other birds: a furnace behind the sky. It struck me that one curious feeling is, that the writing "I," has vanished. No audience. No echo. Thats part of one's death. (VW, *Diary*, 5:293)[47]

The meditation moves from surreal figures to clipped, stark statements of psychological fact, from public event to private casualty.

A novel's reverberations consist in part of an audience's specific comments on the work. More generally consequential is the sense of tradition shared by artist and public, the collective knowledge of rules applicable to and understood by every aspect of English society. These cultural guides operate even when a writer chooses to place herself in opposition to their premises. But in the summer of 1940 Woolf laments that "even the 'tradition' has become transparent" (VW, *Diary*, 5:304). She may encourage a sense of the author's transparency within the preserve of her books—turning her pages over to other authors—but she never openly seeks the insubstantiality caused by her readers' silence. When she delivers a book to the public, she assails a world that she hopes exists, calling on it for a reaction that confirms her presence: "[P]erhaps the walls, if violently beaten against, will finally contain me" (VW, *Diary*, 5:304). In her image of this interchange, she remains ghostly, unseen even by herself until another's eyes and voice give her shape: "I feel tonight still veiled," she muses on the evening preceding the publication of *Roger Fry*. "The veil will be lifted tomorrow, when my book comes out. Thats what may be painful: may be cordial." Whether she feels pain or pleasure is almost incidental. More significant than the opinions of gathered commentators will be Woolf's hoped-for return of identity: "And then I may feel once more round me the wall I've missed—or vacancy? or chill?" (VW, *Diary*, 5:304). Her last questions uncover her certain knowledge that these "walls"—themselves mere figures of speech—furnish scant shelter. The figure, by leaving what might lie within those walls unnamed, exhibits the abyss it is designed to cover: "This little pitter patter of ideas is my whiff of shot in the cause of freedom—so I tell myself, thus bolstering up a figment—a phantom: recovering that sense of something pressing from outside which consolidates the mist, the non-existent" (VW, *Diary*, 5:235).

But in the fall of 1940, as she revises *Between the Acts* for publication, Woolf discovers an alternative if temporary solution to the coincident problems of her nonexistence, her work's invisibility, and her certainty that her audience is only an apparition she has willed into being. In the first chapter of her history of English literature and society, tentatively called "Reading at Random,"[48] she tells the story of an age before individuality, before the vexed and vexing "I," when the artist had no need to search for readers or to expand the book's frame with apparatus. Titled "Anon" in her drafts, this chapter records the passing of that mythical time and the fall into selfhood which is also a fall into publication.

Her uncompleted survey commences with the fanciful portrait of a figure who vanished with the advent of the printed book.[49] Peering behind Caxton and his press, Woolf glimpses her elusive predecessor, Anon, who is hardly more than a voice speaking for a simple audience.[50] Language dutifully serves this straightforward singer as the simplest of vehicles for perfectly uncomplicated narratives: "The story is told with a childs implicit belief. It has a childs love of particularity. Everything is stated. The beauty is in the statement, not in the suggestion. . . . The world is seen without comment" ("Anon," 384).[51] In these legends of queens and enchantresses, knights and kings, language seems transparent because the artist stays quietly subordinate to the material, refusing to gloss what he presents, avoiding any singular point of view. His listeners similarly make the most basic demand: that he give "voice to the old stories" ("Anon," 383). Anon's words would have evaporated as they were spoken, so little importance did their singer attribute to his syllables, had not Caxton "fixed the voice of Anon for ever" in the killing jar that is the printed page ("Anon," 384).

Caxton's specimen, though less lively than Anon's ephemeral song, suggests to Woolf the possibility of a book every bit as open, as hospitable to the world as *Finnegans Wake*. But her ideal pages, rather than being filled to overflowing with scattered samples from the compound languages of men and women, would be absolutely transparent to their surroundings, thus making irrelevant the boundaries between artist and audience, text and gloss, book and world. In his "Lessons," Joyce dismantles the same categories by creating an elaborately divided chapter and then subverting those divisions. Woolf dreams of doing away with the book altogether.[52] Her antibook—by definition impossible to produce—would mime the artistic conditions of a time before print. Malory, though caught by Caxton, nevertheless eludes the book's deadly stasis by avoiding the trap of style: "Of the writer the scholars can find something. But Malory is not distinct from his book. The voice is still the voice of Anon" ("Anon," 385). A writer, cursed with an identifiable voice, must watch as the compositor locks his every line into galleys, setting his name and narrative permanently into print. But immediately after they are spoken, Anon's words belong to everyone. They are alive, buoyant, unattached:

Thus the singer had his audience, but the audience was so little interested in his name that he never thought to give it. The audience was itself the singer; "Terly, terlow" they sang; and "By, by lullay" filling in the pauses, helping out with a chorus. Every body shared in the emotion of Anons song, and supplied the story. ... Anon ... is the common voice singing out of doors, He has no house. He lives a roaming life crossing the fields, mounting the hills, lying under the hawthorn to listen to the nightingale. ("Anon," 382)

In Woolf's hypothetical model, the words themselves dissolve once they have initiated an exchange between their speaker and his environment. They easily accommodate involved readers, not by sending them off to other literatures and languages, not by demanding that they engage in the author's strenuous verbal play, but by calling from them common refrains and recollections of ancient, half-remembered tales. Joyce's strategy of inclusion, partly motivated by a comparable impetus to recover a buried past, remains purely linguistic: each word in *Finnegans Wake* imports as much as it can possibly carry from history and the world's diverse semantic territories. If the book succeeds, these charged words become the shifting foundations for our individually constructed (and continually reconstructed) *Wake*s—attached loosely to Joyce's book as is the apparatus to II.2. Virtually indistinguishable from his environment, Anon welcomes those around him into his songs without necessarily requiring that their contributions be rendered into language at all. Rather than drafting annotations for "Rawmeash, quoshe with her girlic teangue," we may join in a universal chorus: "Terly, terlow."

Woolf fancies that creation during this time before print was equally relaxed. Anon's plots of war, love, and betrayal never seem composed. They repeat the fundamental stories we have told ourselves since childhood. These resonant, viscerally appealing songs fall outside the province of modernism's premeditated designs. Readers still seek to find and invent the meanings of *Finnegans Wake*. Joyce constantly reminded his coterie that "Work in Progress" exacted fantastic physical and intellectual pains from the artist at every stage of its composition. His admirers further spread the message that no one else would dare such a costly undertaking and that the project's importance was commensurate with the struggle involved. Woolf's own novels, even though their difficulty was not so openly advertised, proved as demanding of their author and scarcely less so of her audience. Anon's tale gives way naturally to the nightingale's song.

In Woolf's mythology, Anon's "wandering voice" yields to Spenser's less mellifluous "voice of a man practising an art, asking for recognition, and bitterly conscious of his relation [to] the world, or the worlds scorn" ("Anon," 391). Woolf begins "Reading at Random" with a fable of artistic freedom—or, more to the point, she imagines the freedom from being an artist in 1940—but she does not long allow herself the pleasure of her dream. She draws instead a less comforting sketch of the individual author, compassed by a capricious audience, exposed to a world that is distracting and distracted. Appearance in print challenges the writer to choose his words cautiously because the book endures as the testament of his consciousness, and because it fixes what was a momentary utterance irrevocably "against a background of the past" ("Anon," 385). Woolf's published poet closely resembles Joyce's beleaguered artist in the *Wake*, cruelly uncovered for the public's merciless inspection or its no less damaging indifference:

> The poet is no longer a nameless wandering voice, but attached to his audience. tethered to one spot and played upon by outside influences. Some are visible to himself only; others show themselves only when time has past. As the book goes out into a larger, a more varied audience these influences become more and more complex. According to its wealth, its poverty, its education, its ignorance, the public demands what satisfies its own need—poetry, history, instruction, a story to make them forget their own drab lives. The thing that the writer has to say becomes increasingly cumbered. ("Anon," 390)

Fear of restraint dominates the passage. "Attached," "tethered," and "played upon," the poet cannot range freely through the land, straying among distinct social classes, combining those classes' different words. He has lost "the outsiders privilege to mock the solemn, to comment upon the established" ("Anon," 383). The subject of poetry grows correspondingly confined. Once the artist consents to the fixity of print, he precipitates the claims of a progressively more demanding audience and hears within himself insistent voices commenting on his work at the moment of creation. He has bowed to these and a hundred other circumstantial limitations. And his books provide a painfully objective public record of the changes the world outside has worked on the artist's vision. With the death of Anon, art makes its appearance framed by contingencies.

"Anon" describes both a personal and a historical period; those contingencies are private as well as public. Woolf aches for the time when "self consciousness had not yet raised its mirror" ("Anon," 384). She wistfully points to "the world beneath our consciousness; the anonymous world to which we can still return" ("Anon," 385). But although we can perhaps "forget something that we have learnt when we read the plays to which no one has troubled to set a name," the artist cannot long evade the thoughtful self and its surroundings ("Anon," 398). Countless entries in her journal show Woolf compelling her mind to stay on track after it has been "jangled" by irrelevance (VW, *Diary*, 5:205); over and over, she records the agonizing variety of the world's interruptions. A characteristic entry demonstrates how confused internal and external distractions become when, invigorated and utterly perceptive, Woolf is trying to write:

> And I wish I need never read about myself, or think about myself, anyhow till its done,[53] but look firmly at my object & think only of expressing it. Oh what a grind it is embodying all these ideas, & having perpetually to expose my mind, opened & intensified as it is by the heat of creation to the blasts of the outer world. If I didn't feel so much, how easy it would be to go on— (VW, *Diary*, 4:289)

These wishes illuminate Woolf's yearning for anonymity. They belong beside her vow, formally recorded on 19 December 1932, to "be free & entire &

absolute & mistress of my life by Oct. 1st 1933. Nobody shall come here on their terms; or hale me off to them on theirs" (VW, *Diary*, 4:133). "I will no longer be fettered by any artificial tie," she adds twelve days later, but will learn "[t]o suppress one self & run freely out in joy, or laughter with impersonal joys & laughters" (VW, *Diary*, 4:135). The first-person pronoun evolves unobtrusively into the indefinite "one." She expresses her dream of running free, far from internal and external obligations, in the same journal entry in which she celebrates joining the raggle taggle gypsies as she opens *The Pargiters* to "externality." Following her declaration of independence from herself at the end of 1932, she attempts to effect her escape in large part by relaxing her hold on the novel's form, by making experiments with apparatus that continue as she revises the form of the essay as well. "As a woman I have no country," she declares in *Three Guineas*: this statement is equally a lament and a celebration (*TG*, 109). In a frame of mind that grew increasingly familiar to her during the 1930s, she might have substituted "book" for "country" with no less ambivalence. Woolf's glosses to her greatest polemic represent her deeply equivocal attempt to redeem the condition of writing in a world of cumbrances, to surmount the "blasts of the outer world" by making them part of texts that she sometimes scarcely calls her own.

Woolf's longing to stay impersonal and paradoxically fortified, freed for creation with her consciousness stilled, reverberates elsewhere in modernist aesthetics. Yeats strives to ignore the accidents of individuality, since "if we become interested in ourselves, in our own lives, we pass out of the vision."[54] Eliot proposes his considered evasion of personality.[55] Joyce gradually ascends to the lofty remove of "dramatic" form until he has carried *Finnegans Wake* so far from a single speaker that readers cannot devise an image of the artist from his style. Pound extends an invitation, made first to Tiresias and Elpenor at the "ell-square pitkin," for hundreds of different voices to speak in the space cleared by his long poem. Woolf discloses her own desire for unattainable serenity most clearly with her final description of Anon in "Reading at Random":

> Anonymity was a great possession. It gave the early writing an impersonality, a generality. . . . It allowed us to know nothing of the writer: and so to concentrate upon his song. Anon had great privileges. He was not responsible. He was not self conscious. He is not self conscious. He can borrow. He can repeat. He can say what every one feels. No one tries to stamp his own name, to discover his own experience, in his work. He keeps at a distance from the present moment. ("Anon," 397)

The shift from past to present tense halfway through the passage—"He was not self conscious. He is not self conscious"—while likely to occur in a working draft, suggests how earnestly Woolf seeks the liberty that graces her "Anon." Her definition of anonymity embraces an idiosyncratic meaning: Anon not only hides effectively from a prying audience but also knows how to avoid his own inquisitive mind. In his creative moments he is anonymous to himself. Achieving this asylum from the "I" means accepting a type of death.

The ideal represented by Anon gives appropriately ambiguous shape to

Woolf's fundamental ambivalence about her possession of identity and about her culture's increasingly ruthless manner of asserting its values. An obscured self can be an artist's necessity, a politically admirable ideal, and a terrifying consequence of the silence of readers. Writing can build essential walls to contain an otherwise scattered ego, and those walls can suddenly appear to be the result of the ego's natural bent toward tyranny—at which point writing (including the printed words of others) can be employed to breach the walls it has created. A text can condemn its author to the immobility of print, and it can provide comforting shelter from direct exposure to the public. Apparatus, contracting around kernels of fact, can silence opponents; it can also liberate the text from the limitations of the single position, thereby inaugurating a conversation. The voices of strangers can shatter the design of a sentence or ruin a morning set aside for composition. They can even signal the onset of physical and emotional collapse. Sometimes they can be blessed—glosses for an open book.

# 4

# EZRA POUND
# FINAL PRIMERS

*And how far does anybodies single mind or work matter? Ought we*
*all to be engaged in altering the structure of society?*
                              Virginia Woolf, *Diary*, 2 October 1935

Ezra Pound, determined that his art receive undivided attention, that his
readers not wander from his poem to its margins and then to a space entirely off
the page, repeatedly pronounces against all forms of annotation. As early as
1911, in the second part of "I Gather the Limbs of Osiris," he insists that "the
artist seeks out the luminous detail and presents it. He does not comment" (*SP*,
23).[1] He turns unwillingly in that essay from quotation to his task of exposition:
"As an artist I dislike writing prose. Writing prose is an art, but it is not my art"
(*SP*, 23). Twenty-two years later he promises in the introduction to his *Active
Anthology* (1933) to surround his selections with minimal frames: "The proportion between discussion and the exhibits the discusser dares show his reader
is possibly a good, and probably a necessary, test of his purpose. In a matter of
degree, I am for say 80 per cent exhibit and 20 per cent yatter" (*SP*, 396). When
it comes to his Cantos, he responds angrily to James Laughlin's suggestion that
readers might welcome a preface: "Cantos 52/71 can NOT have a preface in the
book. Cover gives ample space for blurb. The new set is not incomprehensible.
. . . Read 'em before you go off half-cocked."[2] Pound wearily tells Herbert
Creekmore, one in a series of readers asking for the poem's key, to recognize
that art takes precedence over its interpretations: "As to the *form* of *The Cantos*:

All I can say or pray is: *wait* till it's there. I mean wait till I get 'em written and then if it don't show, I will start exegesis" (EP, *Letters*, 323). Only as a last resort, only after the form inheres in the completed work, might a gloss be reluctantly added to make that form "show."[3]

But as Pound proclaims his poetry's freedom from contamination by apparatus, he labors with extraordinary energy on a project of annotation whose scope and detail at times seem to render the glosses of Joyce and Woolf modest by comparison. In this chapter, I assess those elaborate glosses: Pound's "Guides" and *ABC*s; his letters telling correspondents what to read and whom to publish, praise, or slander; his essays that, no matter what their ostensible subject, quickly bring us around to lessons we should already know or should have learned from a previous essay. He always contends that these miscellaneous, vehement directives are peripheral to his artistic labor and to the artistic, economic, historical, or political material on which they comment. Although often dismissively presented by Pound as hastily assembled primers to difficult topics, they constitute an immense body of writing and represent a sustained endeavor that addresses, more clearly than any other collection of writings I know, the complex disjunctions between artist and audience that differently trouble each of the modernists in my study. Throughout his life, with augmented intensity and diminishing clarity from the late 1920s into the 1930s and the early 1940s, Pound works to create and educate an audience so that it will be fit to comprehend the art and politics of the twentieth century and the periods of particular infamy or achievement that preceded the modern era. But, musing in his notes for the *ABC of Reading*, he wryly considers the foreordained failure of an artist who turns pedagogue:

> If he go down from "creation," that is the production of his specific work, aimed at the timeless, he either arrives in agora unseasonably soon, and passes for a lunatic, or he arrives after the battle, even though he be *almost* in time. I mean that by the time [he] . . . has felt he MUST do something about it, i.e. turn man of action, some other "artist," some specialist in action, leader of men, etc, has done the real work, and our scribe arrives in time to get a tardy credit mark from an imaginary high school board of the future.[4]

Driven by the world's corruptions to forsake poetry, Pound perfectly describes his difficulties in knowing how and when to enter the agora and his displacement by those "specialists in action" whose lives have long been devoted to effecting political change. For Pound in the 1930s, those who reshape societies deserve to be called "artists." The "scribe" merely records the results and is subject to the indignity of achieving nothing more than belated recognition by the most mundane of educational institutions. His documentary efforts will be remembered, if at all, by schools, not by governments or grateful citizens whose lives he has improved.

Pound experiences so little success in the classroom in large part because he cannot respect his students sufficiently to teach them, and because he cannot bring himself to embrace the potential reality of a larger community acting in concert with him and thereby roping him irretrievably into the demos, the everyday, the popularly accepted. Michael North explores in detail the ideological binds that lie behind Pound's attempts to preserve his isolation while he earnestly steps onto the reformer's platform. Like any number of disenchanted intellectuals in our century, Pound damns liberal individualism and the disorderly ragbag that is contemporary culture and blesses something more hierarchical, more expressive of an aesthetic and a political sense of measure, adamant all the while that he and a few worthy others be allowed unabridged personal freedom from totalitarian forms of government. And as he tries to imagine a suitably empowered state that will somehow make room for a newly autonomous, newly significant individual, as he idolizes Mussolini because Il Duce represents "both romantic individualism and impersonal order," he turns almost wholly to teaching his impossibly divided subject.[5] Glosses—themselves perfectly divided in their allegiances, equally hospitable to autocrat and anarchist, to regulatory and vagrant impulses in author and reader alike—provide him with an appropriately equivocal pedagogical tool. But Pound deplores this traitorous form's tendency to enact the impossibly estranged political impulses that he is bent on resolving. Ironically, his knowledge that every moment of instruction, every invocation of political and aesthetic coherence, is simultaneously a sign of a divided world and a broken text further provokes Pound into authoritarian positions.

As Pound composes the texts with which I am primarily concerned in this chapter—"How to Read" (1929), the *ABC*s of economics (1933) and reading (1934), the "totalitarian treatise" *Guide to Kulchur* (1938), and the radio broadcasts (1941–1943)—he fills the space around his Cantos with preparatory lessons. The Cantos composed and published during the 1930s are themselves part of his enormous struggle to teach a few basic truths. I briefly survey three volumes of his long poem—*Eleven New Cantos* (1934), *The Fifth Decad of Cantos* (1937), and *Cantos LII–LXXI* (1940)—not to discover isolated points where the prose might be used to explain an obscurity in the poetry but to demonstrate that these Cantos are best understood as a component of the project carried forward in the prose. The juxtaposition of poetry and guides should help to explain why virtually every reader is uncomfortable with this portion of the Cantos. The poetry of the 1930s, difficult to redeem as emotionally compelling or conceptually profound work, constitutes Pound's experiment in banishing his lyrical, meditative self from his art. It is Pound the committed instructor who clips phrases from a vast array of sources to produce a work that seems almost entirely compounded of quotations.

We have observed a number of vanishing acts in this study. Eliot gives Jessie Weston and Sir James George Frazer the task of elucidating *The Waste Land*. Joyce slips to one side as his Exagminators take the stage; he promiscuously gathers others' words for his open *Wake*. Woolf turns *Three Guineas* over to a company of outspoken women and men; she ends her career dreaming of "Anon." In every case, these contrived disappearances depend somehow on the screen provided by the apparatus—a form that allows the author to break the book's rules, to speak with a different voice, or to invite others to speak in this alternately delineated space. But this vanishing point simultaneously becomes a point of utmost visibility. The author's manipulations—effecting radical changes in the reader's experience of the annotated page—signal the strong hand that frames the work we study. Pound's commentary teaches us how we are to weigh particular passages of his difficult prose and poetry and what we must think of society at large; it also tells us that he serves only as an assembler of others' thought. We come once more to the site where modernism actively disavows agency.[6]

Pound practices this energetic renunciation of the "I" in his various roles as anthologist, translator, and journal editor whose selections promote the "new learning," the "new civilization."[7] Quitting the poet's egotistical vocation, he plays the humbler part of the "CONTEMPORARY book-keeper" who maintains the culture's accounts, keeping a "loose-leaf system" of up-to-date ideas in print (*ABCR*, 38; "HR," 18).[8] He moves into the laboratory, choosing "a few hundred or thousand slides" for comparison, or presenting the literary, economic, and political equivalents of "the elements and primary machines in the opening chapters of a text book on physics" (*ABCR*, 22; *SP*, 276). His "IDEOGRAMMIC METHOD OR THE METHOD OF SCIENCE," Pound's designated master key to his poetic and critical procedure, similarly enjoins readers to examine and juxtapose "particular specimens" before they attend to the collator's own conclusions (*ABCR*, 26; *PE*, 121).[9] This method, which Pound promotes heavily from the late 1920s onward, follows logically from his objection to commentary in any of its guises. Since an ideogrammatically produced text bears few traces of its author, the method also partly masks emotional turmoil and confused ideas. First Pound and then his critics routinely deploy the concept of the ideogram when the form of his poetry and prose seems likely to disintegrate.[10]

I do not intend to attempt a resolution of disorder in Pound's work or to gather the pieces under the rubric of a method suggested by Pound. His fragmented associative forms are in large part extraordinarily powerful because of, rather than in spite of, their brokeness. I endeavor to consider the demonstrably scattered prose and poetry of the 1930s on the level of the broken texts themselves. This cluster of Pound's writing, when studied before its theoretical content has been extracted and set in lucid (and differently disturbing) sentences, profoundly frustrates the most basic attempts at interpretation. Tim Redman, in his fine study *Ezra Pound and Italian Fascism*, notes of Pound's economic writings that "the difficulties clear up when his articles are read as a group."[11] It is to some extent true that a clear-headed, patient reader can distill from Pound's prose and poetry coherent critiques, comprehensible proposals, and more or less workable programs; but I much incline to North's emphasis on Pound's failure to make sense of politics and economics.[12] For North, the fissures in Pound's thought and in his texts mirror and betray significant fissures in twentieth-century attempts to resolve conflicts surrounding the polis in our time—conflicts latent in what can be variously designated "rationalism, material progress, liberal democracy."[13] The disorder characterizing so many of Pound's prose explanations is profoundly expressive of his ambivalence toward assuming his self-appointed role as pedagogue, as maker of apparatus, as social critic rather than poet whose work would more comfortably, more elegantly inhabit a just state. In that better state, each poem of Pound's would implicitly testify, as would all other products of the transfigured culture, to an already perfected sociopolitical design. Instead, he writes primers, striving always to be more explicit, to spell each precept carefully, and to repeat each lesson over and over. As we survey the often baffling material Pound writes in lieu of art, we should keep in mind that his primers grow more impenetrable in exact relation to his constant assurances that his comments on the arts and civilization are absolutely simple and direct. Those assurances themselves, particularly in the radio broadcasts, ironically contribute greatly to the opacity of Pound's lessons. All his glosses have behind them his unmistakable voice repeating what it knows, while the very fact of that repetition signifies, even before we look more closely at the content of each pronouncement, his conviction of the parallel failures of the artist, the pedagogue, and his culture to establish a foundation for "Ecbatan, / City of patterned streets" (*C*, 5/17). An opening sentence from one of his radio broadcasts stands as a fitting epigraph for Pound's potentially endless work: "I have to go on tryin' to tell you" (*RS*, 140).

Before examining Pound's instructional texts of the 1930s in detail, we should consider the status he accords his prose — this subordinate, substantial body of his writing. Too often it has been used simply as an intermittently applicable gloss to *The Cantos*, as verification of the poet's insight or pathology, or as a junkyard or gold mine from which critics may salvage quotations or uncover explanations.[14] Pound himself, beginning early in his career, urges us to look first at his poetry.[15] Prose is the vehicle for his efforts at education, but he invariably maintains that his most valuable contributions to culture are poetic. Every word of instruction that he writes, therefore, is in an important sense a maddening waste of the poet's time, a violation of aesthetic principles never justified by the comparative silence that follows each primer's publication. He stipulates that the *Dial* prize of 1928 must be based solely "on Cantos or on my verse as a whole. . . . It wd. be stupid to make the award on prose-basis as my prose is mostly stop-gap; attempts to deal with transient states of Murkin imbecility or ignorance" (EP, *Letters*, 213).[16] His misgiving lest recognition by the *Dial* for "services to literature" be too loosely understood reveals an annotator's abiding concern for the proportions of his oeuvre, the ratio of art to yatter. Once they have performed their menial service, the directives should vanish: "A lot of my prose scribbling is mostly: 'There digge!' Plus belief that criticism shd. consume itself and disappear" (EP, *Letters*, 261).[17] "There is MORE in and on two pages of poetry," he shouts in his *Guide to Kulchur*, "than in or on ten pages of any prose save the few books that rise above classification as anything save exceptions. . . . Man gittin' Kulchur had better try poetry first" (*GK*, 121). The deceptively named *Guide to Kulchur* contains relatively little of value: "[P]rose is NOT education but the outer courts of the same. Beyond its doors are the mysteries" (*GK*, 144-45). With these last laconic tips, the prose *Guide* abruptly turns into an *ignis fatuus*: the hapless reader finds himself or herself following a misleading beacon through inhospitable lands.

In a properly civilized age, a *Guide to Kulchur* would be superfluous; people would naturally "try poetry." The anger that boils beneath almost every sentence of Pound's prose derives in large part from his conviction that circumstances—the barbarousness of our century, the stupidity of readers, the wickedness of those who hold power—have forced him from Parnassus into the classroom.[18] Gertrude Stein's quip that Pound was "a village explainer, excellent if you were a village, but if you were not, not" captures his irrepressible impulse to instruct but misses the style of that instruction: he tends to raze the village before beginning his explanations.[19] Halfway through a brief introduction to Jean Cocteau's writings (1935), Pound breaks off, struck by the infuriating realization that he can depend on his readers' utter misunderstanding:

> I am fed *u p* (up) with young idiots who can't see that history does not exist without economics; who do not know that Bithinian mortgages at 12 per cent are a matter of history; who think that any man can understand history in the book, without economics, or that "l'histoire morale" can get on without economics any more than any other department of history, or that literature keeps its head in a bag. (*SP*, 435)

This sudden squall comes simply from the meditative act of writing rather than from any specific provocation in the preceding paragraph, any special injustice that mars Cocteau's life. By this point in Pound's career, similar outbursts interrupt virtually every page of his prose, regardless of the subject.[20] The characteristic leap from general observation to unexplained "Bithinian mortgages," a leap that almost no one in his audience will make, ensures that Pound's assessment of his readers' inadequacy will be confirmed and ironically warns away those prospective students not already discouraged by being labeled "young idiots."[21]

In spite of his demonstrated unfitness for the dirty job of teaching, however, Pound follows his complaint with a grim statement of mission. "A writer's awareness to relations is vastly other than an impulse to write treatises," he laments. The garbled syntax of this sentence—"awareness to," "vastly other than"—suggests that his thoughts are elsewhere and that revision of this lowly form is out of the question. The breathless, repetitive series of succeeding phrases likewise bespeaks a hasty first draft:

> I write treatises because I am a species of pachyderm, I am a porter of teak, I am a beast of burden because the circumjacent literati are weaklings, they are piffling idiots that can't get on with the job, they can not even write text books. It is necessary to start in the grammar schools, and I can type for eight hours a day.
>
> It is necessary for me to dig the ore, melt it, smelt it, to cut the wood and the stone, because I am surrounded by ten thousand nincompoops and nothing fit to call an American civilisation or a British civilisation; but that is no reason for Cocteau's writing treatises. (*SP*, 435)

Here is a writer who undertakes any job but writing, a man who merely types when he should be creating, who buries himself under his drab burden because no one else possesses the strength required to save civilization. Cocteau owes his liberty to an admirer's sacrifice. Pound's poetry gives way to his textbooks.

Pound's famous gifts as reformer and promoter of the arts—"a poet and an impresario," Wyndham Lewis called him—involved the poet in linguistically contradictory projects long before he championed Cocteau.[22] Reflecting in the early 1940s on a past filled with a remarkable variety of poetry and criticism, he tries to divide his work along simple lines:

> The problem of the word cannot be exhausted in a single lifetime. It consists of at least two parts:
> (1) the word of literary art which presents, defines, suggests the visual image: the word which must rise afresh in each work of art and come down with renewed light;
> (2) the legal or scientific word which must, at the outset, be defined with the greatest possible precision, and never change its meaning. (*SP*, 321)

Language, of course, will not stay thus carefully pigeonholed, nor will these two categories accommodate a random sampling of Pound's poetry and prose. But the aspirations Pound reveals in this passage help explain his frequent frustration with the scattered writing he actually produces. Ideally, words are made of either air and fire or earth. Criticism, so distinct from literary pursuits that it is closer kin to the rigorous disciplines of law and science, should form an unchanging foundation, a solid base on which artists can construct their glorious, ethereal, eternally vital creations.[23]

We shall see Pound's prose filled with habitual gestures toward stability and permanence, but the exigencies of each troubled year demand immediate intervention. "I must get out of the big stick habit," he confesses to Margaret Anderson in 1917, "and begin to put my prose stuff into some sort of possibly permanent form" (EP, *Letters*, 122). He describes his big sticks with a fine display of self-conscious humor that fades in later years as permanence grows more elusive and his failure to effect change becomes increasingly obvious: "I.e. articles which can be reduced to 'Joyce is a writer, GODDAMN your eyes, Joyce is a writer, I tell you Joyce etc. etc.' Lewis can paint, Gaudier knows a stone from a milk-pudding. WIPE your feet!!!!!!" (EP, *Letters*, 122–23). Pound's parody clarifies the fundamental differences between his prose apparatus and the glosses I have examined thus far. He delivers his running commentary with even less faith in his audience and with greater hopes for demonstrable success than either Joyce or Woolf. He does not invent verbal games that exploit and celebrate his readers' tendency to miss the point. Nor does he offer even tentative welcome to the untidy formal consequences that attend his lifelong urge to shape the perceptions and opinions of those readers. When his simple message does not change the world, he repeats it, simplified even further, at greater volume. As the world's deafness persists, he grows more condescending and dictatorial.

Joyce's letters occasionally disclose comparable anger at his public's ignorance, though when most upset he tends to play the part of a gloomy comedian, laughing ruefully at his solitude. But when he portrays the rowdy schoolroom in *Finnegans Wake*, or when he circuitously dispenses his own lessons to the public, he does so in full awareness that even willful misunderstandings perpetuate the rule of language, the disorderly empire of fiction, as they frustrate the lethal simplicities that belong most prominently in his time to political discourse. Woolf, in contrast, shares Pound's horror at the political consequences of impeded communication. She earnestly desires that her annotated *Three Guineas* and her publicly oriented work of the 1930s may at least provoke reflection by addressing, in a revisionary but essentially approachable fashion, issues of general importance in the splintered world beyond the bounds of art. Unlike Pound, however, Woolf takes care to approach that world with rhetorical subtlety: "[I]f I say what I mean in 3 Guineas I must expect considerable hostility. Yet I so slaver & silver my tongue that its sharpness takes some time to be felt" (VW, *Diary*, 5:84). Her outrage sometimes spills unchecked into the pages of her journal, but the same private receptacle also contains her recognition of anger's moral complexity and the need for strategic manipulation of that powerful emotion. Pondering an insulting exchange with E. M. Forster, she realizes how every shock furthers her progress with *Three Guineas*: "[T]hese flares up are very good for my book: for they simmer & become transparent: & I see how I can transmute them into beautiful clear reasonable ironical prose. God damn Morgan. . . . And dear old Morgan comes to tea today, & then sits with Bessy who's had cataract" (VW, *Diary*, 4:298).[24] She is, after all, surrounded by and often emotionally bound to "the enemy," not railing at him from another continent.

Pound, too, is capable of querying his bitter intrusions, and when he does so he uncovers the fears that lie at the heart of his entire enterprise of annotation. In an extraordinary letter of 9 November 1927 to Glenn Hughes, editor of his translation of the *Ta Hio*,[25] Pound proposes to retract the preface he had prepared — a preface that thrust his irritated social analysis into an otherwise measured volume of Confucius' wisdom:

> On reading over my translation of *Ta Hio*, it strikes me that the acrid and querulous preface I had sketched is a bloody impertinence and that any attempt to force local application, talk about need of present America, etc., bloody bureaucracy, etc. etc., would be a damned impertinence. I mean tacking my bloomink preface onto the work itself. (EP, *Letters*, 213)

For a moment, Pound has grown tired of his own voice uttering its familiar, dreary case ("etc. etc.") against contemporary society. Caught in the typically vexed relationship of annotator to annotated text, uneasy at grafting his unnecessary words onto a philosophical stock that has lived for centuries without him, he dismisses himself from his edition, suggesting that Hughes substitute a spare alternative introduction: "In this brochure (or chapbook) Mr. Pound does for the first of the Confucian classics what he did, in *Cathay*, for Rihaku" (EP, *Letters*, 214). This chastened prospectus allows Confucius room to stand unencumbered by his translator's sordid accusations against contemporary enemies. It lets the principles of the *Ta Hio* float free of the "local applications" that increasingly preoccupy Pound at the end of the 1920s. Because his violently maintained convictions threaten to distort every sentence he writes, he is of all people the least fit to gloss the temperate collection of teachings he has translated. "If there be a knife of resentment in the heart or enduring rancor," the *Ta Hio* admonishes, "the mind will not attain precision; under suspicion and fear it will not form sound judgment, nor will it, dazzled by love's delight nor in sorrow and anxiety, come to previsions."[26]

But Pound translates the *Ta Hio* for the same reason that he gathers pages of Chinese and American history into his Cantos—in order that "local applications" occur to his readers at every turn. "Men suffer malnutrition by millions," he writes in an essay of 1937, "because their overlords dare not read the *Ta Hio*" (*SP*, 80). He gives us guides for daily life, not aids for undisturbed meditation, not scholarly documents leading to "a realm of uncertainty, or to a remote grove where contradictions are needless."[27] In the last issue of his journal, *The Exile*, he sends his audience out into a dishonest world with the advice that "[e]thical and economic queries can be solved, usually, by ref. to the *Ta Hio*."[28] The remainder of his letter to Hughes becomes a lament for giving up the gloss, and with it the chance to transmit essential lessons. Unable to resign his place in the book with ease, he returns to the question of the preface three times after his opening paragraph: "Re the preface to *Ta Hio*: I don't think I ought to use Kung as a shoehorn for a curse on American State Dept. and the Wilson–Harding Administrations, etc. At least thass the way I feel this A.M." (EP, *Letters*, 214). His style veers toward the awkwardly colloquial, its forced offhandedness betraying the depth of his regret and distancing this jaded author as far as possible from the man who translated Confucius: "Re preface: Wot's use telling 'em they are damn sick? I mean I prefer trying giving 'em the medicine; if they don't feel better after it or don't feel they needed it, woss use telling 'em?" (EP, *Letters*, 214). The letter concludes with an effort at generalization: "Re *Ta Hio*: Everything one tends to put into a preface merely tends to draw red herrings across trail." He remains only momentarily theoretical, however. He is compelled to offer an abbreviated list of social applications inspired by Confucius before he can relinquish his preface:

> Most of what I had written wd. merely raise irrelevant issues re state of America, damnd perversion of Constitution, sonsovbitches in office, of collapse of Xtianity, goddamnability of all monotheistic Jew, Mohammed, Xtn. buncomb, etc.
> So I
> Cut it aht. If they can't see from the text, they won't see any better from being irritated by my irritability beforehand. (EP, Letters, 215)

He has glimpsed himself in a mirror of his own making—the translated *Ta Hio*—and seen a man who waves his arms wildly when he should be perfectly composed. He applies sarcastic labels to cherished causes: "red herrings"; "irrelevant issues." And yet these issues force their way into his renunciation. The preface, not entirely suppressed but distilled, bitter, broken into four pieces, finds its audience of one: the editor—the man who, of all Pound's readers, least needs to hear it.[29]

Two months before Shakespeare and Company issued *Our Exagmination Round His Factification for Incamination of Work in Progress*, the "Books" section of the *New York Herald Tribune* serialized Pound's "How to Read."[30] To juxtapose these events is to illustrate the striking differences between the two anno-

tative projects. Joyce's title, almost impossible to remember in full, resonates
with private associations; furthermore, it contains a jab at his critics that no one
but him will have even the opportunity of comprehending until the title reappears, tied to "the twelve deaferended dumbbawls," in *Tales Told of Shem and
Shaun* (June 1929). His book is a counter in the game he plays with glosses
throughout his career, a game that mocks and provokes all self-confident acts of
interpretation. The inner circle that attempts to decode "Work in Progress"
finds itself illustrated in a pun on the cover of *Our Exagmination*, where the title
forms a wheel whose spokes are the names of avant-garde artists and critics.[31]
Those who fall within this exclusive ring would not likely be drawn to "How
to Read." The straightforward title assures readers of a guide uncomplicated by
duplicity or coded statements. An editor's note introducing the first installment
of the essay guarantees that readers will see action in the company of "Ezra
Pound, American Poet and critic, who has fired grapeshot at literature from
various parts of Europe for two decades." Here will be no clever conundrums
for the elite. Instead, the irreverent poet will teach a commonsensical method
for approaching the arts.

The *New York Herald Tribune Books* carries a generously assorted cultural
sampling on its newsprint pages. Bracketing "How to Read" are publication
notices for Lytton Strachey's *Elizabeth and Essex*, Benito Mussolini's *My Autobiography*, Felix Salten's *Bambi*, Virginia Woolf's *Mrs. Dalloway*, and A. A.
Milne's *House at Pooh Corner*. An advertisement for Womrath's Library and
Bookshops appeals to frugal readers: "Rent the Book You Want." Closely following the end of Pound's primer is a full-page advertisement similarly, if more
boldly, pitched to readers' inclinations for self-improvement: "ONLY 7,500 SETS
LEFT TO BE SOLD," the headline urges: "A HIGH SCHOOL EDUCATIONAL COURSE
IN 60 HANDY VOLUMES FOR $2.98 POSTPAID TO ANY ADDRESS."[32] Among these
"pocket size" references are "Facts You Should Know About the Classics" and
a basic "Reading Manual and Guide."

Pound equivocally welcomes this democratic context for "How to Read."
Two months before the essay's serialization in the *Herald Tribune*'s review, he
is excited by the idea that he and Louis Zukofsky might start "the book of the
quarter club," an alternative to the Book-of-the-Month Club. He notes that the
series "wd. be an Xcuse for a 50 cent edtn. of 'how to read' which is what I want.
I dont want to tie the little lesson up in a fancy vol. that the pore cant buy"
(*P/Z*, 20).[33] His condescending reference to "the pore" who can scarcely afford
his "little lesson" reveals his inclination to distance himself from his text when
speaking to the few who are already literate. Even the artless title momentarily
shows a contemptuous edge invisible to outsiders. Nevertheless, Pound enter-
tains ardent hopes for the widespread dissemination and reformative powers of
"How to Read": he conceives of this compact introductory essay as the beginning of a prolonged campaign of popular education. In 1931, three years after
the "book of the quarter" scheme, he plans the publication of a relatively inex-
pensive "series of brochures, each volume to sell for fifty cents the copy. The
series will consist of the following volumes: How to Read, etc, etc" (*P/Z*, 115).[34]
"How to Read" does not really belong where it is commonly encountered, in

Eliot's edition of the *Literary Essays of Ezra Pound*. Like much of Pound's prose, it can best be understood in its original environment—set, in this case, on the demotic pages of the *Herald Tribune*'s review.

Joining a long line of American authors who pledge their allegiance to the public, Pound immediately takes sides with his readers against the academy.[35] In his first sentence, he drops "institutions of learning" into sarcastic quotation marks ("HR," 15). In his second paragraph, he sympathizes with "the general contempt of 'scholarship'" and "the shrinking of people in general from any book supposed to be 'good'" ("HR," 15). The people's judgment demonstrates native wisdom: Pound faults the effete, obtuse collection of teachers and poet-asters who have failed to notice "that there is something defective in the con-temporary methods of purveying letters" ("HR," 15). The *Herald Tribune*'s readers finally have an advocate, someone who has lived among the enemy and comes to tell them "what these methods are at the 'centre'" ("HR," 15). This Jamesian plot—the wide-eyed, energetic, solitary American abroad, who uncovers ancient, immense conspiracies that ultimately defeat him—underlies virtually all of Pound's prose from his earliest essays and letters to the radio broadcasts. Each instructional piece must do more than elucidate the funda-mentals of reading or economics, the similarities between Mussolini's Italy and Jefferson's America, organizational principles in history and the arts. It must also alert us to the sinister recurring story that explains why certain books reach the market while others lie unread in the desks of their neglected authors, why museums hang the paintings they do, why civilizations rise and fall. Much later, after we have diligently mastered this elementary knowledge, we may worry ourselves with river names in ALP, or Vico's beautifully patterned history, or cruxes in the Cantos. But first we need to grasp the means by which an artist achieves authority in a diseased society.

"How to Read" opens with Pound's disenchanting exploration of the American university system and his subsequent journey to England, where he finds even "greater darkness" ("HR," 17). From the outset, he stands above his contemporaries—"Already in my young and ignorant years they considered me 'learned'" ("HR," 17)—and yet this fact only points to the crippled state of British national culture, exemplified by the literary weeklies: "It was incredible that literate men ... believed the stupidities that appeared there with such reg-ularity" ("HR," 17). "Embedded in that naïve innocence" that marks citizens of the frontier, he measures the temporal lag between artists and the public and ascribes "the delay to mere time" ("HR," 17).

"But that is not all of the story," an older Pound cynically remarks ("HR," 17). When he provides his agent with what seems a likely solution, "a twelve-volume anthology in which each poem was chosen ... because it contained an invention, a definite contribution to the art of verbal expression," the archaic machinery begins its inexorable process of suppression ("HR," 17). Pound's phlegmatic agent, presented with the anthology proposal, is "courteous":

> [H]e was even openly amazed at the list of three hundred items which I offered
> as an indication of outline. No autochthonous Briton had ever, to his professed

belief, displayed such familiarity with so vast a range, but he was too indolent to recast my introductory letter into a form suited to commerce. He, as they say, "repaired" to an equally august and long-established publishing house. ("HR," 17)

The inflated, portentous verb "repaired," belonging in an overwrought novel of the nineteenth century, signals the baffling of this direct American's enterprise.[36] When the agent returns, Pound's style swerves toward *Huckleberry Finn*. His audience should trust a man whose strongly held opinions incite him to ignore decorum: "I found him awed, as if one had killed a cat in the sacristy" ("HR," 18). The affected pronoun "one," lifted from mannered prose by the unpolished narrator, completes Pound's stylistic attack on the Old World. Having referred in his prospectus to "that doddard Palgrave" and his *Golden Treasury*, on which "the whole fortune of X & Co. is founded," Pound discovers that his ingenuous recommendation for reform has driven him into literary exile: "From that day onward no book of mine received a British imprimatur until the appearance of Eliot's castrated edition of my poems" ("HR," 18). Because the publishing industry has "thousands of pounds sterling invested in electro-plate"—Pound's cautionary tales typically end with a single explanatory key delivered to the reader like a punch line—it will never register the subtle, often sudden changes in an active artist's work ("HR," 18). This introduction to a revolutionary curriculum, "the only one that can give a man an orderly arrangement of his perception in the matter of letters," closes with the paralysis of its author: "Against ignorance one might struggle, and even against organic stupidity, but against a so vast vested interest the lone odds were too heavy" ("HR," 18).

What we are reading, then, is a severely abridged document, testifying in its attenuated form to opposition and unwilling compromise. Less substantial than the "short guide" Pound subsequently proposes to an American publisher, "How to Read" contains hardly enough sustained discussion to warrant the label "essay," which he offers at the end of part 1 ("HR," 22). Like all of Pound's most ambitious prose, it comprises a loosely gathered set of notes, each of which gestures adamantly but disjointedly to a variety of subjects.[37] Its pages fall into splinters: headings and subheadings, short outlines, phrases in parentheses, hastily annotated bibliographies, categories and terms barely tied to quick definitions. "How to Read" is a compendium of forcefully compacted lists that threatens at every moment to burst open, yielding dozens of titles and a score of authors where before there was a manageable handful. The definitions grow more puzzling, more elliptical with study, particularly if we wrestle with each sentence as an earnest reader in 1929 might have tried to do, rather than peering behind the terms for portraits of Pound and his contemporaries or culling phrases to clarify the aims of Pound's poetry.

How are we to follow Pound, for example, as he groups artists into "clearly definable sorts of people, and . . . a periphery of less determinate sorts" ("HR," 23)? "*The inventors*" introduce "certain methods of rhyming" or exhibit "a certain fineness of perception," whereas "*[t]he masters* . . . succeed in pervading the whole" of their work "with some special quality or some special character of their own, and bring the whole to a state of homogeneous fullness" ("HR," 23). "There are three 'kinds of poetry,'" our instructor declares, but his quotation marks cast the fleeting presentation of melopoeia, phanopoeia, and logopoeia into an unsettling shadow ("HR," 25).[38] Does his punctuation divulge a skeptic's wry appraisal of his overly clever demarcations? As he employs his own slippery vocabulary, he illustrates how little his terms advance discussion:

> It is not enough to know that the Greeks attained to the greatest skill in melopoeia, or even that the Provençaux added certain diverse developments and that some quite minor, nineteenth-century Frenchmen achieved certain elaborations.
>
> It is not quite enough to have the general idea that the Chinese (more particularly Rihaku and Omakitsu) attained the known maximum of *phanopoeia.* . . .
>
> You may say that for twenty-seven years I have thought consciously about this particular matter, and read or read at a great many books, and that with the subject never really out of my mind, I don't yet know half there is to know about *melopoeia.* ("HR," 26–27)

I quote at some length in order that the reader may experience the effect of following Pound through a sustained stretch of "How to Read." We sit in the classroom listening as our lecturer ruminates aloud on matters that come to him in midthought. Lost in an incompletely sketched puzzle that only he can appreciate, he forgets his audience and the purpose of his class altogether. Without the heartfelt letters that affirm Pound's absolute seriousness of intent, without an ample number of companion pieces that echo its representative confusion, the whole of "How to Read" might be taken for an elaborate spoof of all attempts to educate the general public—a cruel send-up, from one of the incorrigible authors of *BLAST*, of the *Herald Tribune*'s unwary readers. Insisting that he brings "sense and co-ordination" to literary studies ("HR," 15), Pound creates labyrinthine tangles of syntax and terminology throughout his essay. He carefully refines his classificatory system, designed to allow novices direct and expeditious access to "works where language is efficiently used" ("HR," 23). But anyone bent on following his lead must flounder in the wilderness of Pound's prose:

> Unless I am right in discovering *logopoeia* in Propertius (which means unless the academic teaching of Latin displays crass insensitivity as it probably does), we must almost say that Laforgue invented *logopoeia* observing that there had been a very limited range of *logopoeia* in all satire, and that Heine occasionally employs something like it, together with a dash of bitters, such as can (though he may not have known it) be found in a few verses of Dorset and Rochester. At any rate Laforgue found or refound *logopoeia*. And Rimbaud brought back to *phanopoeia* its clarity and directness. . . . Laforgue is not like any preceding poet. He is not ubiquitously like Propertius. ("HR," 33)

We should keep this exemplary passage in mind (especially its last gnomic sentence) as we consider Pound's descriptions and promotion of "How to Read."

In late 1931 the publication of the "Prolegomena (Collected Prose) of Ezra Pound" seemed likely (*P/Z*, 115). George Oppen, the prospective editor for this series of fifty-cent brochures, repeats Pound's grand summary of the first volume in a letter to Louis Zukofsky: "He [Pound] says, speaking of the advisability of starting with H[ow]. T[o]. R[ead]. that 'it is an introduction to the whole method of my crit. and everything that has heretofore looked like dilletantism and tasting here and there; shifts into place and has its proportion'" (*P/Z*, 116).[39] Pound's emphasis on a newly won order illuminates his slighting reference in the essay itself to his hitherto "unorganized and fragmentary volumes" ("HR," 19); he designs "How to Read" to remedy a haphazard, piecemeal approach to the arts. In the draft notes for this text that is in theory newly coherent, he asks us, as we survey his earlier "scattered prose fragments," to acknowledge that he has labored for his readers without being

> upheld by the professorial salary, of the kind granted to other people when they indulge in research. Hence [his previous essays'] fragmentary form, which has one other case also, my dislike of making books, or of swelling a fragment into the form of a book, merely because in such form with such tumid "completeness" it can pass for a more "serious work." When I ex[h]austed the interest in the subject I stopped.[40]

His second defense of his fractured critical corpus—that he knows when to stop expanding on his pronouncements—urges that any extensive and finely proportioned critical effort receive our suspicious regard; we would pause more fruitfully, employing our time more efficiently, over Pound's terse glosses. It is possible that Pound deleted this justification of his apparatus as he came to emphasize the differences between "How to Read" and his preceding essays and reviews. In particular, his latest guidebook must not seem merely another gathering of pieces since it occupies a crucial position in a contest with Eliot, whose *Selected Essays* appear in September 1932, three months after the comparatively slight first volume of the "Prolegomena."[41] If Pound hopes to change his readers' beliefs, he has to take a place beside the magisterial editor of the *Criterion* at the center of contemporary debate concerning art and politics. He cannot accept his role of wild skirmisher firing "grapeshot at literature" from the fringes of Europe. He requires a portion of the respect accorded Eliot by the public: "[T]he fact that I have a crikikul METHOD ought to be rubbed into the blighted pubk," Pound tells Zukofsky. "[A]nd that yawp (started by Aldington; about Eliot beink the more seerious schorlar or crik or whatever, ought to be spiked. fer the sake of everybodys future income" (*P/Z*, 126). His hardheaded mention of money and his derisive misspellings only partly mask a bid for attention, a cry for students and the power to teach.

Pound's insistence on the coherence of his latest work is an integral component of his plan for "a radical reform in education, and in the whole teaching of literature" (*P/Z*, 128), a methodical program that should maintain, with dependable, "mechanical" action, "the health of thought outside literary circles and in non-literary existence, in general individual and communal life" ("HR," 22). Ironically, it is the enormous ambitions of Pound's educational project that generate the disorder of his prose, turning what he intends to be a single, seamless, encyclopedic summation of knowledge into an extended collection of marginalia, of partial lists and suggestive notes. The disjunctive form of his essays leaves the reader who is unused to Pound's style wondering how these lessons are to be read, although their author invariably argues that he imparts only the most basic ideas in the most simple terms. The hopeful title for the series that "How to Read" inaugurates—"Prolegomena"—comes from the Greek *pro-legein* : to say beforehand or preliminarily. This emphasis on the incomplete, the anticipatory, succinctly conveys the nature not only of the first essay but also of the ensuing work.

We may begin to grasp the overwhelming dimensions of the domain Pound proposes to survey and the effect of this vast arena on the form of his sentences by listening to one of his broadcasts delivered over Radio Rome during the Second World War.[42] Although it is important to recognize that Pound in 1942 has grown more desperate and consequently less intelligible than he was at the beginning of the 1930s, the mechanics of this speech are not fundamentally different from those of his earlier instructional attempts. This particular speech bears the title "Continuity"—a noun that, like Pound's letters on the methodical organization of "How to Read," expresses the concerns that motivate his work but fails to describe the broadcast itself. "Continuity" is so radically fractured that it has been cited by one critic as evidence of Pound's fears for his sanity.[43] The talk begins with a clear disclosure of the anxieties about audience and order that accompany all of Pound's prose: "Had I the tongue of men and angels I should be unable to make sure that even the most faithful listeners would be able to hear and grasp the whole of a series of my talks" (*RS*, 191). Pound's compulsion to "make sure" mirrors the desires of Joyce and Woolf to reach out directly beyond the borders of the book, ascertaining whether readers understand and whether they can be persuaded to accept the unique difficulties of a new undertaking. Pound's method of influence consists, characteristically, of repetition with a typographical yell that he might have reproduced at the microphone: "Nevertheless you may as well make the effort to grasp at least the fact that there IS a sequence in what I am saying, and that the conversation of February coheres with that of April" (*RS*, 191).

Continuity between lessons is tremendously important since dispersed instruction leads to half-taught, partly dysfunctional students, incapable of arranging their lives or their surroundings. And no matter how comprehensive Pound's lectures are, they can never eradicate the students' illiteracy: "PITY is that there is so much else, so much essential else that they are unblissfully UNaware of" (*RS*, 191). Only at this source can the ignorant become whole: "And I honestly do not know where they can get essential parts of that else, except from my broadcasts. And out of them, out of these talks, the young men in England and America will have to build their souls, or at least their minds for tomorrow, or LOSE time, never get into life at all" (*RS*, 191). Given such formidable pressure on every word Pound utters, it is little wonder that he grows frantic, in the middle of his presentation, when he considers the extent of his syllabus and the cruel brevity of his term. We must follow the entire tormented passage to comprehend the magnitude of Pound's dilemma:

[A]fter a hundred broadcasts it is STILL hard to know where to begin. . . . I am held up, enraged, by the delay needed to change a typing ribbon, so much is there that OUGHT to be put into the young American head. Don't know which, what to put down, can't write two scripts at once. NECESSARY facts, ideas, come in pell-mell. I try to get too much into ten minutes. Condensed form O.K. in book, saves eyesight, reader can turn back, can look at a summary. Mebbe if I had more sense of form, legal training, God knows what, could get the matter across the Atlantic, or the bally old channel. Art, economics, pathology. You need to know MORE about all of 'em. Need to GIT out of this war, need to stay out of, or prevent the next one, need to change the stinkin' old system.

ROT in art, art as pathology, university delays. How come class war? What is it the professors don't know? Got to choose between two or four subjects or I will git nothing over in any one talk. (RS, 192)

Pound divides his anger between his listeners and himself; no one can satisfactorily master the pressing subjects at hand. His critical evaluation of his ungainly compendiums does not prevent his sentences from falling apart. Subjects and verbs get lost in his hurry to record information; information evaporates, leaving isolated nouns in mystifying succession ("Art, economics, pathology") and truncated questions that will mean nothing to the empty "American heads" Pound hopes to fill. Composition occurs while we listen; there is no time for reflection on and arrangement of thoughts.

Pound's sense of mission paradoxically constitutes a later manifestation of the scorn for the public that he displays, for example, in the second issue of *BLAST* (1915), where artists lead an audience composed of obedient, contemptible dogs: "Of course the homo canis will follow us. It is the nature of the homo canis to follow. They growl but they follow."[44] But the growls grow fiercer: Are those dogs following or pursuing the artist? Perhaps they are after other game altogether and will dash past him on their way elsewhere. Early in his career Pound proclaims the proud detachment of the avant-garde: "The arts can thrive in the midst of densest popular ignorance" (1913) (*SP*, 110). Readers are an unnecessary luxury. Those living outside the circle of art stumble about in an earlier historic period: "The arts, explorative, 'creative,' the 'real arts,' literature, are always too far ahead of any general consciousness to be of the slightest contemporary use" (1917) (*SP*, 194). But circumstances—war, economic misery, the immediate difficulty of getting his words and the words of his friends printed and circulated—force him to acknowledge his intimate, detested ties to the surrounding populace. Society's destructive power makes it dangerous to ignore: "I have blood lust because of what I have seen done to, and attempted against, the arts in my time" (*SP*, 229). Pound realizes that he must either teach or slaughter this benighted assembly.

The confusion of these incompatible tasks vitiates his enterprise of enlightening the ignorant. Violence and disgust seize his lessons; every new gesture works at cross-purposes to the last. Woolf and Joyce display comparable ambivalence toward their commerce with the public, but not so frequently nor with such impolitic tactlessness as Pound. Those beginning "How to Read" need not be frightened by his erudition: "To tranquilize the low-brow reader, let me say at once that I do not wish to muddle him by making him read more books, but to allow him to read fewer with greater result" ("HR," 16). Similarly clumsy reassurances regularly destroy whatever tranquillity might exist in Pound's classroom; his encouragement is customarily attended by a sneer. In a letter of 1922 addressed to Felix Schelling, who taught Pound freshman English twenty years earlier, Pound argues that "shock troops" must administer the ABCs to unwilling or timid students: "There are things I quite definitely want to destroy, and which I think will have to [be] annihilated before civilization can exist, i.e. anything I shd. dignify with the title civilization" (EP, *Letters*, 181).

In these dark ages, he tells Schelling, the literate few live on the margins, exiled and endangered, hoarding their precious gift of understanding: "I mean all that is left is exiled, driven in catacombs, exists in the isolated individual, who occasionally meets one other with a scrap of it concealed in his person or his study" (EP, *Letters*, 181). These bearers of culture figuratively share God's power to create men and women: "Humanity is malleable mud, and the arts set the moulds it is later cast into" (EP, *Letters*, 181). But mud, not divinity, captures Pound's imagination. He changes his figure for instruction, likening art to a purgative that will cleanse the filthy tracts of twentieth-century thinkers. He wonders how to accomplish this task quickly without killing the patient: "Being intemperate, at moments, I shd. prefer dynamite," he confesses, "but in measured moments I know that all violence is useless (even the violence of language. . . . However, one must know an infinite amount before one can decide on the position of the border line between strong language and violent language)" (EP, *Letters*, 182). He concludes his letter, not surprisingly, thinking of dynamite rather than medicine or temperate language. The teaching artist becomes a miner who must discriminate between "the governed explosion of dynamite in a quarry, useful, O.K.; and the calamitous useless explosion" (EP, *Letters*, 182). With this final figure, people have vanished from Pound's hypothetical classroom. He works more comfortably, more brutally, with stone.

F. R. Leavis is among those who immediately recognized the contradictory aspects of Pound's educational impulses. Even before his *How to Teach Reading: A Primer for Ezra Pound* (1932), he offers a cogent statement of the condition that impels Pound to write "How to Read": the distressing gap between artists and public. "'Civilisation' and 'culture,'" Leavis warns in *Mass Civilisation and Minority Culture* (1930), "are coming to be antithetical terms," each representing a group with competing interests and widely differing capacities to influence events.[45] Leavis notes the "ominous addition" of the label "high-brow" to the modern vocabulary and admits that "the minority is being cut off as never before from the powers that rule the world."[46] Woolf, Joyce, and Pound (along with many other artists writing in the 1930s) would all readily assent to this disturbing analysis, but Pound responds to the prospect of irrelevance with a specific proposal to change the ways of the academy and thereby draws the professional educator's scrutiny. In *How to Teach Reading*, Leavis objects to the difficulties an actual undergraduate would have following Pound's idiosyncratic tutelage. He fears that Pound's abbreviated syllabus, his search across a vast range of literature for isolated technical developments, and his concurrent assurance that we need know only a very few books well in order to establish unshakable "axes of reference" will leave students ignorant of literary tradition and cultural contexts.[47] Those unfortunate enough to complete Pound's course will at best exhibit a "scholarly eclecticism," "a more or less elegantly pedantic dilettantism like that which has its monument in the Cantos."[48] Although Pound ostentatiously bills himself as a man uncontaminated by the university, Leavis accuses him of segregating literary studies from the rest of life, of remaining blind to all but books—a disability that widens the division between highbrows and the masses: "[O]ne cannot be seriously interested in literature and remain purely literary in interests."[49]

This charge of aestheticism vexes Pound throughout his life.[50] It strikes him as an egregious injustice when leveled at his calculatedly red-blooded, no-nonsense efforts as a teacher and provokes his response to Leavis in "Murder by Capital" (1933).[51] Repeating the qualified invitation that he extends to the public in "How to Read," Pound hopefully opens his arms to a general audience at the close of "Murder by Capital": "I don't care about 'minority culture.' I have never cared a damn about snobbisms or for writing *ultimately* for the few" (*SP*, 231). He spurns the embattled highbrows, confirming, by his refusal of their company, Leavis's observation that they are powerless. But even Pound, almost always able to avoid confronting his inconsistencies, must qualify his unconditional declaration: "Perhaps that is an exaggeration," he allows: "Perhaps I was a worse young man than I think I was" (*SP*, 231).

His italicized adverb, "*ultimately*," further tempers his expression of enthusiasm for the masses; repeated three times in the next paragraph, it explains Pound's strategy for crossing to the people's side without forsaking his credentials as a member of the elite: "Serious art is unpopular at its birth. But it ultimately forms the mass culture. Not perhaps at full strength? Perhaps at full strength" (*SP*, 231). His query and tentative assertion betray understandable doubts about this blind faith in time. Over the course of his life, the aging Pound waits for the world to catch up. "It may take another twenty years' education to give that passage a meaning," he comments in an essay of 1938. "Give 'em another 20 or 40," he adds in a barbed footnote of 1959. Writing from St. Elizabeths Hospital in 1946, he tells his old friend Joseph Ibbotson: "25 years time lag / no one understands / simplest phrases." In a sober postscript one year later: "Time lag in Americ. mind / now 40 years instead of 20."[52] Perpetually caught in this debilitating "lag," Pound consoles himself in "Murder by Capital" with the conviction that Leavis's "yatter about art does *not* become a part of mass culture" (*SP*, 231) and the certainty that the public, eager to arrive at ultimate comprehension, prefers demystifying instruction in a familiar style. "Mass culture probably contains . . . the demand for that which is hidden," Pound surmises, conjuring up his ideal readers, all endowed with an appetite for unending exposé. "This sometimes pans out," he explains, "as a demand for colloquial; i.e., living language as distinct from the ridiculous dialect of the present Cambridge school of 'critics'" (*SP*, 231). In a reversal reminiscent of the opening gambit of

"How to Read," Pound has shifted the terms of Leavis's diagnosis, placing the sterile, upper-class "minority culture" at the heart of power while genuine artists join the vigorous but disenfranchised masses in the streets. Pound has Leavis offering an institutional solution, characterized by specialized terminology, shaped by unsavory, largely concealed connections to financial powers that oppose art because it exposes their corruption. Pound remains outside the walls of Cambridge, holding forth, in his fantasy, to a rough-edged but trustworthy crowd in the common tongue.[53]

Pound's Pyrrhic victory over Leavis, however, has necessitated the sacrifice of art. Mass culture never clamors in the present for what Pound calls the "mysterium," cunningly captured in the subtle nets of poetry. Their daily craving for "the colloquial" ironically forces artists to postpone creation of the beautiful lofty things that they hope the masses will someday cherish. Like Woolf's "Anon," this people's Pound has solved the problem of solitude by renouncing artistry, and yet he cannot even comfort himself with Woolf's evanescent dream of careless song. Pound faces this loss with unusually ruthless honesty in "'We Have Had No Battles But We Have All Joined In And Made Roads.'" This essay was published in 1937, along with a number of literary pieces, in an anthology bearing the deliberately anachronistic title *Polite Essays*. "'We Have Had No Battles'" advertises its difference from the "polite essay" (something that a Cambridge professor might produce) by taking its title from an unwieldy, up-to-date quotation that describes the willing labor of the active, organized citizens of Fascist Italy. Pound's essay should be placed beside Woolf's "Leaning Tower." Both are exemplary statements from the 1930s: meditations on the loss of aesthetic sanctuary from writers who once sustained a sense of writing in isolation.

Pound's sense of dispossession is more extreme than Woolf's. He stands on the ground consulting with the man in control about what will replace the broken tower. He realizes, with a wistfulness he does not often confess in this tumultuous era, that he may move and instruct his auditors, but his words can no longer please. "The serene flow of sentence" certainly brings readers more pleasure, he admits, and may even prove "more exciting to the reader than . . . words set down in anger" (*PE*, 55). "But when one is not narrating?" he asks querulously:

> [W]hen one specifies the new life or the new temple? When one talks to the capo maestro, that is to the building foreman as distinct from making architectural pictures that one knows will remain for ever (or for ages) unrealized, one may have other criteria? Risking the END of the reader's interest when the house or palace is up? (*PE*, 55)

Pound has good cause to fear his readers' declining interest in his discussions with the foreman. His poetry and prose of the 1930s and early 1940s have been largely condemned, criticized, or ignored in favor of his earlier and later writings. He follows his own prognosis of his audience's future boredom with a parody of his preaching: "(And an now my deerly beeluvved brevvrem etc. et cetera)" (*PE*, 55).[54] "It may be that my weekly writings are no more articulate than the trumpetings of a terrified elephant," he acknowledges. "I have no specific will to preserve them as written" (*PE*, 52). In this deprecatory mood he offers an indignant, apologetic defense for the awkward apparatus he builds instead of working on his art—the temporary frameworks obscuring our view of his half-constructed *tempio*: "No man who is building anything more than a suburban villa can be expected to have his construction always on the market, always finished, with all the scaffoldings taken down" (*PE*, 49).

With the *ABC*s of economics and reading, issued in 1933 and 1934, Pound continues the struggle I have charted in "How to Read" and related essays, preparing the few readers still willing to follow his uncertified program for their perilous journey through books and the world.[55] The complex pedagogical dynamics we have already observed do not fundamentally change, but in the 1930s and early 1940s Pound's classroom manner grows more shrill. The stakes are raised each week, the deafness of readers worsens daily, and Pound worries more openly about the clarity and effectiveness of his notes for a new society. He manifests mounting concern over his work's integrity through habitual commentary on the lessons as they unfold: he glosses his own scaffolding. These glosses—critiques, digressions, justifications, accusations, reassurances— exist in part for the frustrated reader, but they are no less significant for Pound, who clings tenaciously during these troubled years to the comforting sound of his isolated voice. They regularly interrupt the *ABC*s, and they increase with each year until, in *Guide to Kulchur* and the radio broadcasts, they frequently displace the ostensible subject altogether. We have seen a powerful illustration of this later imbalance in "Continuity."

On the most basic level, the apparatus constitutes an apology for his work, a defense of the very act of writing. It is comparable to the arguments for abandoning poetry to make plans for "the new temple" in "'We Have Had No Battles.'" Pound pauses in his *ABC of Economics* to justify himself: "I go on writing because it appears to me that no thoughtful man can in our time avoid trying to arrange those things in his own mind in an orderly fashion. . . . To separate ideas that are not identical and to determine their relations" (*ABCE*, 247-48). "The man of understanding can no more sit quiet and resigned while his country lets its literature decay," he writes in the *ABC of Reading*, "than a good doctor could sit quiet and contented while some ignorant child was infecting itself with tuberculosis under the impression that it was merely eating jam tarts" (*ABCR*, 33). He feels equally compelled to publish his thoughts on economics: "I shall have no peace until I get the subject off my chest, and there is no other way of protecting myself against charges of unsystematised, uncorrelated thought, dilettantism, idle eclecticism, etc., than to write a brief formal treatise" (*ABCE*, 233).

This prologue to the *ABC of Economics*, containing a concise summary of the anticipated attacks that Pound now knows like old wounds, invites judgments against a work that will prove anything but "systematised." Joyce and Woolf exploit the inherently disruptive nature of annotation; when Pound breaks into his texts, it is often to maintain their wholeness, to tell us that they have "form," even if that form seems indistinguishable from randomness. He expects that his *ABC of Reading* will disappoint those who are accustomed to more traditional textbooks: "You have been promised a text-book, and I perhaps ramble on as if we had been taken outdoors to study botany from the trees instead of from engravings in classroom. That is partly the fault of people who complained that I gave them lists without saying why I had chosen such-and-such authors" (*ABCR*, 45). He provides no obscure pattern, no arcane schema. Nor should his admitted rambling ultimately affect the coherence of the *ABC of Reading*. At the beginning of his second chapter, Pound presents a key to his method, under the heading "APPROACH":

> It doesn't, in our contemporary world, so much matter where you begin the examination of a subject, so long as you keep on until you get round again to your starting point. As it were, you start on a sphere, or a cube; you must keep on until you have seen it from all sides. Or if you think of your subject as a stool or table, you must keep on until it has three legs and will stand up, or four legs and won't tip over too easily. (*ABCR*, 29)

This bit of structural wisdom appeals to him; he repeats it again in chapter 7, and notes, in chapter 8, that he is "[c]oming round again to the starting point" (*ABCR*, 62, 63). He makes an implicit plea for his rough piece of furniture when he reminds his readers that "[a]brupt and disordered syntax can be at times very honest, and an elaborately constructed sentence can be at times merely an elaborate camouflage" (*ABCR*, 34). Pound's excursion through books follows a "contemporary," meandering path because he writes in a slovenly century for an audience that cannot reach consensus on any type of social, political, or aesthetic order. His syntax bears painful witness to the "SOCIAL AND ECONOMIC PROBLEM / ADVANTAGES ACCRUING FROM THERE BEING A 'STYLE OF THE PERIOD'" (*ABCR*, 154). The writers of the seventeenth century, he pointedly notes, "didn't have to start by reforming anything" (*ABCR*, 154). They built virtually without effort, without scaffolding, without the agonizing certainty of separation from their audience, as did Woolf's mythical Anon, Eliot's poets and dramatists of the sixteenth and early seventeenth centuries, Yeats's architects and artificers of Byzantium. They had no cause to interrupt the graceful flow of their sentences as Pound must in his treatises — interruptions that paradoxically demonstrate the integrity of Pound's modern forms: designs for a disheveled age.

Unlike Woolf, who fights authoritarianism with her fractured texts, and unlike the pre-poststructuralist Joyce, Pound does not delight in this formal paradox. He yearns in his politics as in his aesthetics for absolute standards of value, for enforced cultural and political coherence. "The great man," he tells us in *Jefferson and/or Mussolini* (1935), "is filled with . . . the will toward *order*."[56] Confucian thought clarifies the chaos within the self and moves outward to the state, "sorting things into organic categories."[57] Jefferson "set[s] up a civilization in the wilderness."[58] Fascism appeals to Pound, by his own testimony, precisely because it dispels verbal complexities, since it means "at the start DIRECT action, cut the cackle, if a man is a mere s.o.b. don't argue."[59] And Mussolini earns Pound's highest admiration as one who reduces the plural to the singular: "All right, bo', you come along with a card-deck, set card for each clot of theories, demo-liberal, bolshevik, anti-clerical, etc., and make that junk-shop into a nation, a live nation on its toes like a young bull in the Cordova ring."[60] A deck of cards, like any linguistic system, leaves us with only a set of signs for different positions; Mussolini transforms this disarray of theories into a single, organic entity: a bull ready for combat. Pound, who shuffles words instead of making states whole, cannot long suppress his uneasy awareness that his own glosses, in their form and their effects, make him a producer of card decks rather than the creator of a living nation.

Disorder in his *ABC*s reflects the troubled times all too accurately and disturbs the modernist who seeks method more urgently than any of his contemporaries. Kathryne Lindberg, who has given Pound's prose its most extensive treatment to date, argues that Pound's tendency to complicate his guides with contradictory gestures reveals a Nietzschean, proto-Derridean delight in deconstructive illogic and free play: "Fragmentary argument, even the fragment, exceeds the regulating law and cultivates the activity of interpretation." Pound's refusal to build a fully integrated analytical structure is "deliberately (?) ironic."[61] Lindberg rhetorically duplicates her tellingly evasive question mark at important interpretive points throughout her text. She does document in convincing detail Pound's challenge to "the categories and hierarchies of canonical literary criticism and linguistics."[62] Yet she has demonstrable difficulties as she credits him with a conscious strategy of fragmentation. I find Pound less in control, more uneasy victim than confident master of the broken forms, the confusions and mystifications, the double binds that characterize his prose.

Pound's anxieties lie closer to the surface in his *ABC of Economics* than in the *ABC of Reading*. When talking about books, however scattered his observations, he can nevertheless claim, "I am a specialist getting on toward my fiftieth year, with a particular and matured interest in writing and even in literary criticism" (*ABCR*, 170). He can defend his provocative syllabi as "the result of twenty-seven years' thought on the subject" ("HR," 39). Authority to pronounce on economic matters, since unearned, refuses to be so casually summoned. Pound delivers his *ABC of Economics* from a position very near that of a student.

In this jumbled primer, he exhibits many of the protective mannerisms that we might adopt if we were thrust behind the podium without being adequately prepared to lecture.[63] He couches his call for our respect in cynical humor: "I am an expert. I have lived nearly all my life, at any rate all my adult life, among the unemployed" (*ABCE*, 244). His remarks, he insists, "have no claim to be novelties"; they cannot be considered "the whole answer" (*ABCE*, 259, 236). When he does make "a contribution to the subject," it is a personal one: "I pointed out [to C. H. Douglas] that my grandfather had built a railroad . . . from inherent activity, artist's desire to MAKE something" (*ABCE*, 239).[64] The aphorisms with which he cuts his way through obstinate literary matters in his criticism lose their edge in this different jungle. They seem to have less insight supporting them; they take on a blusterous air, the flamboyantly outspoken words of a man who hopes to avoid further questions. "The minute I cook my own dinner or nail four boards together into a chair, I escape from the whole cycle of Marxian economics"; "Goods in the window are worth more than the goods in the basement" (*ABCE*, 239, cf. 243); "Time is not money, but it is nearly everything else" (*ABCE*, 241, cf. 243). Within a few pages he has repeated each of these "gists" as an alternative to additional analysis (*SP*, 354). He assures his pupils, frequently enough to inspire doubts from the skeptical, that the transparently intelligible subject hardly even warrants an *ABC*:

> THE BASES OF ECONOMICS are so simple as to render the subject almost wholly uninteresting.
> The complication of the subject is hardly a complication, it arises
> *A.* from the extreme difficulty of foreseeing what will be wanted;
> *B.* from the rascally nature of certain men. (*ABCE*, 261)

These periodic proclamations of simplicity, strewn everywhere in his prose, attain an incantatory power over the instructor himself. They are talismans to be used whenever the class starts to unravel.

We see him applying them liberally, as well as resorting to heavy annotation, as he tries to explain Douglas's concept of national dividends and the inequities that dividends would remedy. At this point—perhaps the most vexed, most illuminating in the *ABC*s—the chaos at the core of the instruction and Pound's desperate attempts to salvage his lecture come to a cacophonous climax. His obtrusive colloquialism, often exaggerated when he is least sure of himself, makes his initial explanation hilarious:

> And again, if I remember rightly, Major Douglas explained how the wangle was wangled. According to him, if I translate correctly, a certain part of the credit-slips received by the *entrepreneurs* was wormed down a sort of tube, i.e. instead of equalling the cost of the thing made and given for it, it equalled that cost plus part of the machinery used in producing the article (part of the plant).
> And nothing was done against this amount of credit taken in from the public and hidden. It flowed continually down into the ground, down into somebody's pocket. (*ABCE*, 251-52)

The radio broadcasts display more sustained but rarely more profound riddles of clarification. Like the definitions of terminology in "How to Read," this "translation" from Douglas seems to have been written in inordinate haste. The "tube" down which credit is "wormed" or "flows" leads into the ground or a pocket; such language hints that exploitation is an integral part of the capitalists' machinery. But Pound leaves his figure half-conceived, correcting and specifying its import as he writes.

He turns momentarily after his dark sketch of conspiracy to encourage his readers—"All of which requires a bit of thinking"—and to put his discussion back on its basic track: "Manifestly we have seen companies building new plants out of 'profits.' Manifestly we have seen crises" (*ABCE*, 252). Following his two nods to the obvious, Pound characteristically suspends his *ABC* for a direct address to his audience: "The foregoing is perhaps very confusing" (*ABCE*, 252). But he follows this concession with an irreducible nugget on which we can construct a system: "Against every hour's work (human or kilowatt hour), an hour's certificate. That can be the first step. That can be scientific. Ultimately it must be scientific" (*ABCE*, 252). As part of his superstructure threatens to collapse, Pound shores up a portion of his foundation with grammatically simple blocks.

We should not miss the apprehension behind Pound's invocation of scientific procedure. He continues his appeal to order three paragraphs later: "That may sound very vague, but it is nevertheless reducible to mathematical equations and can be scientifically treated. The equations (algebraic equations) *will not mean* merely any old quantity turned out haphazard" (*ABCE*, 253). The repeated word "equations" itself offers a comforting promise of stability and enables Pound to lead us afield again. He inserts a *"Digression Perhaps Unnecessary"* on the value of "a home for each individual" and makes a stab at answering "the questions of *de-* and *in-*flation" (*ABCE*, 253). The latter undertaking reduces him once more to apology: "This looks like a mare's nest or like wilful confusion!" he confesses, and proceeds to jettison Douglas's gnarled ideas: "What the major said fifteen years ago matters less than getting a valid and clear statement" (*ABCE*, 254). After another paragraph, filled with parentheses and "i.e."s, Pound, still not satisfied that he has achieved the desired lucidity, almost wholly discounts his recent strenuous efforts: "Perhaps the only value of these statements is a test value. I mean that I am merely saying 5 and 2 make 7 in place of the other economists' statements that 2 and 5 make 7, to see whether either they or their readers understand their previous statements" (*ABCE*, 254). Motioning now to "other economists" and "their readers," Pound retires from his *ABC*. The text that he has been assiduously straining to arrange and that we have tried to fathom exists solely to determine whether other writers, other readers, know what they have said or purported to understand. The *ABC of Economics* figuratively proves nothing more than the undisputed associative property of addition. We must not expect anything further: "After all, this is a very rudimentary treatise" (*ABCE*, 254), so basic that anyone might have placed its familiar parts on this primer's ordinary page.

Throughout his lessons Pound strives for absolute simplicity, but he worries that his beginning students, left alone with their primers, will confuse the basic with the banal and will discover no evidence of authorship in his guides. Setting down "root ideas" in his journal, *The Exile*, he wonders how he can avoid disappearing from his fundamental works: "The discouraging thing for an artist is that when he emits an 'abstract' or general proposition he can not sign it in the way he signs a poem or a drawing; i.e., saturate it with his own presence in cadence or in proportion."[65] Without the certification of a signature, how will readers discriminate between counterfeit and genuine wisdom?[66] Anyone can "produce something that looks like an idea; the only difference being that one man's statement is true and the other man's buncomb."[67]

The artist is further effaced, equally hard to credit or discredit, when he chooses to produce "ideogrammic" texts, in which even basic commentary signals the anthologizer's trespass on his material. "It would be particularly against the grain of the whole ideogrammic method," he announces in the *ABC of Reading*, "for me to make a series of general statements" (*ABCR*, 59). He urges his Italian audience to employ "the ideogrammic system" before accepting another's pronouncements on art or culture: "True criticism will insist on the accumulation of these concrete examples, these facts, possibly small, but gristly and resilient, that can't be squashed, that insist on being taken into consideration, before the critic can claim to hold any opinion whatsoever" (*SP*, 333-34). Pound selflessly establishes essential anthologies for beginners, developed not "according to Aristotelian logic," he warns in the *ABC of Economics*, "but according to the ideogramic method of first heaping together the necessary components of thought" (*ABCE*, 239). His volumes lack obvious order because the principles of their assembly render the author almost superfluous. His lectures seem unfocused, he explains, because they eschew prescription: "In no case should the student from now on be TOLD that such and such things are facts about a given body of poetry, or about a given poem," Pound stipulates in the *ABC of Reading* (*ABCR*, 80). Students of a given period of history, a society, a government should be accorded the same latitude.[68]

Fifteen pages after granting them freedom from indoctrination, however, Pound declares in his headnote to the "EXHIBITS" section of the *ABC of Reading* that his hobbled audience cannot teach itself solely by poring over ideograms:

> The ideal way to present the next section of this booklet would be to give the quotations WITHOUT any comment whatever. I am afraid that would be too revolutionary. By long and wearing experience I have learned that in the present imperfect state of the world, one MUST tell the reader. I made a very bad mistake in my INSTIGATIONS, the book had a plan, I thought the reader would see it. (*ABCR*, 95)

Pound's temperament has compelled his reappearance. We might recall his constitutional inability to let the *Ta Hio* go without at least a privately articulated preface. The titles of Pound's primers of reading and economics foretell his decision to gloss the exhibits. He admires the energetic dispersal of forms that vorticism entails; he admires, too, the oriental array of ideograms. But in the period of his life with which we are concerned, he endorses the more restricted sequence of the occidental alphabet, in which the ABCs are taught in a succession of letters that follow one another along a single line. So powerful is his opposition to his own practice and its implications that he can write, in 1933, of his respect for the shepherded recipients of the *ABC*s: "[Eliot's] contempt for his readers has always been much greater than mine, by which I would indicate that I quite often write as if I expected my reader to use his intelligence, and count on its being fairly strong" (*SP*, 389).[69] In making this judgment, Pound seems completely unaware that, while he compiles his assorted facts, his exhibits, his hoards of raw material, another part of him busily tags each item with a gloss—anticipating that whoever next comes across this sample will never begin to understand it without a label.

Over the course of the 1930s, while Pound gathers and explains his ideogrammatic gists in essays and books, he adds three volumes—268 pages—to his Cantos. Compared with his frequently contradictory statements concerning the purpose of his prose, his expressed aims for his poetry remain relatively clear, even when the Cantos themselves prove particularly resistant to reading. Working with increasing speed as the decade lurches toward ruin, Pound dedicates his poem to the same educative ends as his prose, thereby exposing himself to the readers' antipathy and reviewers' hostility that he foresaw in "'We Have Had No Battles.'" What might pass for permissible if contentious argument in an *ABC*, his audience largely believes, hopelessly mars Pound's poetry. "[A]s Hitler says, *there are no more islands*," Randall Jarrell writes in a merciless review of 1940. "Mr. Pound has deteriorated with the world. *Cantos LII-LXXI* contains the dullest and prosiest poetry that he has ever written. . . . His talents are primarily lyric—not narrative, certainly not expository or didactic."[70] "The sermon goes on too long," Louis Martz complains; "it is too consistently prosy, flickering, and ragged." Pound's "impatient desire for direct action does heavy damage to the Cantos from XXXI to LXXI."[71] Edwin Muir gives the middle Cantos a more charitable but nevertheless tentative reception: "Why Mr. Pound's criticism of human society required the inclusion of such a mass of detailed matter may become clear when the poem is finished."[72] Pound's audience quickly recognizes, though it generally abhors, the stylistic qualities that set the middle Cantos apart: the amassing of detail, the voluminous quotations, the preaching, the emphasis on exposition, the willful repression of his lyrical impulses. In the main, these Cantos show much less evidence of an author's design and of his poetic ability than *A Draft of XXX Cantos* or the *Pisan Cantos*—the sections of the poem by which they are framed.[73]

The Cantos of the 1930s, like Pound's prose, provide glosses to a culture under attack.[74] Passages in the prose do illuminate portions of the poem, but these fitful explanations simply demonstrate Pound's tendency to repeat, in every open forum, those truths he considers essential, those facts he hopes to embed deeply in our minds. When we cannot follow the highly condensed Cantos, we can sometimes appeal to the essays for an expanded citation of the text from which Pound selected his quotations, but this appeal works because Pound trumpets the same list of indispensable books in his letters, essays, and poetry. In healthier times, Pound would write poetry that was less singlemindedly committed to getting crucial passages from a collection of sourcebooks into print—poetry that would please more and instruct less stridently.[75]

But in the 1930s, pleasure must wait: "[T]he delectet is prone to mean mere literature of escape" (*PE*, 50). He tells Ibbotson, in 1936, that he is busy "fighting hell as incarnate in [/] the Regents of the Bank of France[/]Morgenthau/ Strauss/Rothschild/Sieff[/]Sasoon/Eden/Beckett/Cranbourne[/]the belch of hell, and damned lice of usura.[/] And glllorrry/if Amurika aint touchingly innercent."[76] Waging this war in essays entails finding a publisher; bringing poetry's force to bear requires Pound to defend the propriety of using art as a weapon. He rages to Douglas, also in 1936: "A pimping pseudo intelligentzia which thinks a subject which, provably, interested Aristotle, Dante, and/or almost all the best minds recorded in history, is something which I as a 'poet' ought not to soil me 'ands wiff, such a (fake) intelligentzia ought to be scraped off the wheel."[77] Projected onto an ignoble "intelligentzia," his doubts about dirtying his hands with the recalcitrant material of contemporary life, as Vincent Sherry has demonstrated, signal his "failure to understand society in the best way possible for him—in aesthetic terms."[78] Speaking with comparative moderation but evincing the same defensiveness and despair, he writes to Basil Bunting in the same year that "poetry does not consist of the cowardice which refuses to analyze the transient, which refuses to see it. The specialized thinking has to be done or literature dies and stinks" (EP, *Letters*, 277). And that "thinking" cannot be segregated from verse. Art must police its own messy domain—a policing that irrevocably alters the nature of the domain itself. In Pound's terms, either literature must be policed into exile, or it must die and stink. He registers the torments of this choice in virtually every utterance he makes about art during this decade.

Lobbying in 1933 for the publication of Canto 37 in *Poetry* magazine, Pound justifies the changes in his poem while acknowledging that most of Harriet Monroe's subscribers will not find Martin Van Buren's financial policies suitable matter for an epic: "I know you hate like hell to print me, and that an *epic* includes history and history ain't all slush and babies' pink toes. I admit that economics are *in themselves* uninteresting, but heroism *is* poetic, I mean it is fit subject for poesy." At the close of this letter, he glances momentarily at the sphere he forsakes, half-concealing that glance with rough, coy humor: "(Damn my reppertashun fer writin pretty sentimengs)" (EP, *Letters*, 247). He evades nothing in a candid exhortation to the then-poet laureate, John Masefield, using the changed Cantos as an example of what must be done to pretty words in an ugly decade:

> I have chucked a good many literary scruples, and I hold you responsible at least to think for 24 hours on your responsibility in the face of crass ignorance and of crass falsifications. . . . No man has the right to evade thinking any longer. Least of all those of us who have the word in our keeping.[79]

The careless brutality of "chucked" suits a letter intended to disturb its recipient. "My Dear John Masefield," it begins, turning then immediately to a 1930s cliché that gains sudden, bracing power when uttered by Pound: "Verse is a sword, unused for the most part."

In Canto 46, published in *The Fifth Decad of Cantos* (1936) and subsequently broadcast over Radio Rome on 12 February 1942, Pound shows what he leaves behind when he unsheathes the sword and takes on the enemy.[80] He chose to read only two selections from his poem over the air during the war—this Canto and Canto 45 ("With *Usura*"). His reasons for selecting Canto 45 are obvious: it is the most compact, rhetorically effective statement of the evils of usury that Pound ever composed. Canto 46, continuing the campaign against economic villainy, proves a more meditative choice. Before mustering a familiar collection of evidence against private banks, this Canto explores, in its first twenty lines, the origins and consequences of Pound's allegiance to his mission. In introductory comments briefly prefacing his reading, he promises the radio audience that the poem "contains things or at least hints at things that you will have to know sooner or later," and he offers them typically condescending reassurance: "I am feedin' you the footnotes first in case there is any possible word that might not be easily comprehended" (*RS*, 34).[81]

The beginning of the Canto, as though anticipating this annoying later frame, addresses our likely resistance to such heavy-handed instruction. Perhaps we bridle at "E.P. speaking" on the radio (*RS*, 38) or at the insistent rhythms and reductive truth of Canto 45. Any one of a hundred different didactic lines in the preceding Cantos could have driven us to conclude, with Louis Martz, that the sermon should end. But Pound bids us pause:

> And if you will say that this tale teaches. . .
> a lesson, or that the Reverend Eliot
> has found a more natural language . . . you who think
> you will
> get through hell in a hurry . . .
>
>                                  (*C*, 46/231)

"Reverend Eliot"—the title reverberates with disdain—may provide Christian comfort or poetry and prose in a tempered style. He may offer escape to those troubled by Pound's stringent lessons. Pound fumes particularly, as William Chace has pointed out, at the possibility that Eliot's religious beliefs will suggest to readers in the mid-1930s "a means of transcending history."[82] Pound vows that his Cantos will offer no sanctuary, no soothing words, no illusory detour around the inferno.

And yet, in the seven lines succeeding this forbidding announcement, he gives his readers the very lyricism that they desire. The poet looks away from the hell he would analyze with relentless specificity, away from the task that others say has spoiled his poem, and into the sky:

> That day there was cloud over Zoagli
> And for three days snow cloud over the sea
> Banked like a line of mountains.
> Snow fell. Or rain fell stolid, a wall of lines
> So that you could see where the air stopped open
> and where the rain fell beside it
> Or the snow fell beside it.
>
>                                  (*C*, 46/231)

He looks also to *The Waste Land*—its shower of rain followed by sunlight over the Starnbergersee, its snow-covered mountains. This scene, however, this style, perhaps the Reverend himself, belong to a time when one could linger upon clouds or ponder the integrity of one's faith. Pound has a more relevant piece of history to recall. He shatters the serene composition of rain, snow, and air with a bald enumeration of the time he has spent learning the economic lessons we too must master so that conscientious artists can return to song: "Seventeen / Years on this case, nineteen years, ninety years / on this case" (*C*, 46/231). He will repeat portions of this résumé throughout the Canto, dismissing reverie from the courtroom, summoning the authority to deliver the closing arguments in his case against fiscal corruption.[83]

As Canto 46 accounts for the shift toward quotation and prosaic summary that marks much of Pound's production during the 1930s, it displays the stylistic agility of the poetry and prose of the two preceding decades. After the august investigative lawyer's interruption of verse, we hear a voice from rural America describing one of Pound's early conversations with the economist C. H. Douglas in the office of A. R. Orage's journal, *The New Age*.[84] This emblematic exchange—the moment of Pound's awakening to the full dimensions of his public responsibility, the source of seventeen years of *ABC*s—must be told in the accent of a common man. Pound brings himself onto the stage first, a student too busy pursuing essential knowledge to worry about his ungainly appearance:

> An' the fuzzy bloke sez (legs no pants ever wd. fit) "IF
> that is so, any government worth a damn can
> pay dividends?"
> The major chewed it a bit and sez: "Y—es, eh . . .
> You mean instead of collectin' taxes?"
> "Instead of collecting taxes."
>
> (*C*, 46/231)

Like the *ABC*s in the simplicity of its message as well as its manner, this dialogue invites readers into a room where everything is aboveboard and anybody can add her or his two cents to the discussion. It is stylistically opposed to what Pound portentously calls "the place of control" in the *ABC of Economics*: "a dark room back of a bank, hung with deep purple curtains" (*ABCE*, 237).[85]

In the surrounding Cantos, Pound tears down curtains and illuminates dark rooms, using the quintessentially American linguistic methods that punctuate his prose. With colloquialism and simplification as his blunt instruments, he makes a continual verbal assault on bureaucratic hierarchy, on governmental obfuscation, on Jews and Buddhists, on individuals (living or historical) who have caught his damning eye, and ultimately, as he does in his *ABC*s, on difficulty itself. This plain poetry belongs on the shelf next to "How to Read," the pamphlet for "the low-brow reader."[86] Chinese history, abridged from Pound's precipitous reading for the easily muddled student, flows in predictable waves: "war, taxes, oppression / backsheesh, taoists, bhuddists / war, taxes, oppressions" (*C*, 54/281), or "change, tartars more tartars" (*C*, 55/299).[87] Behind this repetitive sketch of the eras' passing, as many of Pound's readers have demonstrated, lies a philosophy of patterned, cyclical history. Framed by our examination of the pedagogical methods of Pound's prose, lines like these also demonstrate the translation of Pound's pedagogy into poetic terms. We will remember "Hiang-yu" because he wears the stamp of a modern enemy, a "bloody rhooshun" (*C*, 54/276) ; "HAN-OU," by contrast, "was for huntin', huntin' tigers, bears, leopards" (*C*, 55/278). We can readily fix the events of K'ang Hsi's era: they occur "(a bit before Tommy Juffusun's)" birth (*C*, 60/330). Here is history for forgetful people in a hurry:

> And the 46 tablets that stood there in Yo Lang
> were broken and built into Foé's temple (Foé's, that is
>                                   goddam bhuddists.)
> this was under Hou-chi the she empress.

OU TI went into cloister
        Empire rotted by hochang, the shave-heads, and
Another boosy king died.

(*C*, 54/284)

"Foé," "hochang," "shave-heads"—all violent shorthand for Buddhists, all vivid, memorable tags that the slowest students will understand. "Likewise 'TAOzers,'" Pound writes to Faber's production department about these Cantos: "I want in every way to get into reader's head I am speaking disrespectfully of Taoist" (*EP, Letters*, 329). We could as easily leave the *ABC of Reading* thinking that he applauded nineteenth-century criticism or Milton's Latinate English.

Pound guides us no less firmly through American history, using John Adams as the preeminent exhibit.[88] Readers of the prose will immediately recognize the style and the nature of the teachings in these Cantos. Defending Adams from allegations of greed brought against him by the Massachusetts administrator Thomas Hutchinson, Pound nails shut the case in a parenthesis: "(Re which things was Hutchinson undoubtedly scro- / fulous ego scriptor cantilenae / Ez. P)" (*C*, 64/360). A slightly altered version of this curious certification—half invocation of classical authority, half proof that we could be holding a note signed by a neighbor—accompanies a passage that weighs Hamilton and Adams in Pound's Manichaean balance:

and as for Hamilton
we may take it (my authority, ego scriptor cantilenae)
that he was the Prime snot in ALL American history
        (11th Jan. 1938, from Rapallo)
But for the clearest head in the congress
                                1774 and thereafter
                pater patriae
the man who at certain points
                made us
at certain points
                saved us
by fairness, honesty and straight moving

ARRIBA ADAMS<br>(*C*, 62/350)

Even when Adams rummages in the arcana of English law, carrying the Cantos into snarls of Britain's legal history and statutes in Latin, his example encourages Americans to educate themselves, to untangle what has been deliberately obscured by those in power. In his library at night, armed with "the only complete set of British Statutes" in the colonies, "preparing the next day's paper, cooking up paragraphs, / articles, working the political engine," he fights a battle employing the weapons Pound hopes his modern readers will learn to wield (*C*, 64/359). Adams's scholarly decisions to "follow the study / rather than gain of the law" and to start by scrutinizing the oldest document of his profession—"I began with Coke upon Littleton" (*C*, 63/352)—invariably propel him into direct political action. They do not leave him stranded in the ineffectual academy.[89] Pound's Adams, though deeply lettered and intellectually scrupulous, supports the simplifications and the pragmatism that characterize instruction in the Cantos and the *ABC*s. Pound has called him from the archives to play a pedagogic role. He echoes Pound's fears that the United States has been the victim of infiltration: "a few foreign liars, no Americans in America" (*C*, 70/410). He agrees, in a now familiar accent, that "our trouble is iggurunce / of money especially" (*C*, 70/411). Pound delights that his teaching partner also "(found Milton a dithering idiot, tho' said this with / more circumspection)" (*C*, 68/395).[90]

The bulk of Pound's poetry written during this decade differs from the prose primarily in the quantity and disposition of matter forced onto each page. The same emphatic, simplistic historian who lays out China's dynasties and Adams's career has told us in previous lessons that "[r]eading Crabbe is a bit like trying to go somewhere on Fulton's first steamboat; he does, nevertheless, get you somewhere"; that "Rochester is London, 1914"; that "Wordsworth got rid of a lot of trimmings, but there are vast stretches of deadness in his writings"; that "Voltaire was at WORK shovelling out the garbage, the Bourbons, the really filthy decayed state of French social thought" (*ABCR*, 178, 172, 73, 186). Now, at the opening of *The Fifth Decad of Cantos*, worried that we will not digest the details of Siena's fiscal policies, he gives us a nudge: "(All of this is important)"; five pages later he still doubts our capacities: "get that straight" (*C*, 42/209, 214). "There is *no intentional* obscurity," Pound assures a reader of the Cantos in 1939: "There is condensation to maximum attainable. It is impossible to make the deep as quickly comprehensible as the shallow" (EP, *Letters*, 322-23). In 1913 the imagist Pound had cautioned poets against using superfluous words that might muddy the instantaneous perception of "an intellectual and emotional complex" ("HR," 4). Twenty years later he distills pages of history in order that the world not fight another war.

Confucius, adept at paring a subject to the bone, realizes this grand ambition in the *Ta Hio*, or "Great Digest," an apt subtitle for the 1930s Cantos.[91] Pound explains in a headnote to his translation that Confucius "had two thousand years of documented history behind him which he condensed so as to render it useful to men in high official positions. . . . China was tranquil when her rulers understood these few pages."[92] If Pound has mastered Confucius' model, if his Cantos are to be politically "useful," *The Fifth Decad of Cantos*, along with *Eleven New Cantos* (1934) and *Cantos LII–LXXI* (1940), will have to be "clearer than the preceding ones" (EP, *Letters*, 294), though hundreds of difficult pages lie behind each lucid line. He must put a library onto note cards that others can comprehend. His confession at the beginning of "How to Read" persists, querying this daunting goal: "I have been accused of wishing to provide a 'portable substitute for the British Museum,' which I would do, like a shot, were it possible. It isn't" ("HR," 16).

The pile of books sifted by the determined poet (brought back out of the stacks by those who have worked to decipher his omnibus) includes Father Joseph de Mailla's *Histoire générale de la Chine* (ten volumes), *The Works of John Adams* (ten volumes), *The Writings of Thomas Jefferson* (twenty volumes), *The Autobiography of Martin Van Buren*, the *Correspondence of John Adams and*

*Thomas Jefferson*, and the nine-volume history of il Monte dei Paschi, the seventeenth-century bank of Siena. Pound saves more than time by gathering passages from these documents: he assembles an anthology of writings otherwise unavailable to the public. The same corrupt publishing industry that boycotts Pound's own poetry and prose and refuses his collection of innovative poetry in "How to Read" deliberately deprives citizens of texts crucial to the understanding of how they are governed. Pound's letters of the 1920s and 1930s broach scores of proposals for "editions of the gists of J. Adams, Jeff, Madison, Jackson, Van Buren, Johnson, etc."[93] He defends Canto 37 to Harriet Monroe by appealing to her civic duty as a publisher: "Van Buren was a national hero, and the young ought to know it. . . . CAN'T keep the Van B. out of print any longer. . . . As there are a few clean and decent pages in the nashunul history, better print 'em" (EP, *Letters*, 247).

The *Cantos*—only one part of Pound's comprehensive response to the dire need for textbooks—presents "gists" in a radically compressed format, a format that makes Pound's prose guides seem rich with explanation. A complete translation of "Donna mi priegha" (Canto 36) precedes the excerpts in Canto 37 from Van Buren's worthy struggle against the bank. Incriminating quotations from weapons manufacturers follow Van Buren in Canto 38, along with a corrective handful of lines taken from an essay on Douglas that Pound previously published in the *New English Weekly* and a nineteen-line quotation, slightly emended, from an article by Douglas in the *New Age*.[94] This largely uncaptioned anthology, this ark filled with a small portion of what must be conserved for the New World, belongs, like the *ABC*s, to a genre peculiar to Pound: the primer for specialists. The poet turned editor, unable to anticipate his readers' distress at this elliptical construction, credits himself with producing a work wholly divested of innovation. In his furious reply to Laughlin that "Cantos 52/71 can NOT have a preface" since "[n]obody can summarize what is already condensed to the absolute limit," he claims that his utterly straightforward work is revolutionary in its simplicity: "The Point is that with Cantos 52/71 a NEW thing is. Plain narrative with chronological sequence."[95] The "NEW thing" is not structurally innovative, not an artist's ingenious variation on some older aesthetic design. It does not fall into any of the six categories for poetry that Pound outlines in the *ABC of Reading*; it is not a guide to "the mysteries" or "the SECRETUM," as he calls the realm of faith in two letters from 1939 (EP, *Letters*, 327, 329). His apology for the poem in a letter of 1937 recalls his repeated disavowals of novelty in the *ABC*s: "I don't expect, in the end, to have introduced ethical novelties or notions, though I hope to light up a few antient bases" (EP, *Letters*, 293). Writing to George Santayana in December 1939, one month before the last volume of the 1930s Cantos appears in print, Pound sums up his work in distinctly down-to-earth terms: "I have also got to the end of a job or part of a job (money in history) and for personal ends have got to tackle philosophy or my 'paradise'" (EP, *Letters*, 331). This is poetry—the noun describes the degree of compression on a given page—designed to reform individuals and governments "by the infusion of certain known facts condensable into a few pages" (*SP*, 328): poetry that works, like the prose, in the shortest imaginable class period.

Halfway through *Guide to Kulchur* (1938), Pound breaks into the midst of yet another harangue against England in order to consider the futility of his speech: "For the 300th time I repeat that it is quite useless telling these things to people who do NOT want to hear them" (*GK*, 228). This remark, a monument to vain persistence, flies wide of an audience. Those who cultivate deafness will miss the 300th reprimand just as surely as they did the first and the 299th; those who hear have been forced to sit through 299 inappropriate repetitions. The only person to whom the admonition can sensibly refer is Pound.[96] Not only do Pound's glosses on his apparatus for reform grow more frequent and more obtrusive as the decade progresses, but they increasingly sound like the words of a man who is talking to himself rather than trying to explain how readers might approach his instruction. Both Joyce and Woolf create the illusion that they leave their books in others' annotating hands. Pound, as we have seen, labors unsuccessfully to exclude himself from his exhibits of gristly fact; he objects in theory to his habitual practice. But the final irony of his project to supply relevant notes for the building of a new society manifests itself in *Guide to Kulchur* and the radio broadcasts. Once he has stepped openly to the front of his texts, freely admitting his observations as part of those texts' splintered structures, his commentary uncovers his darkest convictions: analysis and education have taken precedence over poetry to no avail. Wherever the artist chooses to stand, however he decides to present himself, it is his readers who have vanished, and with them his power. These increasingly pronounced fears become, as with Joyce and Woolf, more and more frequently the subject of the apparatus itself: in his glosses Pound often glances at the failure of his glosses.[97]

*Guide to Kulchur* and the radio broadcasts attempt to apply to a wider field the principles of the earlier guides. Like Woolf and Joyce in their work of the 1930s, Pound aspires to an ideal of inclusiveness, though he brings heterogeneous material into his texts so that he may demonstrate its reduction and simplification: "I am at best trying to provide the average reader with a few tools for dealing with the heteroclite mass of undigested information hurled at him daily and monthly and set to entangle his feet in volumes of reference" (*GK*, 23). Replacing those ponderous volumes with this comparatively tidy book, Pound advertises the *Guide*'s novelty to those who know his previous compendia: "[T]hese are notes for a totalitarian treatise," he advises. "I am in fact . . . not simply abridging extant encyclopedias or condensing two dozen more detailed volumes" (*GK*, 27). In similar defensive asides throughout *Guide to Kulchur* and the broadcasts, he discloses his constant sense of hostile auditors by naming the criticisms he anticipates even as he claims their irrelevance.

Pound explicitly denies that *Guide to Kulchur* duplicates any aspects of "How to Read" or *ABC of Reading*. Referring to the earlier two books, he writes, "I was avowedly trying to establish a series or set of measures, standards, voltometers, here I am dealing with a heteroclite set of impressions" (*GK*, 208). The unbalanced terms of this comparison (which merely states that guidelines differ from data, a cardinal principle in all three works) indicate Pound's difficulties in making a qualitative distinction between these kindred tools for sorting through books and other artifacts of culture. Although vastly different

in tone, his grandiose evocation of a "totalitarian" synthesis differs little in practice from his promise that on mastering our *ABC*s, we can venture through literature or economics, confident that we have the "T squares" to analyze whatever we encounter (*ABCR*, 87).[98] A less dramatic assertion later in the *Guide*
gives a clearer representation of its method: "If I have said it ten times in other
books and not yet in this book it shd. be repeated here and in all books for a
decade UNTIL it enter the popular mind" (*GK*, 246).

The radio broadcasts openly proclaim their affinities with the 1930s textbooks: "I have said before, said it in poetry and said it in prose" (*RS*, 179).
"There is no item in this present talk that I have not mentioned in preceding
communications," Pound wearily reminds us, "but the historic importance of
every one of these items is so tremendous, and the difficulty of getting them
[in] their sequence, their cumulative significance into the public head is so difficult that I should be justified [in] repeating them ten times over" (*RS*,
265–66). He begins a talk titled "The Keys of Heaven" with an epitome of his
pedagogical style and procedure: "I suppose if I go on talking to you kids LONG
enough I will get something into your heads" (*RS*, 162).

For my purposes, it is the number and nature of the glosses that most significantly distinguish the broadcasts and the *Guide* from Pound's earlier work.
Questions regarding audience, authority, and form—questions around which I
have focused my discussions of Joyce, Woolf, and Pound—haunt almost every
written or spoken sentence in Pound's last two major prose undertakings before
the end of the war and his imprisonment interrupt his teaching. In these dis-
orienting texts the reader must pause again and again as Pound shakes free of
the particular point to deliberate altogether broader issues. Like the content of
his lessons, Pound's notes on his effectiveness repeat themselves. He returns to
exhaustively studied clusters of familiar anxieties about the clarity of his sentences and the existence of his fearfully elusive audience. "Let the reader be
patient," he writes in a half-reprimand, half-plea just after starting to measure
"Kulchur" in his *Guide*: "I am not being merely incoherent. I haven't 'lost my
thread' in the sense that I haven't just dropped one thread to pick up another
of different shade. I need more than one string for a fabric" (*GK*, 29). The qualifier "merely" only partly conceals a confession of disorder. When pressed by his
own awareness of that disorder to demonstrate the unity of this text, Pound
resorts to metaphor, just as he did in the *ABC*s. But here, not entirely comforted
by threads and fabric, he ushers his readers to the door of his study, pointing to
tangible proof of design: "I may, even yet, be driven to a chronological catalogue
of greek ideas, roman ideas, mediaeval ideas in the occident. There is a perfectly
good LIST of those ideas thirty feet from where I sit typing" (*GK*, 29). Preparatory to heading back into the Analects, Christian thought, and the fascist historical sense—and as an alternative to reading this serviceable list aloud—
Pound reiterates his overall objective of discrimination: "I am trying to get a
bracket for one kind of ideas, I mean that will hold a whole set of ideas and
keep them apart from another set" (*GK*, 29).

As specific complexities threaten to throw his texts out of balance, Pound
retreats, calling up reasonable generalities to preserve the impression of a plan.

"Do I ramble?" he asks in one of his broadcasts. "One can't just isolate an idea. If it is real, it is bound to have bits of fact and sidelights clingin' to it" (*RS*, 250). Pound reverts to bedrock, to inarguable propositions for himself even more than for others. A truth culled from the *Ta Hio*, for example, takes on private significance: "Any man's clarity must start inside his own head. I therefore propose to put my own ideas in order, and to communicate that order in the hope that it assists the hearer in finding out where he or she is" (*RS*, 175).[99]

The inward-turning nature of this proposal, meaningless to anyone but Pound until that order speaks for itself, is also a feature of a critical moment in *Guide to Kulchur*. Pound begins by debating the efficacy of his teaching and then wonders how firmly he grasps his own ideas: "'I wish,'" yodeled Lord Byron "'that he wd. explain his explanation.'" That was in another country and a different connection, but I admit that the foregoing pp. are as obscure as anything in my poetry. I mean or imply that certain truth exists" (*GK*, 295). He answers the charge of obscurity with the comment that "truth exists." Careful not to claim that he has actually expressed that truth, he moves to metaphorical grounds in this gloss on his *Guide*: "Certain colours exist in nature though great painters have striven vainly, and though the colour film is not yet perfected" (*GK*, 295). This figure offers Pound temporary respite from the alarming thought that his tool for the average reader will be indistinguishable from the "heteroclite mass" it was supposed to simplify.[100] He shifts finally into the first-person plural, a voice with the appearance of objectivity that nevertheless allows the "I" to assess itself: "Truth is not untrue'd by reason of our failing to fix it on paper. Certain objects are communicable to a man or woman only 'with proper lighting,' they are perceptible in our own minds only with proper 'lighting,' fitfully and by instants" (*GK*, 295). The dimensions of the dimly lit classroom dwindle, considerations of men and women fading in "our own mind."

The possessive adjective also combats Pound's overwhelming sense of solitude and impotence—a sense that accompanies his earliest addresses to a heedless public. His need to find a circle, a "we," increases as he is denied access to publication, rudely treated in reviews, and ignored by the economists and politicians he seeks to educate.[101] Ignored, that is, with an exception that he muses on in *Guide to Kulchur*. When Pound talked with Mussolini on 30 January 1933, Mussolini asked the poet, "Why do you want to put your ideas in order?" (*GK*, 105, 182).[102] Pound explains the enigmatic question as an illustration of the "Boss's" incisiveness—penetrating, "unhesitant to the root," what were in this case the vagaries of Pound's economic explanations (*GK*, 105). It is at least a souvenir from a conversation between the worlds of politics and the arts, a conversation for which Pound had yearned for years. But the question contains at its cruel core Pound's fear that the ideas he tries to hold, the exhibits he wants to arrange, the facts he needs to muster are scattered beyond recovery. And, perhaps worse than this fear, which Pound can at least continue to fight by renewing his efforts at internal clarity, Mussolini's question potentially conveys absolute indifference. A poet has no more need for orderly ideas than any other negligible, powerless citizen has; the organization, when required, will come from Il Duce. Why should anyone arrange his thoughts when no one listens?

Speaking into a microphone brings the intimately related issues of audience and order into painful convergence for Pound. The voice conjures a community; it solicits a response with a force unmatched by the printed page. The possibility that someone listens as Pound utters each word, and that he or she might stop listening at any point, makes him debilitatingly sensitive to the form of every broadcast. "I am taking my whole time on one point durin' this little discourse," he says, eager to repair past mistakes. "Sometimes I try to tell you too much. I suspect I talk in a what-is-called incoherent manner" (*RS*, 227). The criticism, only partly admitted, is deserved: "'[C]ause I can't (and I reckon nobody could) tell where to begin. What knowledge one can consider as pre-existed in the mind of the AVERAGE American listener" (*RS*, 227). Woolf's similar complaint—"No audience. No echo"—lies close to this query, as does Joyce's allied fear that no one but his critics follows his work in progress: "His producers are they not his consumers?"

Just before "the American pressmen left Rome," Pound heard how his lessons would be received: "[A]n experienced well broken journalist said: don't worry, there'll always be some fellow in a newspaper office sitten there, trying to get something for his column or something" (*RS*, 227). The United States Foreign Broadcast Intelligence Service, rather than "some fellow," diligently recorded Pound's commentaries, and yet we should also preserve the journalist's vision of this single writer, bored or desperate to meet a deadline, tuned in to Pound.[103] The image exactly captures modernism's severely reduced stage at the end of its first generation's period of greatest achievement. Pound stands, like Joyce and Woolf, in a space partly constructed, partly resisted, carefully measured by his apparatus. He hears nothing from those for whom he writes his notes. He doubts, in a broadcast he names "As a Beginning," whether even the last listener exists, since opponents and allies alike remain quiet. So vivid is this present silence that time itself—its passing largely measured by our hearing voices other than our own—seems to have stopped. Have we been brought to a beginning or an end? "Have you no eyes, no history and no memories? No eyes, no knowledge or memory of your own history, and no memory of events that have happened before you?" (*RS*, 151). Pound waits again among the shades he summoned in Canto 1, except these cannot speak back, no matter how much blood flows in the fosse. Still he keeps talking, sending his glosses into air.

# NOTES

## Introduction

1. I cite quotations of Eliot's notes to *The Waste Land* by page and line number.

2. Eliot, *Use of Poetry*, 30.

3. Important studies addressing the literature and politics of the 1930s are Valentine Cunningham, *British Writers of the Thirties*; James Gindin, *British Fiction in the 1930s*; Lucy McDiarmid, *Saving Civilization*; Samuel Hynes, *Auden Generation*; and the essays collected in Frank Gloversmith, ed., *Class, Culture and Social Change*.

4. Pound, *The Exile* 3 (1928): 108.

5. Lee Patterson, "Introduction," 787.

6. Over the past two decades, theorists have written from a wide variety of perspectives on marginalia and, more often, on figuratively marginal forces that operate within the compass of an always divided, always polysemous book. Three studies, focused primarily on medieval and early modern glosses, are of particular interest: Evelyn Tribble, *Margins and Marginality*; Stephen Barney, ed., *Annotation and Its Texts*; and the fall 1992 issue of the *South Atlantic Quarterly*, ed. Lee Patterson. David Stern's "Midrash and Indeterminacy" represents another suggestive path for theorizing the gloss. Writings by Jacques Derrida, Roland Barthes, Walter Benjamin, and Mikhail Bakhtin more generally helped me to frame this study. Of especial relevance are Derrida's "Parergon," "Living On," and *Glas*; Barthes's *S/Z* and *Pleasure of the Text*; and Bakhtin's *Dialogic Imagination* and *Rabelais and His World*. Another important reference point for considering modern glosses is Benjamin's Arcades project; Susan Buck-Morss describes and explicates this project in *Dialectics of Seeing*. The most provocative single piece on apparatus that I know is Lawrence Lipking, "Marginal Gloss."

7. For a discussion of the publishing history of *The Waste Land*, see Lawrence Rainey, "Price of Modernism." Daniel Woodward discusses the early editions of the poem in "Notes on the Publishing History and Text of *The Waste Land*."

8. Eliot, *Use of Poetry*, 150–51.

9. Pound, "T. S. Eliot," 24.

10. In Michael Grant, ed., *Critical Heritage*, 1:158–59.

11. Richard Poirier, *Renewal of Literature*, 130. Poirier, though he consistently underestimates the complexity of modernist apparatus, provides a searching discussion of modernism and difficulty in *Renewal of Literature*, chap. 2. See also Allon White, *Uses of Obscurity*.

12. Grant, *Critical Heritage*, 1:199.

13. It is in the eighteenth century, with the quarrel between the ancients and the moderns, that many of the issues surrounding the modern gloss arise—particularly those related to an expanded readership and the creation and cultivation of a particular audience. For a detailed discussion of the battle of the books and the nature and effects of Augustan apparatus, see Joseph Levine, *Battle of the Books*.

14. Eliot, "Frontiers of Criticism," 121.

15. Hugh Kenner, *Eliot*, 151. After Eliot, Kenner makes the best-known argument against critical attention to the notes.

16. Peter Ackroyd, *Eliot*, 317.

17. Eliot, "Frontiers of Criticism," 117.

18. Ibid., 131.

19. Ibid., 121.

20. In fact, the poem was accompanied by notes as it circulated in typescript among Eliot's friends. A. Walton Litz writes in *"The Waste Land* Fifty Years After": "In this sense, the original notes were an integral part of the poem, not unlike the elaborate chart of symbolic correspondences and Homeric parallels that Joyce circulated privately for the benefit of the first readers of *Ulysses*" (9).

21. Eliot, "Frontiers of Criticism," 121.

22. See Stanley Sultan's discussion of "The Frontiers of Criticism," in *Eliot, Joyce and Company*, 163–66. He questions Eliot's disavowal of the notes but concludes that they are nothing more than an instance of "literary trifling or play" in *The Waste Land* (166).

23. Eliot's repudiation of his notes should be considered a part of his campaign, begun almost immediately after *The Waste Land* was published, to distance himself from the poem. See Ronald Bush, *Eliot*, chaps. 5 (sec. 3) and 6. For a discussion of Eliot's renunciation in terms of the changing poetics of modernism, see Michael Levenson, *Genealogy of Modernism*, 210–20.

24. For a full discussion of the marketing of *The Waste Land*, see Rainey, "Price of Modernism."

25. Eliot, "Frontiers of Criticism," 121.

26. Ibid.

27. Ibid., 122.

28. Clive Bell, *Old Friends*, 119–20.

29. Eliot, *Sacred Wood*, 54.

30. Ibid.

31. Luke Menand discusses the notes' explanatory inadequacy in the context of a wider survey of Eliot's "philosophical critique of interpretation" in *Discovering Modernism*, 89.

32. Eliot, *Selected Essays*, 20.

33. Oscar Wilde, *Artist as Critic*, 365, 370.

34. Eliot, *Selected Essays*, 20.

35. In *Discovering Modernism*, Menand provides an illuminating discussion of Eliot's early critique, in his dissertation on Bradley, of the possibility of objectivity (chap. 2). Jeffrey Perl, in *Skepticism and Modern Enmity*, further clarifies the philosophical foundations and extent of Eliot's skepticism.

36. Eliot, *Selected Essays*, 22.

37. Ibid., 21.

38. Perl, *Skepticism and Modern Enmity*, 84, 69.

39. Eliot, *Selected Essays*, 21.

40. Eliot, *After Strange Gods*, 42, 59.

41. Ibid., 65.

42. Throughout *Concept of Modernism*, Astradur Eysteinsson pursues our century's contrasting constructions of modernism as that which is purely aestheticist, evasive of all sociopolitical matters, and as an artistic movement that always remains culturally engaged.

43. Eliot, *Use of Poetry*, 154.

44. Ibid., 152. Pound makes a comparable assertion, probably in 1933, on a draft sheet for his *ABC of Reading*: "[A]n illiterate with a love of justice is probably a better literary critic than a half educated professor with an axe edge 'needing' attention / or a journalist suffering from INF/CX/[inferiority complex]" (Pound, drafts for *ABCR*).

45. Eliot, *Use of Poetry*, 153, 154.

# Chapter 1

1. The publication date for Herbert Gorman's *James Joyce* differs from the copyright date. Gorman's biography was published on 15 February 1940; its copyright date is 1939.

2. All quotations pertaining to the drafting of Joyce's political parables are taken from galley page 81 and the insert that is taped to that page.

3. Cheryl Herr, *Anatomy*, 7. I should state clearly here that I choose Herr's book precisely because it is one of the most exciting and useful works of a fairly new category of studies on Joyce; I urge simply that developing culturally and sociologically sophisticated readings need not compel us to leave the author out of the picture.

4. Ibid., 9–10.

5. Ibid., 7–8. Buttressing her criticisms of Ellmann and Manganiello, Herr quotes from a review of Manganiello's *Joyce's Politics* by Sidney Feshbach in the *James Joyce Quarterly*. The texts she and Feshbach discuss are Richard Ellmann, *Consciousness of Joyce*, and Dominic Manganiello, *Joyce's Politics*.

6. Herr, *Anatomy*, 8.

7. James Longenbach, *Wallace Stevens*, 11.

8. Valentine Cunningham discusses the difficulties of maintaining neutrality during the 1930s in "Neutral?" Cunningham's discussion focuses largely on Eliot, who is what Cunningham calls a "false neutral."

9. Willard Potts has already performed this survey with admirable lucidity and thoroughness in "Joyce's Notes."

10. For discussions of Irish neutrality before and during the Second World War, see R. F. Foster, *Modern Ireland*, 559–63. See also Robert Fisk, *In Time of War*.

11. Michael Lennon, "James Joyce," 649. Potts discusses the Gorman biography as "an opportunity for responding to this attack by Lennon" ("Joyce's Notes," 96).

12. Lennon, "James Joyce," 649.

13. Joyce, *Critical Writings*, 159, 163, 166.

14. Ibid., 172. Joyce makes his most forceful charge of his country's willingness to betray itself in *Critical Writings*, 162–63. See also his discussion of the pernicious effects of Irish romanticism in "The Soul of Ireland" (1903) (*Critical Writings*, 102–5).

15. Joyce, *Critical Writings*, 243.

16. Withholding taxes is of course itself a dangerous and time-honored form of political protest—a protest against the polis itself. That Joyce so construed his refusal can be seen in the fifth stanza of his satirical poem "Dooleysprudence" (Richard Ellmann, A. Walton Litz, and John Whittier-Ferguson, eds., *James Joyce*, 120–22). Ell-

mann discusses the poem in *JJ*, 423–25; Gorman frames the one stanza he quotes in more explicitly political terms (Gorman, 240–41).

17. Joyce, *Portrait*, 215.

18. Frank Budgen quotes "Dooleysprudence" in *James Joyce*, 201. The quotation follows Budgen's description of the Carr dispute; it seems tacked on (perhaps at Joyce's suggestion) to the end of Budgen's chapter. Although I do not intend to discuss Joyce's involvement with the production of Budgen's book, I note Paul Léon's comment to Harriet Shaw Weaver about Joyce's eager participation in revisions: "It is a long time since I have seen Mr. Joyce so interested in anything as he has been in this work making suggestions, remembering points etc. Even after Mr. Budgen's departure he kept dictating me various suggestions to be wrought in the text" (JJ, *Letters*, 3:286).

19. Joyce alludes to Finley Peter Dunne's character Mr. Dooley, the Irish-American bartender whose skeptical analysis of politics and manners perfectly suits the Mr. Dooley of Joyce's song. Dunne's Dooley flourished between the late 1890s and the First World War.

20. In his song commemorating the Carr–Joyce feud, "The C. G. Is Not Literary," Joyce records the irony of his becoming entangled in court over a play by his infamous countryman: "[T]he bully British Philistine once more drove Oscar Wilde" (Gorman, 256). Margot Norris discusses at length the complex bonds between Wilde and Joyce in chapter 3 of *Joyce's Web*.

21. Hélène Cixous, *Exile*, 261. See *JJ*, 426–28, 440–41, 445, 452; and Brenda Maddox, *Nora*, 155–56. The Carr–Joyce feud is central matter for Tom Stoppard's *Travesties*.

22. Maddox, *Nora*, 155.

23. Ellmann gives an account of the gift in *JJ*, 405–6; he says it was from Edmund Gosse that Joyce received the "hint" about favors owed to the Crown (*JJ*, 423).

24. Budgen, *James Joyce*, 200; Gorman, 255.

25. Budgen, *James Joyce*, 200; Gorman, 255–56.

26. Budgen, *James Joyce*, 200.

27. Lennon, "James Joyce," 651.

28. Ibid., 643, 648, 648. Although some of Lennon's charges against John Joyce can be made to stick, John Joyce was in fact secretary of the United Liberal Club (*JJ*, 16). Gorman infuriated Joyce by taking as true Lennon's assertion that John Joyce was "befriended by Conservative party interests" (Gorman galleys, 36). Joyce strikes this phrase, substitutes his own (see Gorman, 11), and writes to Gorman in the galley margin: "[T]his is completely false and seems to have been taken also from M. Lennons [*sic*] poisonous article!" (Gorman galleys, 36).

29. Edith Rockefeller McCormick, patroness of Carl Jung and a number of artists, began offering anonymous financial support to Joyce in February 1918 (Joyce discovered her identity shortly thereafter). For reasons that have never been wholly clear, she stopped her monthly stipend to Joyce in October 1919 (*JJ*, 422, 466–69; Gorman, 264–65).

30. As with my discussion of Herr's book, I choose Norris's study of Joyce precisely because I admire so much of its theory, so many of its readings; what I see as its flaws are thus part of the most sophisticated work being done on Joyce.

31. Norris, *Joyce's Web*, 24.

32. Ibid., 31.

33. Ibid.

34. Joyce, *Dubliners*, 74, 84.

35. Budgen, *James Joyce*, 20.

36. Joyce, *Dubliners*, 73. Seamus Deane, in "Joyce and Nationalism," suggests that for Joyce, whose linguistic achievements allowed him to "[discover] the fictive nature of politics," "the finite nature of historical fact was supplanted by the infinite, or near infinite, possibilities of language" (181, 168). But Joyce achieves no such poststructural aesthetic nirvana; he lives much more firmly tied to the world, as his apparatus and his texts everywhere reveal.

37. Norris, *Joyce's Web*, 8.

38. Ibid., 23.

39. Ibid.

40. Ibid., 7, 20.

41. In "Modernist Under Siege," Ronald Bush points out that the New Criticism, "a movement more univocally conservative than modernism ever was," remains largely responsible for many post–New Critical readings of the modernists' sociopolitical engagements (6). Speaking of Yeats's work, he notes that "the interesting thing about many recent Marxist and postmodernist critics of Yeats is that rather than questioning the New Critics' assumptions, they accept them and reverse their valence" (6).

42. Michael North, in *Political Aesthetic*, is eloquent on the effect of the aesthetic and political tensions in the work of three canonical modernists: "I feel that modernism still has a claim on our interest precisely because it does not make good sense, because we find in it more of the unfinished business of our time than in any other literature" (viii).

43. In chapter 4 of *Concept of Modernism*, Astradur Eysteinsson provides a detailed and incisive discussion of the theoretical problems involved in maintaining this divide between the modern and the avant-garde. He gives particular attention to the theory of Peter Bürger throughout the chapter. Bürger's *Theory of the Avant-Garde* is crucial to an understanding of Norris and important to my own discussion. See also Andreas Huyssen, *After the Great Divide*; and Renato Poggioli, *Theory of the Avant-Garde*.

44. For a list of episodes from "Work in Progress" published in *transition*, see James Spoerri's *Check List*, 7.

45. In "Elliot Paul's *transition* Years," Arnold Goldman discusses Paul's editorial role and his contributions to the journal.

46. Marvin Magalaner and Richard M. Kain, *Joyce*, 244. For a measured, persuasive response to Magalaner and Kain, see Maria Jolas, "Joyce's Friend Jolas." See also the discussion of Joyce, Jolas, and *transition* in Gorman (341–42), and recall that Joyce read and approved Gorman's glowing account of Jolas and *transition*.

47. Hugh Kenner, *Dublin's Joyce*, 360.

48. "Joyce's Notes," Potts's essay on Joyce's revisions to the Gorman biography, focuses more fully than I do in this chapter on Joyce's energetic participation in the creation of his image as hardworking artist and loyal father, husband, and son.

49. Dougald McMillan, *transition*, 183.

50. "Literary works do not know themselves, and cannot *be* known, apart from their specific material modes of existence/resistance. They are not channels of transmission, they are particular forms of transmissive interaction" (Jerome McGann, *Textual Condition*, 11).

51. It is important to place the editorial statements in *transition* in the context of other nineteenth- and twentieth-century manifestos. An admirable study of the genre is Marjorie Perloff's *Futurist Moment* (esp. chap. 3). Kay Boyle suggests that the avant-garde in the 1930s reflected its sense of crisis in the rhetoric of its various proclamations: "This was a serious business, and if one laughed a good deal over café tables, one did not laugh very loudly on the printed page" (Robert McAlmon and Kay Boyle, *Being Geniuses*, 239).

52. Valentine Cunningham usefully discusses the literal and figurative importance of "frontiers" to writers of the decade in *British Writers of the Thirties*, chaps. 11, 12.

53. Eugene Jolas's unpublished autobiography, "Man from Babel," dwells at length and with insight on political matters, particularly as he discusses his life and the fortunes of *transition* during the 1930s. For a published glimpse of the political Jolas, see McAlmon and Boyle, *Being Geniuses*, 303.

54. McMillan, *transition*, 191; see also 201n.11.

55. In his autobiography, Jolas recalls that Joyce voiced the same concern even more anxiously: "'This book of mine must appear before the war comes,' [Joyce] said wearily. 'Otherwise no one will read it'" ("Man from Babel," draft A, box 6, folder 147).

56. Jolas recalls Joyce's telling him that "all the characters in my books belong to the lower middle classes, and even the working class; and they are all quite poor" ("My Friend James Joyce," 14). According to Jolas, Joyce was nettled by a Marxist attack from the Russian critic Karl Radek. For excerpts from Radek's review, see Robert H. Deming, ed., *Critical Heritage*, 2:624–26.

57. See also Gorman, 23–24, 27–28 (the dark past of Clongowes Wood); 49–51 (Dublin and the Irish mythos); 228 (the "Time-Spirit" of Europe); 339–40 (the "Time-Spirit" of the 1930s).

58. An insightful discussion of the deliberate crossing of myth and political program in fascist ideology in Germany during the first half of the twentieth century can be found in Jeffrey Herf, *Reactionary Modernism*.

59. Budgen, *James Joyce*, 152.

60. Jolas, "Man from Babel," draft E, box 9, folder 197.

61. For brief biographies of Eugene Jolas, see McMillan, *transition*, chap. 1; see also McAlmon and Boyle, *Being Geniuses*, 303–4.

62. Jolas, "Man from Babel," draft A, box 6, folder 147.

63. Ibid., draft E, box 9, folder 196.

64. Philippe Sollers, "Joyce & Co," 108.

65. David Bennett, "Periodical Fragments," 498. Throughout his book on modernist politics and aesthetics, North offers a much more carefully discriminating discussion of the "contradictions of liberalism," showing how schismatic and unifying forces contend in our century's political fields. North finds in fascism "the explosive coalescence of the left and right wings of anti-liberal thought" (*Political Aesthetics*, 4, 5).

66. Bennett, "Periodical Fragments," 494. Bennett ends his essay with congratulatory words for postmodern little magazines "grounded not in universals but in difference" (500), implying that the pages of *transition* were filled with ideologically consistent documents all representative of a program promoted by Jolas.

67. I take the phrase from Kenneth Burke's essay "Rhetoric of Hitler's 'Battle.'"

68. Wyndham Lewis, *The Enemy*, 18. For an unremittingly hostile assault on the "naive philosophy of linguistic nihilism" supposedly promoted by Jolas, see Michael Finney, "Eugene Jolas." Finney's essay repeats the most common charges made against *transition* almost from the journal's inception.

69. V. F. Calverton, *Modern Quarterly*, 281. The issue of Calverton's *Modern Quarterly* featuring arguments from both sides (*transition* is represented by Jolas, Stuart Gilbert, and Robert Sage) is an important document in the assessment of the political position of *transition*. Calverton's was the line taken against *Finnegans Wake* by Communist critics. See, for example, in Deming, ed., *Critical Heritage*, essays by Dmitri Mirsky (2:589–92); V. Gertsfelde (2:616–18); and Margaret Schlauch (2:722–24).

70. See Robert Short, "Politics of Surrealism." North provides us with a usefully

complicated portrait of political ideologies, focusing specifically on the status of fascism, in his *Political Aesthetic*, 158ff.

71. For a persuasive reading of this episode as Joyce's farewell to Jolas and *transition*, see McMillan, *transition*, 225–30. Nathan Halper offers a myth-centered interpretation in "James Joyce and the Russian General." Jean-Michel Rabaté offers a psychopolitical reading in chapter seven of *James Joyce, Authorized Reader*, chap. 7. See also Edward Kopper's "'. . . but where he is eaten.'"

# Chapter 2

1. *transition* 23 contains the episode from II.2 published separately in 1937 as *Storiella as She Is Syung* (*FW*, 260–275.2; 304–8).

2. Dougald McMillan compares Jolas's principles to those of Joyce in his study of the journal (*transition*, 193–200). The primary difference lies in Jolas's focus on the unconscious as creative source. Joyce clearly dissociated himself from the surrealists and from other schools founded on a psychological basis. "Joyce's interest was not in 'soaking loose' what was in the unconscious but in a conscious use of language to pierce beneath the normal level at which we respond to words" (199).

3. The commercial origins of the manifesto as well as its later design—"less to move the masses to action than to charm and give pleasure to one's coterie"—are discussed in Marjorie Perloff, *Futurist Moment*, 114, 94–96. Her entire third chapter, "Violence and Precision: The Manifesto as Art Form," provides a suggestive background for reading *transition*. Renato Poggioli also usefully discussed the formation of an audience for experimental art in *Theory of the Avant-Garde*, chaps. 2, 5.

4. When Petitjean engages in specific textual criticism of "Work in Progress," he is just as confident, though his single paragraph of explication is magnificently confused and confusing (*t* 23 [1935]: 140). And yet Joyce, probably swayed by Petitjean's adulation, writes to Budgen on 25 April 1934: "A young Frenchman Armand Petit Jean has written a book, an amazing study of W.i.P. . . . He is only 20 and began it 3 years ago!" Unfortunately the book never appeared (JJ, *Letters*, 3:303 and n. 3).

5. Bridges had sent Joyce his latest volume of poetry, *The Testament of Beauty* (Oxford: Clarendon Press, 1929), with, Joyce tells Harriet Weaver, "an inscription expressing his full sympathy with what I am trying to do" (JJ, *Letters*, 1:288).

6. The letter is full of animals: "capriciously" comes from *caper*, meaning "goat." Stuart Gilbert had not read this letter when he wrote in his preface to *James Joyce's Ulysses*, "[T]he ideas, interpretations and explanations put forward in these pages are not capricious or speculative, but were endorsed by Joyce himself" (10).

7. See, for example, Gorman, 16, 35, 45, 71, 198, 274, 332–34. I include only footnotes in this list—all of them added by Joyce to Gorman's galleys.

8. On 3 September 1920, Joyce sent a "scheme" composed only of chapter titles and section divisions to John Quinn (JJ, *Letters*, 1:145). He forwarded a much more elaborate schema on 21 September 1920 to Carlo Linati and, in November 1921, lent a similar key to Valery Larbaud for an upcoming lecture that Larbaud was to deliver on *Ulysses* at Shakespeare and Company Bookstore (JJ, *Letters*, 1:146–47; *JJ*, 519–23). A second, somewhat different version circulated among Joyce's intimates until it appeared, in a slightly abbreviated form, as a cornerstone of Gilbert's *James Joyce's Ulysses*, 41. Gorman also received a copy of this second plan for use in his biography of Joyce. The three schemata are reproduced and compared in the appendix to Richard Ellmann's

*Ulysses on the Liffey*. The Gorman–Gilbert schema is discussed in H. K. Croessmann, "Joyce, Gorman, and the Schema of *Ulysses*." I choose not to treat the *Ulysses* schemata in my own text because the details have been thoroughly discussed by a large number of critics writing on *Ulysses*, and because they are not part of Joyce's work of the 1930s.

9. J. Mitchell Morse wittily characterizes the "weapons" Joyce deployed against his readers: "exile, cunning and publicity" ("On Teaching *Finnegans Wake*," 66).

10. Perloff writes that, in an era of manifestos and avant-garde theoretical programs, "[t]o talk about art becomes equivalent to making it" (*Futurist Moment*, 90). Perloff is speaking specifically of the early period of Italian manifesto making (1909–1915), but her comment applies equally to subsequent modernist theoretical endeavors. See also Geoffrey Hartman, "Literary Commentary as Literature."

11. Sylvia Beach, *Shakespeare and Company*, 183.

12. Beach, in *Shakespeare and Company*, describes the arrival of Slingby's protest, mistakenly identifying the source for the name as Edward Lear's poem "The Jumblies" (183). "Slingby" is the name of one of the children in Lear's poem "The Story of the Four Little Children Who Went Round the World."

13. The first assertion that Dixon was an authentic contributor to *Our Exagmination* came in 1979 from Thomas Goldwasser, "Who Was Vladimir Dixon?" I have published an expanded biographical and textual study of Dixon's relationship with Joyce and Beach in "The Voice Behind the Echo."

14. I owe to A. Walton Litz my tentative identification of the "Mrs. Kennedy" who appears in Sylvia Beach's account books for *Our Exagmination*. Litz discovered her name frequently on the book checkout sheets from the Shakespeare and Company Bookstore (which also served its patrons as a library).

15. Jacques Mercanton, "Hours of James Joyce," 213.

16. I presented this portion of my chapter at the "Finnegans Wake: Contexts" conference in Leeds, England (1987). Suzette Henke, in "Exagmining Beckett & Company," also briefly discusses this addition of the Exagminators to the *Wake*.

17. The typescript is dated in *JJA* 53:97, 8.8. I quote from the typescript; the passage in the *Wake* (*FW*, 284.18–22) reads "pregross" rather than "procress."

18. The words ending in "-tion" are added in Joyce's hand on pages from *transition* in 1936 (*JJA* 46:455). The holograph additions are dated in *JJA* 46:441.

19. These "sigla" are the shorthand symbols by which Joyce designated the associative clusters that stand in some sense for "characters" in *Finnegans Wake*. The Twelve and their sigillum are discussed in Roland McHugh, *Sigla of Finnegans Wake*, 8, 101–5. McHugh lays out a number of possible mythological and historical predecessors for the Twelve and briefly describes a number of their structural functions in the *Wake*. The Twelve are also sketched in Adaline Glasheen, *Third Census*, 292–93. Joyce focuses briefly on them—"the component partners of our societate"—in the seventh of the twelve riddles of I.6 (*FW*, 142.8–29).

20. William Jenkins provides a brief but illuminating discussion of the Twelve as "non-entities" or "zeros" in "Zerothruster," 123–24. His other note on the Twelve, "From Solation to Solution," linking the "-tion" words associated with the Twelve to Gilbert and Sullivan's librettos, is less helpful. Neither essay focuses on *Our Exagmination*.

21. Joyce's challenge can be found, somewhat altered, in *FW*, 284.11–14. The section of "Work in Progress" that appeared in *transition* 11 was to become *FW*, 282.6–304.3. This section was later published as part of *Tales Told of Shem and Shaun* (Paris: Black Sun Press, 1929), titled "The Muddest Thick That Was Ever Heard Dump" (John J. Slocum and Herbert Cahoon, *Bibliography*, A36).

22. Giambattista Vico, *New Science*, 118, 8. There are dozens of studies exploring

ties between Joyce and Vico. A recent (and fruitful) one is John Bishop, *Joyce's Book of the Dark*, chap. 7.

23. The additions germane to this discussion are reproduced in *JJA* 62:120–25. I quote directly from the galleys. The passage in the *Wake* (*FW*, 497.1–3) reads "incamination" rather than "incammination."

24. The description should also be read as a challenge to the critical skills of Budgen, who was writing an article on the *Wake* when Joyce offered this characterization of II.2. Joyce's comment, in a letter to Budgen, has become permanently attached to the chapter. Anyone reading Joyce's letters realizes that dozens of his pronouncements have remained similarly connected to other chapters and passages in his work. His label of "most difficult" generally begins discussions of the chapter without itself being queried or, in most cases, attributed to Joyce.

25. Shari Benstock discusses the failure of the notes as guides in "At the Margins of Discourse," 212. In "Conjunctions," Susan Shaw Sailer suggests an entirely opposite, and I think unproductive, approach—promising to "discover the connection[s]" between the glosses and the central text. While she finds connections—as one can with any two pieces of the *Wake* placed side by side—she does not, to my satisfaction, demonstrate the kind of overarching pattern to the glosses that she promises. In "Talmud Another Source?" Richard Schuster finds the Talmud relevant to the form of II.2.

26. The first seven lines of II.2, and the accompanying marginalia and notes, are discussed in fairly detailed conceptual terms, with emphasis on the Viconian cycles latent in the opening, in Lawrence Lipking, "Marginal Gloss," 651–55.

27. Fritz Senn, "Dynamics of Corrective Unrest," 71.

28. Joseph Campbell and Henry Morton Robinson, *Skeleton Key*, 163. This shadowy character takes the name "Professor Jones"—the title and surname supposedly allude to Ernest Jones, author of *Hamlet and Oedipus*—in Glasheen, *Third Census*, 147; and William York Tindall, *Reader's Guide*, 171.

29. I cite notes to II.2 by note number, preceded by L (left), R (right), or F (footnote), according to the note's location on the page.

30. The opening note in the left margin combines a comment Beckett made when Joyce told him John Joyce's story about Buckley and the Russian general with the militant refrain of "Follow me up to Carlow" (*JJ*, 398 and note; JJ, *Letters*, 3:428–29). Joyce employs the song and his father's story to satirize nationalist sentiment.

31. *Wake* critics generally agree that Shem/Dolph has the italics and Shaun/Kev the roman small caps from 260 to 287, that the "halftime" occurs on 287 to 293, and that the brothers "switch sides" (though not typefaces) from 293 to 308. Glasheen clearly lays this out in *Third Census*, xlix.

32. Ur, the reputed home of Abraham, was one of the oldest cities of ancient Sumer. It was being excavated by a team from the British Museum from 1922 to 1934, while Joyce was composing II.2. Chaldea was the land of the Semitic people who were known as the founders of astronomy and astrology. The Chaldeans were also legendary masters of sorcery and other occult sciences.

33. Joyce, *Portrait*, 192.

34. Ibid., 192, 193.

35. See also Stephen's discovery of "foetus" carved on the desk in *Portrait* (89) as well as his own idiosyncratic class in the second chapter of *Ulysses*. In the latter example, Stephen might be said to annotate his own lesson with obliquely related material (his definition of "pier"; his riddle) from his wandering mind.

36. The misspelled "hesitancy" evokes Richard Pigott, an Irish journalist whose

forged letters linked Parnell to the Phoenix Park assassinations of 1882. Pigott was suspected by the Parnellite Kevan Egan of being the forger when Egan noticed the same misspelling, "hesitency," in one of the published forgeries and in a letter from Pigott that Egan possessed (Malcolm Brown, *Politics of Irish Literature*, 329; see also Glasheen, *Third Census*, 234). I gloss the word to point out that Dolph's noteplay has nothing to do with the subject this word should evoke in a student at his lessons, or, for that matter, in a student of the *Wake*'s leitmotifs.

37. Ronald Buckalew points out that the Irish pronunciation of English tends to make "the words written *tin* and *thin* . . . homophones" ("Night Lessons," 100). Thus "thight" readily becomes "tight." Buckalew discusses English spelling and pronunciation in more detail on 100–102.

38. The label—"letter"—is Joyce's (*JJA* 52:227).

39. Oscar Wilde, *The Importance of Being Earnest*, act 2.

40. Grace Eckley offers a more innocent reading of Issy's memory. Eckley has Issy "recalling the noble and dedicated teacher who instills faith and hope" in his students (*Children's Lore*, 182).

41. "Verve," like "verb," derives from *verbum*, which, in Old French, became *verve*, meaning "fantasy." "Vie" comes from *invitare*: to invite.

42. The woman's position and the words from the stable here suggest several similar passages in Joyce's work where a man is "ridden" by a woman. See *U*, 15.1072–73, 2943–49; and Joyce, *Selected Letters*, 182.

43. Derek Attridge comments astutely on the "great deal" of narrative in the *Wake*, noting that "the longer the span, however, the more rarefied the narrative, and the more limited are its satisfactions *as* narrative" (*Peculiar Language*, 215).

44. Examples are ubiquitous. One of the most confident (and the illustration is specifically relevant) is Eckley's chapter on II.2, "Childlight in the Studiorium," in *Children's Lore*. She assures us that "a certain context of familiarity enables readers to recognize the 'voice' or consciousness that dominates specific passages" (188), though Eckley's deliberate vagueness about the "certain context" and her quotation marks around "voice" suggest some of the difficulties latent in her argument for recognizable identities. Although Benstock is much more careful in her treatment, she too, in her pieces on II.2, attributes more consistency, more narrative substance, to the characters than I find warranted.

45. The most impressive attempt to fit all Issy's pieces together is John Gordon's detailed monograph *Notes on Issy*. Although Gordon convincingly assembles a number of themes around Issy, he does not even attempt to make an unbroken link between her and the footnotes to II.2

46. Although no child speaks like Kev, Stanislaus Joyce, by his own account, often struck his older brother James as unusually solemn and unchildlike. Insofar as Stanislaus is a model for parts of Kev/Shaun's composite character, he may have been a partial inspiration for the tone of Kev's marginalia. In *My Brother's Keeper*, Stanislaus recalls that he was "dubiously accepted . . . as my brother's rather taciturn henchman." His brother James "used to say that [Stanislaus] reminded him of a sluggish saurian, whose scaly hide occasionally reflected glints of light" (176, 149).

47. Benstock, "At the Margins of Discourse," 224.

48. A. Walton Litz cautions readers that "the *Finnegans Wake* manuscripts . . . offer the tempting security of 'intentions,'" but that they stand "in no absolute relationship to the finished work" ("Uses of *Wake* Manuscripts," 103). But the manuscripts in this case do offer crucial evidence on the genesis of Joyce's annotative "technique" and also help to explain the effect of those annotations on the reader. The most detailed account of

Joyce's prolonged, difficult labor on II.2, essential for my own study of the drafts, is David Hayman, "'Scribbledehobbles.'" Hayman slightly emends his account in his preface to *JJA* 52:vii–xviii. See also his *'Wake' in Transit*, 14, 46–47.

49. The appearance of the manuscript page suggests that Joyce added "he who" after he had written "there will be," and that he simply forgot to delete "there."

50. Issy's sixth note on 275, "Traduced into jinglish janglage for the nusances of dolphins born," first entered the draft of the chapter as an addition on a later typescript, following "the parrotbook of Dates" (*JJA* 52:183).

51. Hayman discusses the development of the "nodes" of "Work in Progress" throughout *"Wake" in Transit*. Litz was the first to study Joyce's compositional method in any detail; his conclusions, in *Art of James Joyce*, fit well with Hayman's later, more detailed studies. Litz was also the first to notice that Joyce's revisions tended to be of a different order from the initiating passages to which they were attached: "[T]he original units are almost always 'narrative' in the conventional sense, whereas the revisions introduce analogies and connections which are essentially 'static'" (*Art of James Joyce*, 101). Although he speaks here of the "Anna Livia Plurabelle" episode (I.8), his observation applies also to II.2.

52. Hayman argues that Joyce's primary concern when he began to draw notes from his draft was "an expression of Issy's views" ("'Scribbledehobbles,'" 113). He comments in his preface to the first *Archive* volume of II.2 that "the central section of the chapter (§§ 4–5) . . . went through five drafts before [Joyce] more or less simultaneously discovered both the format for *Storiella as She Is Syung* (§§ 1–3, 9) and the textbook format" (*JJA* 52:ix–x). Hayman's preface also reinforces my earlier contention that the annotative form is an apt figure for the composition of *Wake*: "The first-draft material we have been describing is generally found under one of several headings (for example 'Letter,' 'Te Deum,' 'Insertion'). The first drafts of passages that later became *Storiella* were composed piecemeal under the same headings. . . . This suggests that after a certain point he no longer tried to compose sequences, but rather concentrated on the elaboration of a relatively simple idea in a brief paragraph, which he later considerably expanded and often radically reordered or rewrote" (*JJA* 52:xiii).

53. *Storiella* comprises *FW*, 260–75 and 304–8. It appeared, without the title, in *transition* 23 (1935). The same section is published as *Storiella as She Is Syung* (London: Corvinus Press, 1937). This is the beginning and the end of the chapter. See James Spoerri, *Check List*, 7, 15; and Slocum and Cahoon, *Bibliography*, A46, C70.

54. Illustrations of Joyce's continuing preoccupation with betrayal and isolation are everywhere in his work. His first poem, "Et Tu Healy," concerned Ireland's treachery against Parnell (*JJ*, 33). See also the 1912 essay "The Shade of Parnell" and his poem "The Holy Office" (1904), in which he stands "self-doomed, unafraid, / Unfellowed, friendless and alone" (*Critical Writings*, 223–28, 152). Stephen Dedalus lives in perpetual conviction of treachery. See also Bloom's trial in "Circe" (*U*, 15.775ff.).

55. *JJ*, 315–16; Joyce, *Dubliners*, 218–22; Joyce, *Exiles*, 57–63; 65; *U*, 16.1468–69.

56. Hayman, *"Wake" in Transit*, 62–63.

57. David Hayman, "Shadow of His Mind," 77.

58. Hayman, *"Wake" in Transit*, 148.

59. Shari Benstock, *Textualizing the Feminine*, 59. Benstock dissevers Issy and Lucia in "The Genuine Christine," 192–93n.4.

60. Benstock, *Textualizing the Feminine*, 59. Bonnie Kime Scott discusses the connections between Lucia and Issy in appropriately cautious terms: "It seems obvious that Issy is modeled to some extent upon Joyce's own daughter, Lucia. . . . Yet it does not necessarily follow that she must share Lucia's schizophrenia or what Hélène Cixous takes to

be Lucia's 'tragically violent jealousy' over her parents' mutual companionship" (*Joyce and Feminism*, 185).

61. Benstock, *Textualizing the Feminine*, 61.

62. Benstock, "At the Margins of Discourse," 219.

63. Lipking, "Marginal Gloss," 633. Lipking's assertion of Kev's interpretive competence accords uneasily with Kev's role in II.2. He is less able than his brother at his studies. The central episode in the chapter shows us the depths of Kev's ignorance as his brother Dolph gives him a basic anatomy lesson.

64. Ibid., 634.

65. Ibid.

66. Vicki Mahaffey discusses authority in the *Wake*, with specific reference to the geometrical figure at the heart of II.2, in *Reauthorizing Joyce* (32–50), emphasizing Joyce's unmasking of the brutal simplifications behind all models of authority that elevate a single person, a single gender, or any one element of society and "[marginalize] its counterpart" (49).

67. The dream may be found in the Herbert Gorman Papers. Ellmann reproduces it in *JJ*, 549. He changes the pronouns from third to first person and omits a phrase (which I quote on p. 74) about John Joyce vaulting fences. Eugene Jolas alludes to the dream in his recollection of Joyce, "My Friend James Joyce," 16. A more recent discussion of the dream may be found in Patrick McGee's *Paperspace*, 172–75.

68. Although the "astronomical climax" of Joyce's explanation suggests that "the last episode" might mean "Ithaca" (written after "Penelope"), Gorman tells us that Joyce was inspired to compose Molly's repetitive monologue "by the viewing of an astronomical film depicting the starry circling heavens at night" (282). "Penelope" is the more appropriate site for the battle recorded in Joyce's dream.

69. Pound grew uneasy with the experimental nature of *Ulysses* after he read "Sirens" in 1919 (JJ, *Letters*, 1:126). See also Forrest Read, *Pound/Joyce*, 157–60. Pound had almost no patience with *Finnegans Wake*, writing his often-quoted judgment in 1926 that "nothing short of divine vision or a new cure for the clapp can possibly be worth all the circumambient peripherization" (JJ, *Letters*, 3:145).

70. Gorman, 282–83; *JJ*, 549–50. By way of introducing his dream, Joyce tells Gorman, "I think I told you the dream that led up to the writing of Molly Bloomagain" (Herbert Gorman Papers).

71. The infantilized Bloom stands trial and is punished by Bello (*U*, 15:942; *U*, 15:2882ff.). Joyce puts himself in a comparable position with Nora (Joyce, *Selected Letters*, 188–89).

# Chapter 3

1. For a useful description of 1930s fiction that is more directly, often more simply "engaged" than Woolf's writing during this decade, see H. Gustav Klaus, "Socialist Fiction in the 1930s." Also important for providing a sense of the poetry, fiction, and politics of the decade are Valentine Cunningham, *British Writers of the Thirties*; and James Gindin, *British Fiction in the 1930s*.

2. Carolyn Heilbrun, in her essay "Virginia Woolf in Her Fifties," has noted that Woolf's "most interesting introspection about herself as a writer came in the last period [the 1930s], when she underwent an inner debate between her ideas about art and her feminism" (241). Heilbrun's essay, focusing on the insights and authority that come with age, offers an interesting, if somewhat underhistoricized, uncontextualized characteri-

zation of Woolf's final decade as a writer — one that is significantly different from other analyses of Woolf in the 1930s.

3. Since the early 1980s, studies of Woolf have revealed the depth and sophistication of her sociopolitical commitments — commitments that began in earnest at least as early as 1910. Even her earliest fiction cannot accurately be said to be the work of an aesthete. See, for example, Naomi Black, "Virginia Woolf and the Women's Movement"; Alex Zwerdling, *Virginia Woolf and the Real World*; and the essays collected by Mark Hussey in *Virginia Woolf and War*.

4. Zwerdling proposes that *"The Pargiters, The Years,* and *Three Guineas* were in effect responses to the new pressure to write propagandistically, in a style that violated Woolf's natural instincts. Jointly, they represent a temporary loss of confidence in the more indirect satiric methods she had perfected over the previous decade" (*Virginia Woolf and the Real World*, 48). This explanation belongs with a large body of Woolf criticism that I think mistakenly understands her break with the novels of the 1920s as a falling off, "a temporary loss," rather than emphasizing the powerful innovations Woolf made in her later work.

5. I do not discuss the notes to *Flush* because, with the exception of the long note about Elizabeth Barrett's maid, Woolf's apparatus to this book works in a comparatively straightforward manner to flesh out its mock-historical form.

6. Toril Moi discusses connections between Woolf's politics and the formal characteristics of her work (though not her apparatus) in the introduction to *Sexual/Textual Politics*. Moi takes issue with Elaine Showalter's often-cited attack on Woolf's feminism in *Literature of Their Own*, chap. 10. Showalter's failure to study "the narrative strategies" of *A Room of One's Own* and *Three Guineas*, Moi argues, "is equivalent to not reading [the texts] at all" (*Sexual/Textual Politics*, 10).

7. In *Arguing with the Past*, Gillian Beer presents a particularly nuanced analysis of the politics of narrative (in novels and in historical accounts) in Woolf's work (chaps. 7, 8, 9).

8. Beer, speaking of Woolf's transvaluation of historical narrative in *Orlando*, cautions us against dismissing alternative histories as trivial: "If Virginia Woolf moves away from facts and crises it is because she denies the claim of such ordering to be all-inclusive. Escape is not necessarily a form of retreat or failure. Escape can mean freedom and the trying out of new possibilities after imprisonment" (*Arguing with the Past*, 127).

9. I cite Woolf's notes to *A Room of One's Own* and *Three Guineas* by page and note number.

10. I base my assertion on the evidence of the unannotated "Women and Fiction" (collected in *Granite and Rainbow*), which is the earliest printed version of *Room*; I assume that the apparatus to *Room* developed as Woolf expanded and revised her Cambridge talks for publication as *A Room of One's Own*. In her speeches Woolf might, of course, have delivered as conversational asides (an oral gloss, as it were) some of the material with which she annotated *Room*.

11. In "The Authority of Anger," Brenda Silver provides us with a revealing study of the complex reception of *Three Guineas*. Silver points out how often the anger and the arguments of Woolf's text were evaded, "subsumed in praise of the art" (348), in part a sign that readers attended too little to the incendiary notes, in part a sign that Woolf's partial concealment of her anger at the back of her book proved successful. Silver continues her work on the reception of Woolf's polemic in "*Three Guineas* Before and After," an essay that surveys the correspondence that Woolf maintained concerning *Three Guineas* after its publication.

12. Compare this scene in the British Museum with that in *Jacob's Room*, where

"Miss Julia Hedge, the feminist," watches an undergraduate easily accomplishing his task. Unable fully to criticize his methods, Julia works herself into an envious frenzy: "Death and gall and bitter dust were on her pen-tip" (106).

13. For Vera Brittain's account of the speech, see her column in *The Nation*. Woolf's speech was later published in a shortened form with the title "Professions for Women" in *The Death of the Moth and Other Essays* (B. J. Kirkpatrick, *Bibliography*, A27). Black provides a helpful description of the nature of this society in "Virginia Woolf and the Women's Movement," 189–90.

14. In *World Without a Self*, James Naremore discusses *The Waves* as the "ultimate refinement of Virginia Woolf's so-called subjective novels" (175).

15. For a striking discussion of Woolf's consideration of self and selflessness before and after *The Waves*, see Daniel Albright, *Personality and Impersonality*, chap. 3.

16. Quentin Bell, *Virginia Woolf*, 2:257.

17. Ibid. Woolf refers in this passage to her unsigned obituary for her Greek teacher, "Miss Janet Case: Classical Scholar and Teacher," published in the *Times* on 22 July 1937 (Kirkpatrick, *Bibliography*, C351). Her memoir of Julian Bell is dated 30 July of the same year.

18. Eugene Jolas, "My Friend James Joyce," 13.

19. There are numerous studies of *The Pargiters*, commencing with the introduction by Mitchell Leaska to his published edition of the draft. The most extensive examination is Grace Radin, *Virginia Woolf's "The Years."* Another important early study is Jane Marcus, "Pargetting *The Pargiters*." One of the most recent considerations of the draft occurs in Pamela Caughie, *Virginia Woolf and Postmodernism*, 94–108. See also Charles Hoffmann, "Woolf's Manuscript Revisions of *The Years*." I focus less on the details of the essays and the fictional episodes than on the theoretical status of this draft—that is, the considerations it inspired in Woolf's journals, and the importance it has for my discussion of Woolf's apparatus.

20. In *Writing and Gender*, Sue Roe offers a particularly insightful psychologically based analysis of why Woolf had such difficulties composing *The Years* (see esp. 129).

21. Compare Woolf's observation in "Character in Fiction" (July 1924) that "the Edwardians were never interested in character in itself; or in the book in itself. They were interested in something outside. Their books, then, were incomplete as books, and required that the reader should finish them, actively and practically, for himself" (Woolf, *Essays*, 3:428).

22. All quotations from *The Pargiters* retain the brackets and italics that Leaska uses to signal editorially supplied readings (in brackets) and restored deletions (in brackets and italics).

23. Woolf, *To the Lighthouse*, 76.

24. In early 1931, Woolf began systematically to clip, copy, and collect in bound notebooks material germane to her work on *The Pargiters* (and, later, *Three Guineas*). See Brenda Silver's introduction to *Virginia Woolf's Reading Notebooks*, esp. 22–23, and her essay "*Three Guineas* Before and After." Patricia Laurence also discusses the nature of Woolf's notebooks in "Facts and Fugue of War."

25. Lucio Ruotolo offers an extended Bakhtinian view of Woolf's "aesthetic of interruption, her recurring impulse to break derived sequences of art and politics" (*Interrupted Moment*, 231). Ruotolo sketches a portrait of Woolf as an anarchist that obscures the complexity of her political writings. Anne Herrmann, in *Dialogic and Difference*, presents what seems to me the most sophisticated Bakhtinian reading of Woolf's texts. Roe proposes a reading of interruptions in Woolf's text from a largely psychoanalytic point of view in *Writing and Gender*, esp. 52–53.

26. *Novels of Virginia Woolf*, Alice van Buren Kelly's extended study of the "fact and vision" dichotomy in Woolf's work, maintains that the categories are distinct, though often interpenetrating. Both Laurence and Caughie have written more recently on the same opposition in Woolf's work of the 1930s, with Laurence holding that "Woolf's distinctions between fact and fiction are firm" and Caughie asserting, more fruitfully I believe, that Woolf confronts the instability of the categories throughout the decade (Laurence, "Facts and Fugue of War," 230; Caughie, *Virginia Woolf and Postmodernism*, 94–96).

27. In chapter 2 of *Dialogic and Difference*, Herrmann discusses a number of theoretical issues raised by Woolf's choice of the epistolary form for *Three Guineas*.

28. Woolf emphasizes this fiction (and her awareness that it is only a fiction) in *A Room of One's Own* by interrupting her lecture: "I am sorry to break off so abruptly. Are there no men present? . . . We are all women, you assure me?" (*ROO*, 85; see also *ROO*, 115). Zwerdling discusses the unacknowledged audience of men in Woolf's feminist work in *Virginia Woolf and the Real World*, chaps. 8, 9. Lynne Hanley, in "Woolf and the Romance of Oxbridge," suggests that Woolf has lost all faith in the possibility of communicating with men by the time she writes *Three Guineas*.

29. Madeline Hummel discusses the letters in *Three Guineas* in "From the Common Reader to the Uncommon Critic."

30. In *Virginia Woolf and the Real World*, Zwerdling emphasizes "Woolf's acute sense of her audience's potential hostility" (257) as the explanation for the apparatus to *Three Guineas*. Although her defensiveness is obviously a motivating factor, the reasons for the form of this book are considerably more complex.

31. Beverly Ann Schlack offers an intriguing, if limited, view of the function of Woolf's extensive citations, claiming that *Three Guineas* intentionally subjects readers to an experience all feminists undergo: "the sheer crushing weight of lengthy citations in the text, followed by verbose, dissertationese footnoting. All overwhelm us with what is to be, like the tactic of scorn itself, *unanswerable* evidence" ("Woolf's Strategy of Scorn," 149).

32. Woolf probably refers to the preface to *Pendennis*, where Thackeray laments that, since Fielding, no novelist "has been permitted to depict to his utmost power, a MAN. We must drape him, and give him a certain conventional simper. Society will not tolerate the Natural in our Art."

33. Woolf's note on maids in *Three Guineas* bears comparison with her extended biographical sketch in *Flush* of Lily Wilson, Elizabeth Barrett's maid (168–74): "typical of the great army of her kind—the inscrutable, the all-but-silent, the all-but-invisible servant maids of history" (174).

34. In chapter 9 of *Virginia Woolf and the Real World*, Zwerdling provides a detailed and sensitive analysis of Woolf's "twin needs" in her feminist works: "to vent her anger about the subjection of women and to conciliate the male audience she could never entirely ignore" (243). For Zwerdling, Woolf's notes are a place where she can "quarantine" her anger (262).

35. Laurence discusses these photographs, maintaining—too simply, I believe—that "the newspaper and the photograph, the public arts, represent fact and authority in her essay" ("Facts and Fugue of War," 238).

36. Jane Marcus briefly discusses the propagandistic effect of the four photographs included in *Three Guineas* in "No More Horses," 274–75. These photographs further provoked an already furious Q. D. Leavis, who, in her famously hostile review of *Three Guineas*, "Caterpillars of the Commonwealth Unite!" (1938), found them "evidently selected with malice" (384).

37. Mussolini embraced the desire of martial Italians since the turn of the century—"Revenge for Adowa"—as a perfect screen for his imperialist program. Adowa was the town in Ethiopia where the Italian army, attempting to annex Ethiopia as a colony, was defeated on 1 March 1896.

38. Woolf, "Artist and Politics," 227. This essay first appeared as "Why Art To-Day Follows Politics," *Daily Worker*, 14 December 1936, 4 (Kirkpatrick, *Bibliography*, C347).

39. Woolf, "Artist and Politics," 228.

40. Ibid. This opinion by no means came easily to Woolf. The sentence from which I quote begins, "*He is forced* to take part in politics" [my emphasis]. See, for another example, her letter to Ethel Smyth on 25 July 1936, telling how she "was hauled out to Committees and meetings and abused and rooked and at last resigned, and now will never sign a petition or even read a report let alone attend a conference again" (VW, *Letters*, 6:60). She does, however, conclude the letter with the lament that "one cant, alas, entirely withdraw."

41. Woolf, "Leaning tower," 134. "The Leaning Tower" was first published in *Folios of New Writing* (1940), a collection edited by John Lehmann (Kirkpatrick, *Bibliography*, C372).

42. Woolf, "Leaning Tower," 153.

43. Katherine Hill, in "Virginia Woolf and Leslie Stephen," demonstrates how "The Leaning Tower," like many of Woolf's politically focused essays, reveals the influence of Leslie Stephen's literary criticism.

44. Woolf, "Leaning Tower," 154.

45. In "Common Reader" Alex Zwerdling proposes that Woolf grows increasingly impatient about the "compromise between absolute freedom of self-expression and the need always to worry about the responses of an audience," and that she therefore moves in her last years toward composing "something we might call the literature of solitude" (9). Although I agree to some extent with this construction of Woolf's work at the end of her life, Zwerdling seems to propose that this "literature of solitude" indicates a solution to the problem of audience. I see no such solutions in Woolf's late writing.

46. Woolf refers here to joint suicide by means of carbon monoxide inhalation, which she and Leonard discussed several times in the summer of 1940. She first mentions it in her journal of 15 May: "What point in waiting? Better shut the garage doors" (VW, *Diary*, 5:284).

47. Roe makes the point that "[P]aradoxically, the anonymity she was experiencing as a result of her lost audience was coinciding with the bringing of *herself* into play, in her fiction: with 'A Sketch of the Past,' such images as suggest her own desire, her own distress, come to take on discernible significance" (*Writing and Gender*, 58).

48. Woolf's journal records the beginnings of this survey in September 1940 (VW, *Diary*, 5:318, 320). The compositional history of this unfinished book is discussed by Brenda Silver in the introductory sections and notes to "'Anon' and 'The Reader.'"

49. Walter Benjamin, "The Storyteller" (1936), forms an interesting, temporally proximate meditation on a world before the age of print, a companion piece to Woolf's "Anon."

50. Although Woolf writes that Anon was "sometimes man; sometimes woman," she applies the masculine pronoun to Anon throughout her essays ("Anon," 382). To avoid confusing shifts between "she" and "he," I have followed her example here and in my discussions that frame quotations where Woolf uses the masculine pronoun.

51. I quote Woolf's draft from Silver's transcription. For Silver's editorial policy, see her introduction to "'Anon' and 'The Reader,'" 364–65.

52. Maria DiBattista notes Woolf's obsession with "an unwritten novel that would

express the great unsaid of life" and her objections (obviously not shared by Joyce) to language itself ("Joyce, Woolf and the Modern Mind," 109).

53. Woolf was working on *The Pargiters* (later *The Years*) when she wrote this entry, dated 18 March 1935, in her diary.

54. W. B. Yeats, "Anima Hominis," 341.

55. I refer to Eliot's well-known recommendation, presented most memorably in "Tradition and the Individual Talent," that the artist practice the "extinction of personality" (*Selected Essays*, 7). The statement and the essay present only part of Eliot's agenda for poetry. Sanford Schwartz offers a balanced survey of the "dialectical relationship between personal and impersonal aspects" of Eliot's poetry theory in *Matrix of Modernism*, 73. See also Schwartz's entire chapter 2 and his discussion of "Tradition and the Individual Talent" (169–73). Ronald Bush usefully complicates the image of the "impersonal" Eliot in *Eliot*, chap. 4.

# Chapter 4

1. "I Gather the Limbs of Osiris" first appeared in twelve parts in *New Age*, from November 1911 to February 1912 (Donald Gallup, *Pound*, C25–C43). This extended essay, an "illustration of 'The New Method' in scholarship," began not with Pound's theoretical description of that method (as William Cookson's reprint of the essay in *Selected Prose: 1909–1965* suggests), but with his translation of "The Seafarer."

2. Noel Stock, ed., "*Verse Is a Sword*," 265. This letter is dated February 1940. As Gallup reveals in *Pound*, Laughlin only partly heeded Pound's stipulation: "The first 500 copies have an envelope pasted to the inside back cover containing a pamphlet, *Notes on Ezra Pound's Cantos: Structure and Metric* (Norfolk, Connecticut: New Directions [1940]). . . . This consists of two essays, 'Notes on the Cantos,' by H. H. [*i.e.* James Laughlin], pp. 5–12, and 'Notes on the Versification of the Cantos,' by S. D. [*i.e.* Delmore Schwartz]" (A47b).

3. Pound's antagonism toward explanation of his poetry is in part a legacy of his Symbolist inheritance. See James Longenbach, *Stone Cottage*, chap. 3.

4. Pound, drafts for *ABCR*.

5. Michael North, *Political Aesthetic*, 166. North discusses in some detail how fascism promised to resolve these contradictions for Pound (158–77; and see introduction). See also Jeffrey Herf, *Reactionary Modernism*.

6. At the Ezra Pound Centennial Conference in Orono, Maine (1985), I spoke to a poet who openly modeled his work on a Poundian principle of quotation. "I haven't written an original line in ten years," he told me proudly.

7. *GK*, 151; Pound, *The Exile* 3 (1928): 108.

8. This analogy from the financial sphere appealed to Pound. The *ABC of Reading* evokes the "book-keeper" again (*ABCR*, 75), and he reappears in *Guide to Kulchur*, where Pound passes on "a tip from the book-keepers. The loose leaf system is applied in effective business" (*GK*, 56). In a letter of 15 October 1938, Pound tells John Crowe Ransom of the need for "a loose-leaf reference system of vital essays or articles printed during the present couple of decades" (EP, *Letters*, 318).

9. Virtually every critic of Pound discusses his use of ideograms. The most useful analysis for my purpose occurs in Ronald Bush, *Genesis of Ezra Pound's Cantos*, 10–20, where Bush charts the process by which, from 1927 onward, the "ideogrammic method . . . achieved the prominence of an official program" (13). Michael Bernstein, in *Tale of the Tribe*, presents a lucid description of the ideogrammic ideal: "The poet . . . does not

invent anything . . . ; like any epic bard he merely arranges what is already there, apparently letting the tribe's own history narrate itself for the edification (judgment) of its hearers, the truth of the narration guaranteed by the poet's strategic refusal to assume the role of sole, originating source of articulation" (38–39). As we shall see, Pound cannot maintain the distance from his poem or the faith in the reader that this method requires. Bernstein also notes that Pound "wanted the text to give the impression of the tribe's own heritage narrating itself, of the different historical voices addressing us as if without the mediation of one unique narrator or controlling author" (171).

10. A relatively recent illustration of faith in ideogrammatic organization may be found in Marianne Korn's *Pound*, where she presents *Guide to Kulchur* as a key to the method of all the prose: "The explication of the ideogrammic method, and its exemplification, are to be found in Pound's last prose book . . . his *Guide to kulchur.* . . . As allusive as a poem, *Kulchur* can be seen as a vast ideogram containing units of reference to cultural fact, document, and event; in most places it does leave to the reader the task of synthesizing the presented detail and forming inductive conclusions which are the 'meaning' of the book" (123–24).

11. Tim Redman, *Pound and Italian Fascism*, 99.

12. See particularly North's preface, introduction, and chapter on Pound in *Political Aesthetic*.

13. North, *Political Aesthetic*, 2. William Chace, in *Political Identities*, also addresses the ways in which Eliot and Pound, among other modernists, relied on aesthetic form and particular visions of a corresponding political order as an antidote to twentieth-century liberal democracies (see esp. his conclusion).

14. With the exception of desperate reviewers looking for assistance, Hugh Kenner was one of the first critics of "bring all that unknown prose to the service of a newcomer to the poetry" (*Poetry of Ezra Pound*, 7). Reading Pound's prose undoubtedly furthers our understanding of his poetry, but Kenner's preface to the reissued edition of his study of Pound misleadingly suggests that the prose provides a set of easily employed keys: "What Pound said in an essay, he exemplified in a poem. What he'd cited here, he incorporated there" (7). Subsequent studies of Pound's poetry have tended to follow Kenner's emphasis, using quotations from the prose as guides to cruxes in *Personae* or *The Cantos*.

15. Examples abound. See, for illustration, "A Retrospect" ("HR," 3–14); see also "Vortex. Pound," where Pound declares that "elaboration, expression of second intensities, of dispersedness belong to the secondary sort of artist" (Wyndham Lewis, ed., *BLAST*, 154).

16. For discussion of the *Dial* award, see Noel Stock, *Life*, 272–73; and Humphrey Carpenter, *Serious Character*, 441.

17. "There digge" points to an anecdote that Pound used to illustrate the powers of scientific reasoning as developed by the anthropologist Leo Frobenius: "Frobenius looked at two African pots and, observing their shapes and proportions, said: if you will go to a certain place and there digge, you will find traces of a civilization with such and such characteristics" (*GK*, 60–61). For a full discussion of Pound's interest in Frobenius, see Kathryne Lindberg, *Reading Pound Reading*, chap. 5.

18. All his life, Pound worked to keep these circumstances from interfering in other artists' lives. The most famous example is his "Bel Esprit" fund-raising project, designed first to free Eliot from the necessity of working at Lloyd's Bank, and ultimately to "restart civilization" by forming an international endowment for the arts. See EP, *Letters*, 172–73; Timothy Materer, *Pound/Lewis*, 130; Stock, *Life*, 244–46; Carpenter, *Serious Character*, 408–12.

19. Gertrude Stein, *Autobiography of Alice B. Toklas*, 200. Randall Jarrell also queries

Stein's mot: "Gertrude Stein was most unjust to Pound when she called that ecumenical alluder a village explainer: he can hardly even tell you anything (unless you know it already), much less explain it. He makes notes on the margin of the universe; to tell how just or unjust a note is, you must know that portion of the text yourself" ("Review of *Section: Rock-Drill*," in *Critical Heritage*, ed. Eric Homberger, 438–39).

20. Wendy Flory, in *American Ezra Pound*, employs Sacvan Bercovitch's idea of the "American Jeremiad" to help explain Pound's furious crusade for social change (5–12).

21. When Pound instructed individuals rather than an amorphous, general audience, his lessons, though sometimes intimidating, were more affectionately delivered. For personal accounts from those who attended the "Ezuversity," see Marcella Booth, "Through the Smoke Hole"; Booth, "Ezrology"; James Laughlin, *Pound as Wuz*; Mary de Rachewiltz, *Discretions*; and Kenner, *Poetry of Ezra Pound*, prefaces by Laughlin and Kenner. Pound's letters are filled with tutorials; see, for example, those to Iris Barry and Mary Barnard in EP, *Letters*.

22. Wyndham Lewis, *Blasting and Bombardiering*, 253. In *Time and Western Man*, Lewis calls Pound "this sensationlist half-impresario, half-poet" (37).

23. Ian Bell, in *Critic as Scientist*, provides us with a careful study of the scientific analogy in Pound's criticism, focusing on Pound's years in England, from 1910 to 1920.

24. Woolf was angry over a discussion with Forster about whether women should be allowed to sit on the board of the London Library (VW, *Diary*, 4:297–98 and n.6).

25. Pound's translation of this book of the Confucian classics was first published, without a preface, in 1928 as one of the "University of Washington Chap-books, Edited by Glenn Hughes" (Gallup, *Pound*, A28). The first English edition was not issued until 1936 (Gallup, *Pound*, A28b). Pound's original subtitle, *The Great Learning*, carries pedagogical connotations absent from the revised subtitle, "The Great Digest," which Pound employed in a later version (1948) of the text (Gallup, *Pound* A58). John Nolde traces Pound's increasing attraction to Chinese poetry and philosophy and discusses the history of Pound's version of the *Ta Hio*. Nolde points out that Pound's first "translation" of *The Great Learning* "was not really a translation at all but a paraphrase of Pauthier's *Quatre Livres* [a nineteenth-century French translation] . . . , a marginal work at best" ("Pound and the *Ta Hio*," 81). Nolde also shows how Pound sought "to carve out an historical niche for himself as the first American Confucian" (84).

26. Pound, *Confucius*, 51–53. Pound's increasing attraction to Chinese wisdom from the late 1920s onward, resulting in his Chinese history Cantos (half of the volume of *Cantos LII–LXXI* [1940]) and his translations of the *Ta Hio* (1928), the *Chung Yung* (1947), and *The Analects* (1950), constitutes an extraordinarily dramatic instance of the psyche's attraction to its opposite. Flory comments on Pound's search for psychological order through Confucianism in *American Ezra Pound*, 176. In chapter 2 of *Tale of the Tribe*, Bernstein discusses the place of Confucius in Pound's pursuit of a doctrine that will bring order to the Cantos.

27. Pound, *Jefferson and/or Mussolini*, 60.

28. Pound, *The Exile* 4 (1928): 109

29. Pound does not provide an afterword for the public when his new version of the *Ta Hio* is incorporated in the anthology *Confucius: The Unwobbling Pivot, and The Great Digest* (Gallup, *Pound*, A58). He implores his reader to "keep on re-reading the whole digest until he understands HOW these few pages contain the basis on which the great dynasties were founded and endured" (Pound, *Confucius*, 89). The note also locates the book in place and time: "D.T.C., Pisa;/5 October–5 November, 1945" (Pound, *Confucius*, 89).

30. "How to Read" first appeared in three installments—in the *New York Herald*

*Tribune Books* for 13, 20, and 27 January 1929—as "How to Read, or Why: Part I: Introduction"; "Part II, or What May Be an Introduction to Method"; and "Part III, Conclusions, Exceptions, Curricula" (Gallup, *Pound*, C735–37).

31. For a copy of the first edition's cover, see Figure 2. I present an alternative interpretation of the cover on p. 53.

32. *New York Herald Tribune Books*, 27 January 1929, 13.

33. Pound's letter proposing the "book of the quarter" is dated 2 November 1928.

34. The description comes from a letter George Oppen wrote to Zukofsky, who in turn quoted it to Pound. For a discussion of Oppen's project to have French printers produce books that might otherwise not be published, see Mary Oppen, *Meaning A Life*, 130–31.

35. Frank Lentricchia, in "Pound's American Book of Wonders," perfectly expresses another aspect of Pound's ambivalent turn toward the common reader—a particularly American irony of Pound's endeavor in *The Cantos*: "In a[n American] culture that cannot read him . . . Pound would write a poem that his culture needs to read in order to make itself truly a culture" (396).

36. I owe to Robert Spoo the observation that Pound might have chosen "repaired" in this passage after being alerted to the verb's tonal characteristics by Wyndham Lewis, who criticizes Joyce's use of the same verb in the opening of chapter 2 of *Portrait* (Lewis, *Time and Western Man*, 196–7). Lewis published his critique of Joyce in 1927, less than two years before the appearance of "How to Read." The verb "repaired," of course, later plays a central part in Hugh Kenner's *Joyce's Voices*, illustrating what Kenner calls the "Uncle Charles Principle."

37. James Longenbach, in chapter 2 of *Modernist Poetics of History*, demonstrates the "subtle design" of Pound's earliest extended critical work, *I Gather the Limbs of Osiris* (46). It should be noted, however, that the structure is a segmented, even an annotative one: poetry and prose alternate over the course of the twelve installments in which the essay was printed. "How to Read" and the prose texts of the 1930s demonstrate how difficult the gathering of pieces into wholeness becomes as the territory over which Pound ranges grows larger and events challenge his faith in that wholeness with increasing violence. In *Guide to Kulchur*, he briefly refers to the myth of Isis and Osiris, using it as shorthand for the labor of organizing a life: "Our husky young undergraduates may start their quest of Osiris in a search for what was the PRADO" (*GK*, 111).

38. As time grows shorter and the material to cover more vast, Pound becomes increasingly impatient at having to define his literary categories. The classes of writers and the kinds of poetry receive almost completely unintelligible treatment in an introductory textbook Pound composed in Italian in 1942, *Carta da Visita* (Gallup, *Pound*, A50a, b). See "A Visiting Card," the translation of this essay in *SP*, 319, 321.

39. Pound planned that his criticism would also be issued in folio (*P/Z*, 85). He desired a mass audience, but he was equally concerned that his work be preserved in a grander, less accessible form that suited its stature. See also his delight in the 400 franc edition of *A Draft of XVI. Cantos* (EP, *Letters*, 187, 190; Gallup, *Pound*, A26).

40. Pound, typescript of "How to Read."

41. Pound's *Prolegomena I* actually contains the first two parts of the projected series: "How to Read" and *The Spirit of Romance*. "Later volumes of *Prolegomena* were planned to include the second part of *The Spirit of Romance* and other prose work of Ezra Pound, but the publishers went out of business before the plans could be realised" (Gallup, *Pound*, A33b). In his prefatory note to the first volume of *Prolegomena*, Pound is at pains to distinguish "How to Read" from the essays on specific authors that will follow (see *P/Z*, 127–28; *Prolegomena*, 47). Eliot's *Selected Essays* was published on 15 September 1932.

42. Pound's radio broadcasts are briefly discussed in numerous books on Pound. A recent biographical discussion appears in Carpenter, *Serious Character*, 583–97. A more detailed use of the content of the broadcasts occurs throughout Robert Casillo, *Genealogy of Demons*.

43. Flory, *American Ezra Pound*, 127–28. Flory provides an illuminating discussion of the radio broadcasts, largely using them to indicate the depth of Pound's evasion of reality, in her chapter "Pound and Mussolini." See also Vincent Sherry, *Radical Modernism*, 194–95.

44. Pound, "Chronicles," in *BLAST 2*, ed. Lewis, 85.

45. F. R. Leavis, *Mass Civilisation*, 26.

46. Ibid., 25. This sense of the elite's cultural isolation pervades innumerable literary and critical texts of the 1930s. See Valentine Cunningham, *British Writers of the Thirties*, chap. 3.

47. F. R. Leavis, *How to Teach Reading*, 6–11, 48–49.

48. Ibid., 45, 17.

49. Ibid., 21.

50. Dudley Fitts, reviewing *A Draft of XXX Cantos* in 1931, concludes that Pound indulges in "pure pedantry. . . . Mr. Pound's attitude *is* the pedantic, unreal attitude. Throughout the poem he has substituted book-living for actual life" (Homberger, ed., *Critical Heritage*, 255). For similar criticisms collected in Homberger's anthology, see John Gould Fletcher (1920), 173; Geoffrey Grigson (1933), 262; Delmore Schwartz (1938), 313–14; John Wain (1960), 454. See also Lewis, *Time and Western Man*, chap. 15.

51. Ezra Pound, "Murder by Capital," *Criterion* 12 (July 1933): 585–92 (Gallup, *Pound*, C951).

52. Vittoria Mondolfo and Margaret Hurley, *Letters to Ibbotson*, 114, 122.

53. In 1953 Pound circulated *A Manifesto* to academics in America and England. The document, signed by ten professors, urged basic reforms in the university. It is reproduced, with a note by Margaret Bates, in "EP: Maker of Connections," 114–15.

54. Pound similarly parodies himself at the end of his radio broadcast for 19 June 1942: "Dearly beeloved brevrem, this is ole Ezry speaking. You probably do not doubt it. You probably have derived that belief from the intrinsic nature of the discourse even if you tuned [in] after the announcement of what was comin'" (*RS*, 178).

55. *ABC of Economics* was published on 6 April 1933; *ABC of Reading* was published on 24 May 1934 (Gallup, *Pound*, A34, A35). The jacket copy to the *ABC of Economics* explains its origins: "Mr Ezra Pound was asked to deliver ten lectures in an Italian university—on economics, not on the mummified muses. This is his necessary evisceration and clarification of the subject; a concise introduction to 'volitionist economics.'" Gallup adds that "the lectures referred to, announced as 'An Historic Background for Economics,' were given [in] . . . Milan, 21–31 March 1933" (*Pound*, A32).

56. Pound, *Jefferson and/or Mussolini*, 99.

57. Pound, *Confucius*, 31.

58. Pound, *Jefferson and/or Mussolini*, 66.

59. Ibid., 70.

60. Ibid., 66–67.

61. Lindberg, *Reading Pound Reading*, 125, 169.

62. Ibid., 47.

63. Flory, who explains and even, in part, defends Pound's economic agenda with exemplary clarity and depth in chapter 2 of *American Ezra Pound*, finds Pound unqualified to teach the subject unassisted: "He suppressed any awareness that the talent and effort necessary to produce good poetry and the expertise and influence necessary to

reconstruct the economic systems of the West were of a different order of magnitude and that to have succeeded in the first was no guarantee of success in the second" (84).

64. Cf. Pound's characterization of Mussolini as an artist of the act: "Treat him as *artifex* and all the details fall into place. Take him as anything save the artist and you will get muddled with contradictions" (*Jefferson and/or Mussolini*, 34).

65. Pound, *The Exile* 4 (1928): 1.

66. A number of critics have worked fruitfully with Pound's search for certainty on the shifting grounds of the written word, making much of the particular, related instabilities of the signature, of the signs that we call money, and of authorship itself. For especially strong examples, see Jean-Michel Rabaté, *Language, Sexuality and Ideology*; Andrew Parker, "'Economy' of Anti-Semitism"; Maud Ellmann, "Floating the Pound"; and Richard Sieburth, "In Pound We Trust."

67. Pound, *The Exile* 4 (1928): 1. It is ironic and revealing that Pound chooses *The Exile* to express the concern that readers will overlook his presence: every page of the journal that contains his miscellaneous ideas is saturated with his personality. For a discussion of the inception and career of the only journal that Pound controlled absolutely, see Barry Alpert, "Ezra Pound, John Price, and *The Exile*."

68. Focusing his discussion on Pound's scorn for and practice of "Germanic" methods of scholarship, North explores the ways in which this tension between particular example and general precept is a reflection of the tensions between individual and community in Pound's thinking (*Political Aesthetic*, 128–35, passim). See also Reed Dasenbrock, *Literary Vorticism*, where Dasenbrock finds that the new element of the 1930s Cantos is Pound's "stress on the general statement" (205).

69. This passage occurs in "Prefatio Aut Cimicium Tumulus," published first in the *Active Anthology* (1933) (Gallup, *Pound*, B32). Pound's judgment against Eliot introduces an extremely defensive review of Eliot's *Selected Essays*, which had been published the previous year.

70. Homberger, *Critical Heritage*, 348–49. Jarrell's review originally appeared in the *New Republic* 103 (1940): 798–99.

71. Homberger, ed., *Critical Heritage*, 366. Martz's review originally appeared in the *Yale Review* 38 (1948): 144–48.

72. Homberger, ed., *Critical Heritage*, 348. Muir's review originally appeared in *Purpose* 12 (1940): 149–50.

73. Both Bernstein and Dasenbrock offer fine discussions of the middle Cantos and the contradictory structural imperatives implicit in Pound's desire to reveal a transhistorical order at work in history (*Tale of the Tribe*, 115–20; *Literary Vorticism*, 206–13). Both writers examine the ways in which, with his promise that this order is coming to fruition again even as the poem is being written, Pound ties his vision destructively to the events of the Second World War. In *Radical Modernism*, Vincent Sherry notes that, because Pound believes so strongly in "the evident truth of these prior texts" quoted at such length in the middle Cantos, "[a]esthetic embellishment of these texts appears almost irrelevant" to Pound (189; see also 188–96).

74. There is a handful of Cantos from this decade in which Pound provides a glimpse of a world outside documents, or a realm—paradise or inferno—outside history (Cantos 36, 39, 47, 49, and the pair of *Usura* Cantos, 45, 51), but their dramatic difference from the surrounding poem serves to emphasize the comparatively one-dimensional nature of the Cantos written during this period. The three volumes of 1930s Cantos are also marked by distinct characteristics, but they differ less from one another than they do from *A Draft of XXX Cantos* or the *Pisan Cantos* and those that followed.

75. In chapter 1 of *Pound's Cantos Declassified*, Philip Furia provides a suggestive

overview of the Cantos' "attempt to recover and recirculate lost documents" (2). Bernstein discusses Pound's attempt in the Cantos to maintain a "constant and precarious balance between the two codes: the historically analytic and explanatory elements (the 'prose tradition' of the great novels recaptured for verse) and the mythological, intuitive insights, the religious revelations of universal truths (traditionally the rightful domain of verse)." He finds the two "explanatory systems . . . all too often, mutually exclusive" (*Tale of the Tribe*, 24, 98). Although I find Bernstein's analysis of the Cantos extremely illuminating, I place Pound's tendency to analyze and explain in the context of Pound's own prose and his educative designs rather than at the remove of the novelists' prose tradition. Discussion of Pound's prose is almost wholly absent from Bernstein's treatment of the Cantos. I also find a dramatic difference in the Cantos from 31 to 71; Bernstein focuses on the change in Pound's work marked by the *Pisan Cantos*.

76. Mondolfo and Hurley, *Letters to Ibbotson*, 25.

77. Stock, ed., *"Verse Is a Sword,"* 264.

78. Sherry, *Radical Modernism*, 195–96.

79. Stock, ed., *"Verse Is a Sword,"* 263.

80. Canto 46 was published in the first of New Directions' annual collections, *New Directions in Prose and Poetry* (Norfolk, Conn.: New Directions, 1936); and in *New Democracy* 6 (March 1936): 14–16 (Gallup, *Pound*, C1280, C1301).

81. Pound provides Canto 45 with an equally patronizing radio gloss, later printed in Olga Rudge's short collection of broadcasts, *"If This Be Treason"* (Gallup, *Pound*, A59). In addition to explaining the Canto, Pound complains that he is unfairly singled out as an incomprehensible poet: "Why people pick on me for obscurity and NEVER pick on Mr. Eliot is *to me* a mystery" (Rudge, *"If This Be Treason,"* 26).

82. Chace, *Political Identities*, 72. Sherry convincingly proposes that some of Pound's attack on Eliot here is motivated by Pound's own fears that the rarefied language of the immediately preceding Usura Canto (45) is ultimately limited by its archaisms, "that [Pound's] own poetic lexicon is practically useless and useless practically; that it is unable to 'teach a lesson'" (*Radical Modernism*, 192).

83. I have already noted Pound's habit of adding up the years he has been at work on a literary project. During the mid-1930s, he begins to tally up his economic credentials in letters and essays, citing the same "17 years of . . . curiosity" in "When Will School Books......?" (*Delphian Quarterly* 20 [1937]: 18), an essay written two years after Canto 46. Carroll Terrell suggests that "ninety" "refers more generally to the *bellum perenne* against Geryon and Usura" (*Companion*, 1:180).

84. This meeting, usually dated 1918, is described in Stock, *Life*, 221–22; and Carpenter, *Serious Character*, 356–59. The most lucid discussion of Douglas's economics (and his interactions with Orage) may be found in Flory, *American Ezra Pound*, chap. 2. In that chapter, Flory tells us that Orage delivered Pound's first lessons in economics in "the basement of the A.B.C. restaurant in Chancery Lane" (48).

85. Sherry's important analysis of the demotic, the colloquial, in Pound's poetry is apposite here. The common tongue of this Canto "recalls the poet persistently to the inane indeterminacies of history—that raucous sphere in relation to which all answers appear peripheral, contingent, provisional" (*Radical Modernism*, 193–94).

86. Discussing the Ur-Cantos, Bernstein suggests that "Pound's constant intrusions, his compulsion to annotate, give sources and indicate connections," come from a need to "refer everything in the poem back to his need for an appropriate *persona*" (*Tale of the Tribe*, 167). Since Bernstein pays comparatively little attention to the 1930s Cantos, he does not discuss how Pound's motives for glossing his poetry change completely in the middle Cantos, where Pound intrudes to guide his readers' interpretations.

87. John Driscoll, in his study of Pound's sources and techniques in the China Cantos, shows that these are "taken almost entirely" from Father Joseph de Mailla's *Histoire générale de la Chine* (*China Cantos*, 19).

88. Pound's method of working with the historical documents pertaining to John Adams has been exhaustively documented in Frederick Sanders, *John Adams Speaking*. In his prologue to Sanders's book, Carroll Terrell suggests the extent of Pound's labor: "From six thousand pages of letters, documents, memoirs, and reflections written by John Adams, Ezra Pound excerpted eighty pages which he wove into the twenty-five hundred line fabric of poetry known as 'The Adams Cantos.'"

89. Cf. Pound's advice, in *ABC of Reading*, that the students "will . . . find it always advantageous to read the oldest poem of a given kind that he can get hold of" (*ABCR*, 47).

90. In fact, Pound takes considerable liberties with Adams's reservations about a passage from Milton's *Ready and Easy Way to Establish a Free Commonwealth* (Terrell, *Companion*, 1:323). North offers an incisive discussion of how and why Pound's various heroes all resemble one another in so many respects in *Political Aesthetic*, 151.

91. Dasenbrock, in *Literary Vorticism*, provides a fine discussion of the differences between Pound's middle Cantos and the *Pisan Cantos* in terms of Pound's shift from a Confucian to a Taoist mode of understanding (220–32).

92. Pound, *Confucius*, 19.

93. Stock, ed., *"Verse Is a Sword,"* 265.

94. For bibliographic citations of Pound's and Douglas's prior publication of material in Canto 38, see Terrell, *Companion* 1:157–58.

95. Stock, ed., *"Verse Is a Sword,"* 265.

96. Lionel Kelly discusses Pound's troubled relationship with his audience and notes that Pound often seems to address himself. Kelly calls the book a "guide to Pound," and finds it "tenaciously unified in subject" ("Book as Ball of Light," 290).

97. Redman provides some apposite examples of Pound's Italian audience being baffled by his pronouncements in print and on the air in *Pound and Italian Fascism*, 163–64, 169–70. The pressman and friend of Pound, Odon Por, wrote to Pound in 1936 that the Italian minister of the press "can't put you on the wireless—because you said strange things before" (170).

98. Matthew Little, in "Pound's Use of the Word *Totalitarian*," argues that the connotations of "totalitarian" were not primarily political for Pound; he does point out, however, that the word was used in Italian Fascist propaganda, whereas the Germans rarely used the term.

99. See similar passages in the *Ta Hio* (Pound, *Confucius*, 31, 151).

100. Pound's *Guide* is beset by theoretical contradictions as well as complexity and confusion, a fact discussed by Michael North in "Where Memory Faileth." Since "the really crucial limitation of the paideuma is that it cannot be learned at all," North writes, "literary didacticism is, at the very least, beside the point" (153, 158). "As a teacher," he adds, "Pound must attempt to re-create consciously what should ideally be an unconscious, natural possession, transmitted without teaching and in fact unteachable" (155).

101. In chapter 6 of *Pound and Italian Fascism*, Redman offers the best account of Pound's comparatively small community of kindred souls in the 1930s.

102. Presented with a copy of the Cantos, Mussolini supposedly responded in a manner no less difficult to interpret, though Pound proudly memorializes that response in the opening of Canto 41: "'MA QVESTO,' / said the Boss, 'è divertente,' / catching the point before the aesthetes had got there" (*C*, 41/202). For a brief account of the meeting between Pound and Mussolini, see Carpenter, *Serious Character*, 490–91. Redman dis-

cusses the meeting at greater length in *Pound and Italian Fascism*, 95–98. North also fruitfully analyzes Pound's relation to Mussolini in *Political Aesthetic*, 155–77.

103. The Foreign Broadcast Intelligence Service, a monitoring unit of the Federal Communications Commission, recorded all broadcasts from Radio Rome, including Pound's speeches (*RS*, xii).

# WORKS CITED

Ackroyd, Peter. *T. S. Eliot: A Life*. New York: Simon and Schuster, 1984.

Albright, Daniel. *Personality and Impersonality: Lawrence, Woolf, and Mann*. Chicago: University of Chicago Press, 1978.

Alpert, Barry S. "Ezra Pound, John Price, and *The Exile*." *Paideuma* 2 (1973): 427–48.

Attridge, Derek. *Peculiar Language: Literature as Difference from the Renaissance to James Joyce*. Ithaca: Cornell University Press, 1988.

Bakhtin, Mikhail. *The Dialogic Imagination*. Edited by Michael Holquist. Translated by Caryl Emerson and Michael Holquist. Austin: University of Texas Press, 1981.

———. *Rabelais and His World*. Translated by Helene Iswolsky. Bloomington: Indiana University Press, 1984.

Barney, Stephen A., ed. *Annotation and Its Texts*. New York: Oxford University Press, 1991.

Barthes, Roland. *The Pleasure of the Text*. Translated by Richard Miller. New York: Hill and Wang, 1975.

———. *S/Z: An Essay*. Translated by Richard Miller. New York: Farrar, Straus and Giroux, 1974.

Bates, Margaret. "EP: Maker of Connections." *Paideuma* 6 (1977): 114–15.

Beach, Sylvia. *Shakespeare and Company*. London: Faber and Faber, 1960.

Beckett, Samuel, et al. *Our Exagmination Round His Factification for Incamination of Work in Progress*. Paris: Shakespeare and Company, 1929. Reprint. New York: New Directions, 1972.

Beer, Gillian. *Arguing with the Past: Essays in Narrative from Woolf to Sidney*. London: Routledge, 1989.

Bell, Clive. *Old Friends*. London: Chatto and Windus, 1956.

Bell, Ian F. A. *Critic as Scientist: The Modernist Poetics of Ezra Pound*. London: Methuen, 1981.

Bell, Quentin. *Virginia Woolf: A Biography*. 2 vols. New York: Harcourt Brace Jovanovich, 1972.

Benjamin, Walter. "The Storyteller." In *Illuminations*. Edited and introduced by Hannah Arendt. Translated by Harry Zohn. New York: Schocken Books, 1969.

Bennett, David. "Periodical Fragments and Organic Culture: Modernism, the Avant-Garde, and the Little Magazine." *Contemporary Literature* 30 (1989): 480–502.

Benstock, Shari. "At the Margins of Discourse: Footnotes in the Fictional Text." *PMLA* 98 (1983): 204–25.

————. "The Genuine Christine: Psychodynamics of Issy." In *Women in Joyce*. Edited by Suzette Henke and Elaine Unkeless. Urbana: University of Illinois Press, 1982.

————. *Textualizing the Feminine: On the Limits of Genre*. Norman: University of Oklahoma Press, 1991.

Bernstein, Michael André. *The Tale of the Tribe: Ezra Pound and the Modern Verse Epic*. Princeton: Princeton University Press, 1980.

Bishop, John. *Joyce's Book of the Dark: Finnegans Wake*. Madison: University of Wisconsin Press, 1986.

Black, Naomi. "Virginia Woolf and the Women's Movement." In *Virginia Woolf: A Feminist Slant*. Edited by Jane Marcus. Lincoln: University of Nebraska Press, 1983.

Booth, Marcella. "Ezrology: The Class of '57." *Paideuma* 13 (1984): 375–88.

————. "Through the Smoke Hole: Ezra Pound's Last Year at St. Elizabeths." *Paideuma* 3 (1974): 329–34.

Brittain, Vera. Account of Virginia Woolf's 1931 speech to the Society for Women's Service. *The Nation*, 31 January 1931, 571.

Brown, Malcolm. *The Politics of Irish Literature: From Thomas Davis to W. B. Yeats*. Seattle: University of Washington Press, 1972.

Buckalew, Ronald E. "Night Lessons on Language." In *A Conceptual Guide to Finnegans Wake*. Edited by Michael H. Begnal and Fritz Senn. University Park: Pennsylvania University Press, 1974.

Buck-Morss, Susan. *The Dialectics of Seeing: Walter Benjamin and the Arcades Project*. Cambridge, Mass.: MIT Press, 1991.

Budgen, Frank. *James Joyce and the Making of Ulysses*. London: Grayson, 1934. Reprint. Bloomington: Indiana University Press, 1960.

Bürger, Peter. *Theory of the Avant-Garde*. Translated by Michael Shaw. Minneapolis: University of Minnesota Press, 1984.

Burke, Kenneth. "The Rhetoric of Hitler's 'Battle.'" *Southern Review* 5 (1939): 1–21. Reprinted in *The Philosophy of Literary Form: Studies in Symbolic Action*. Baton Rouge: Louisiana State University Press, 1941.

Bush, Ronald. *The Genesis of Ezra Pound's Cantos*. Princeton: Princeton University Press, 1976.

————. "The Modernist Under Siege." In *Yeats: An Annual of Critical and Textual Studies*. Ithaca: Cornell University Press, 1988.

————. *T. S. Eliot: A Study in Character and Style*. New York: Oxford University Press, 1984.

Calverton, V. F. *The Modern Quarterly: A Journal of Radical Opinion* 5 (1929).

Campbell, Joseph, and Henry Morton Robinson. *A Skeleton Key to Finnegans Wake*. New York: Harcourt Brace Jovanovich, 1944. Reprint. New York: Penguin Books, 1977.

Carpenter, Humphrey. *A Serious Character: The Life of Ezra Pound*. Boston: Houghton Mifflin, 1988.

Casillo, Robert. *The Genealogy of Demons: Anti-Semitism, Fascism, and the Myths of Ezra Pound*. Evanston: Northwestern University Press, 1988.

Caughie, Pamela. *Virginia Woolf and Postmodernism: Literature in Quest and Question of Itself*. Urbana: University of Illinois Press, 1991.

Chace, William M. *The Political Identities of Ezra Pound and T. S. Eliot*. Stanford: Stanford University Press, 1973.

Cixous, Hélène. *The Exile of James Joyce*. Translated by Sally A. J. Purcell. New York: David Lewis, 1972.

Croessmann, H. K. "Joyce, Gorman, and the Schema of *Ulysses*: An Exchange of Letters—Paul L. Léon, Herbert Gorman, Bennett Cerf." In *A James Joyce Miscellany: Second Series*. Edited by Marvin Magalaner. Carbondale: Southern Illinois University Press, 1959.

Cunningham, Valentine. *British Writers of the Thirties*. New York: Oxford University Press, 1988.

———. "Neutral?: 1930s Writers and Taking Sides." In *Class, Culture and Social Change: A New View of the 1930s*. Edited by Frank Gloversmith. Sussex: Harvester Press, 1980.

Dasenbrock, Reed Way. *The Literary Vorticism of Ezra Pound and Wyndham Lewis: Towards the Condition of Painting*. Baltimore: Johns Hopkins University Press, 1985.

Deane, Seamus. "Joyce and Nationalism." In *James Joyce: New Perspectives*. Edited by Colin MacCabe. Sussex: Harvester Press, 1982.

Deming, Robert H., ed. *James Joyce: The Critical Heritage*. 2 vols. New York: Barnes and Noble, 1970.

de Rachewiltz, Mary. *Discretions*. Boston: Little, Brown, 1971.

Derrida, Jacques. *Glas*. Translated by John P. Leavey, Jr., and Richard Rand. Lincoln: University of Nebraska Press, 1990.

———. "Living On: Border Lines." In *Deconstruction and Criticism*. Edited by Harold Bloom, et al. New York: Seabury Press, 1979.

———. "Parergon." In *The Truth in Painting*. Translated by Geoff Bennington and Ian McLeod. Chicago: University of Chicago Press, 1987.

DiBattista, Maria. "Joyce, Woolf and the Modern Mind." In *Virginia Woolf: New Critical Essays*. Edited by Patricia Clements and Isobel Grundy. New York: Barnes and Noble, 1983.

Driscoll, John. *The China Cantos of Ezra Pound*. Uppsala: Uppsala University, 1983.

Eckley, Grace. *Children's Lore in Finnegans Wake*. Syracuse: Syracuse University Press, 1985.

Eliot. T. S. *After Strange Gods: A Primer of Modern Heresy*. London: Faber and Faber, 1934.

———. "The Frontiers of Criticism." In *On Poetry and Poets*. New York: Farrar, Straus and Giroux, 1961.

———. *The Sacred Wood*. New York: Methuen, 1986.

———. *Selected Essays of T. S. Eliot*. New York: Harcourt Brace Jovanovich, 1978.

———. *The Use of Poetry and the Use of Criticism: Studies in the Relation of Criticism to Poetry in England*. London. Faber and Faber, 1933.

———. *The Waste Land*. In *The Complete Poems and Plays: 1909–1950*. New York: Harcourt Brace Jovanovich, 1971.

Ellmann, Maud. "Floating the Pound: The Circulation of the Subject of *The Cantos*." *Oxford Literary Review* 3 (1979): 16–27.

Ellmann, Richard. *The Consciousness of Joyce*. New York: Oxford University Press, 1977.

———. *James Joyce*. Rev. ed. New York: Oxford University Press, 1982.

———. *Ulysses on the Liffey*. London: Faber and Faber, 1972.

Ellmann, Richard, A. Walton Litz, and John Whittier-Ferguson, eds. *James Joyce: Poems and Shorter Writings*. London: Faber and Faber, 1991.

Eysteinsson, Astradur. *The Concept of Modernism*. Ithaca: Cornell University Press, 1990.

Feshbach, Sidney. Review of *Joyce's Politics*, by Dominic Manganiello. *James Joyce Quarterly* 19 (1982): 208–13.

Finney, Michael. "Eugene Jolas, *transition*, and the Revolution of the Word." In *In the Wake of the Wake*. Edited by David Hayman and Elliott Anderson. Madison: University of Wisconsin Press, 1978.

Fisk, Robert. *In Time of War: Ireland, Ulster and the Price of Neutrality: 1939–45.* Philadelphia: University of Pennsylvania Press, 1983.

Flory, Wendy Stallard. *The American Ezra Pound.* New Haven: Yale University Press, 1989.

Foster, R. F. *Modern Ireland: 1600–1972.* New York: Penguin Books, 1989.

Furia, Philip. *Pound's Cantos Declassified.* University Park: Pennsylvania University Press, 1984.

Gallup, Donald. *Ezra Pound: A Bibliography.* Charlottesville: University Press of Virginia, 1983.

———. *T. S. Eliot: A Bibliography.* London: Faber and Faber, 1952.

Gilbert, Stuart. *James Joyce's Ulysses.* London: Faber and Faber, 1930. 2d ed., rev. New York: Knopf, 1952.

Gindin, James. *British Fiction in the 1930s: The Dispiriting Decade.* New York: St. Martin's Press, 1992.

Glasheen, Adaline. *Third Census of Finnegans Wake: An Index of the Characters and Their Roles.* Berkeley: University of California Press, 1977.

Gloversmith, Frank, ed. *Class, Culture and Social Change: A New View of the 1930s.* Sussex: Harvester Press, 1980.

Goldman, Arnold. "Elliot Paul's *transition* Years: 1926–28." *James Joyce Quarterly* 30 (1993): 241–75.

Goldwasser, Thomas A. "Who Was Vladimir Dixon? Was He Vladimir Dixon?" *James Joyce Quarterly* 16 (1979): 219–22.

Gordon, John. *Notes on Issy.* Colchester: A Wake Newslitter Press, 1982.

Gorman, Herbert. *James Joyce.* New York: Farrar and Rinehart, 1939.

Grant, Michael, ed. *T. S. Eliot: The Critical Heritage.* 2 vols. London: Routledge and Kegan Paul, 1982.

Halper, Nathan. "James Joyce and the Russian General." *Partisan Review* 18 (1951): 424–31.

Hanley, Lynne T. "Virginia Woolf and the Romance of Oxbridge," *Massachusetts Review* 25 (1984): 421–36.

Hartman, Geoffrey. "Literary Commentary as Literature." In *Criticism in the Wilderness: The Study of Literature Today.* New Haven: Yale University Press, 1980.

Hayman, David. "'Scribbledehobbles' and How They Grew: A Turning Point in the Development of a Chapter." In *Twelve and a Tilly: Essays on the Occasion of the Twenty-Fifth Anniversary of Finnegans Wake.* Edited by Jack P. Dalton and Clive Hart. London: Faber and Faber, 1966.

———. "Shadow of His Mind: The Papers of Lucia Joyce." In *Joyce at Texas: Essays on the James Joyce Materials at the Humanities Research Center.* Edited by Dave Oliphant and Thomas Zigal. Austin, Tex.: Humanities Research Center, 1983.

———. *The "Wake" in Transit.* Ithaca: Cornell University Press, 1990.

Heilbrun, Carolyn. "Virginia Woolf in Her Fifties," In *Virginia Woolf: A Feminist Slant.* Edited by Jane Marcus. Lincoln: University of Nebraska Press, 1983.

Henke, Suzette A. "Exagmining Beckett & Company." In *Re-Viewing Classics of Joyce Criticism.* Edited by Janet Egleson Dunleavy. Urbana: University of Illinois Press, 1991.

Herf, Jeffrey. *Reactionary Modernism: Technology, Culture, and Politics in Weimar and the Third Reich.* New York: Cambridge University Press, 1984.

Herr, Cheryl. *Joyce's Anatomy of Culture.* Urbana: University of Illinois Press, 1986.

Herrmann, Anne. *The Dialogic and Difference: 'An/Other Woman' in Virginia Woolf and Christa Wolf.* New York: Columbia University Press, 1989.

Hill, Katherine C. "Virginia Woolf and Leslie Stephen: History and Literary Revolution." *PMLA* 96 (1981): 351–62.

Hoffmann, Charles G. "Virginia Woolf's Manuscript Revisions of *The Years.*" *PMLA* 84 (1969): 79–89.

Homberger, Eric, ed. *Ezra Pound: The Critical Heritage.* London: Routledge and Kegan Paul, 1972.

Hummel, Madeline M. "From the Common Reader to the Uncommon Critic: *Three Guineas* and the Epistolary Form." *Bulletin of the New York Public Library* 80 (1977): 151–57.

Hussey, Mark, ed. *Virginia Woolf and War: Fiction, Reality, and Myth.* Syracuse: Syracuse University Press, 1991.

Huyssen, Andreas. *After the Great Divide: Modernism, Mass Culture, Postmodernism.* Bloomington: Indiana University Press, 1986.

Hynes, Samuel. *The Auden Generation: Literature and Politics in England in the 1930s.* Princeton: Princeton University Press, 1982.

Irigaray, Luce. *This Sex Which Is Not One.* Translated by Catherine Porter. Ithaca: Cornell University Press, 1985.

Jenkins, William. "From Solation to Solution." *A Wake Newslitter* 7 (1970): 3–11.

———. "Zerothruster and the Twelve Morphios." *A Wake Newslitter* 6 (1967): 123–24.

Jolas, Eugene. "Man from Babel." Beinecke Library, Gen. MSS 108, drafts A (box 6) and E (box 9).

———. "My Friend James Joyce." In *James Joyce: Two Decades of Criticism.* Edited by Seon Givens. New York: Vanguard Press, 1948.

———. ed. *transition* 1–27 (1927–1938).

Jolas, Maria. "Joyce's Friend Jolas." In *A James Joyce Miscellany.* Edited by Marvin Magalaner. New York: James Joyce Society, 1957.

Joyce, James. *The Critical Writings of James Joyce.* Edited by Ellsworth Mason and Richard Ellmann. New York: Viking Press, 1959.

———. *Dubliners.* Edited by Robert Scholes and A. Walton Litz. New York: Penguin Books, 1976.

———. *Exiles.* Introduction by Padraic Colum. New York: Penguin Books, 1977.

———. *Finnegans Wake.* Corrected ed. New York: Viking Press, 1958.

———. *Finnegans Wake, Book I, Chapters 4–5: A Facsimile of Drafts, Typescripts, and Proofs.* Edited by David Hayman, Danis Rose, and John O'Hanlon. New York: Garland, 1978.

———. *Finnegans Wake, Book II, Chapter 2: A Facsimile of Drafts, Typescripts, and Proofs.* Vol. 1. Edited by David Hayman, Danis Rose, and John O'Hanlon. New York: Garland, 1978.

———. *Finnegans Wake, Book II, Chapter 2: A Facsimile of Drafts, Typescripts, and Proofs.* Vol. 2. Edited by David Hayman, Danis Rose, and John O'Hanlon. New York: Garland, 1978.

———. *Finnegans Wake, Book III: A Facsimile of the Galley Proofs.* Edited by David Hayman, Danis Rose, and John O'Hanlon. New York: Garland, 1978.

———. *Letters of James Joyce.* Vol. 1. Edited by Stuart Gilbert. Vols. 2, 3. Edited by Richard Ellmann. New York: Viking Press, 1957, 1966.

———. *A Portrait of the Artist as a Young Man.* Edited by Chester G. Anderson. New York: Viking Press, 1968.

———. *Selected Letters of James Joyce.* Edited by Richard Ellmann. New York: Viking Press, 1975.

———. *Ulysses: The Corrected Text*. Edited by Hans Walter Gabler, with Wolfhard Steppe and Claus Melchior. Preface by Richard Ellmann. London: The Bodley Head, 1986.

Joyce, Stanislaus. *My Brother's Keeper: James Joyce's Early Years*. Edited by Richard Ellmann. Introduction by T. S. Eliot. New York: Viking Press, 1958.

Kelley, Alice van Buren. *The Novels of Virginia Woolf: Fact and Vision*. Chicago: University of Chicago Press, 1973.

Kelly, Lionel. "*Guide to Kulchur:* The Book as Ball of Light." *Paideuma* 15 (1986): 279–90.

Kenner, Hugh. *Dublin's Joyce*. Bloomington: Indiana University Press, 1956. Reprint. New York: Columbia University Press, 1987.

———. *Joyce's Voices*. Berkeley: University of California Press, 1978.

———. *The Poetry of Ezra Pound*. Lincoln: University of Nebraska Press, 1985.

———. *T. S. Eliot: The Invisible Poet*. New York: McDowell, Obolensky, 1959.

Kirkpatrick, B. J. *A Bibliography of Virginia Woolf*. 3d ed. Oxford: Clarendon Press, 1980.

Klaus, H. Gustav. "Socialist Fiction in the 1930s: Some Preliminary Observations." In *The 1930s: A Challenge to Orthodoxy*. Edited by John Lucas. New York: Barnes and Noble, 1978.

Kopper, Edward A, Jr. "'. . . but where he is eaten': Earwicker's Tavern Feast." In *A Conceptual Guide to Finnegans Wake*. Edited by Michael H. Begnal and Fritz Senn. University Park: Pennsylvania State University Press, 1974.

Korn, Marianne. "E. P.: The Dance of Words." *Paideuma* 15 (1986): 243–51.

———. *Ezra Pound: Purpose/Form/Meaning*. London: Middlesex Polytechnic Press, 1983.

Laughlin, James. *Pound as Wuz*. St. Paul, Minn.: Graywolf Press, 1987.

Laurence, Patricia. "The Facts and Fugue of War: From *Three Guineas* to *Between the Acts*." In *Virginia Woolf and War: Fiction, Reality, and Myth*. Edited by Mark Hussey. Syracuse: Syracuse University Press, 1991.

Leavis, Frank Raymond. *How to Teach Reading: A Primer for Ezra Pound*. Cambridge: Minority Press, 1932.

———. *Mass Civilisation and Minority Culture*. Cambridge: Minority Press, 1930. Reprint. Darby, Penn.: Arden Library, 1979.

Leavis, Q. D. "Caterpillars of the Commonwealth Unite!" In *The Importance of Scrutiny*. Edited by Eric Bentley. New York: George W. Stewart, 1948.

Lennon, Michael. "James Joyce." *Catholic World* 132 (1931): 641–52.

Lentricchia, Frank. "Ezra Pound's American Book of Wonders." *South Atlantic Quarterly* 92 (1993): 387–415.

Levenson, Michael H. *A Genealogy of Modernism: A Study of English Literary Doctrine, 1908–1922*. Cambridge: Cambridge University Press, 1984.

Levine, Joseph M. *The Battle of the Books: History and Literature in the Augustan Age*. Ithaca: Cornell University Press, 1991.

Lewis, Wyndham. *Blasting and Bombardiering*. Berkeley: University of California Press, 1967.

———. *The Enemy: A Review of Art and Literature* 3 (1929).

———. *Time and Western Man*. New York: Harcourt, Brace, 1928.

———, ed. *BLAST*. London: John Lane, 1914. Reprint. Santa Barbara, Calif.: Black Sparrow Press, 1981.

———. *BLAST 2*. London: John Lane, 1915. Reprint. Santa Barbara, Calif.: Black Sparrow Press, 1981.

Lindberg, Kathryne. *Reading Pound Reading: Modernism After Nietzsche*. New York: Oxford University Press, 1987.

Lipking, Lawrence. "The Marginal Gloss." *Critical Inquiry* 3 (1977): 609–55.

Little, Matthew. "Pound's Use of the Word *Totalitarian*." *Paideuma* 11 (1982): 147–56.

Litz, A. Walton. *The Art of James Joyce: Method and Design in Ulysses and Finnegans Wake*. New York: Oxford University Press, 1964.

———. "Uses of the *Finnegans Wake* Manuscripts." In *Twelve and a Tilly: Essays on the Occasion of the Twenty-Fifth Anniversary of Finnegans Wake*. Edited by Jack P. Dalton and Clive Hart. London: Faber and Faber, 1966.

———. "*The Waste Land* Fifty Years After." In *Eliot in His Time: Essays on the Occasion of the Fiftieth Anniversary of The Waste Land*. Edited by A. Walton Litz. Princeton: Princeton University Press, 1973.

Longenbach, James. *Modernist Poetics of History: Pound, Eliot, and the Sense of the Past*. Princeton: Princeton University Press, 1987.

———. *Stone Cottage: Pound, Yeats, and Modernism*. New York: Oxford University Press, 1988.

———. *Wallace Stevens: The Plain Sense of Things*. New York: Oxford University Press, 1991.

Maddox, Brenda. *Nora: The Real Life of Molly Bloom*. Boston: Houghton Mifflin, 1988.

Magalaner, Marvin, and Richard M. Kain. *Joyce: The Man, the Work, the Reputation*. New York: New York University Press, 1956.

Mahaffey, Vicki. *Reauthorizing Joyce*. New York: Cambridge University Press, 1988.

Manganiello, Dominic. *Joyce's Politics*. London: Routledge and Kegan Paul, 1980.

Marcus, Jane. "'No More Horses': Virginia Woolf on Art and Propaganda." *Women's Studies* 4 (1977): 264–89.

———. "Pargetting *The Pargiters*." In *Virginia Woolf and the Languages of Patriarchy*. Bloomington: Indiana University Press, 1987.

Materer, Timothy, ed. *Pound/Lewis: The Letters of Ezra Pound and Wyndham Lewis*. New York: New Directions, 1985.

McAlmon, Robert, and Kay Boyle. *Being Geniuses Together: 1920–1930*. New York: Doubleday, 1968.

McDiarmid, Lucy. *Saving Civilization: Yeats, Eliot, and Auden Between the Wars*. Cambridge: Cambridge University Press, 1984.

McGann, Jerome J. *The Textual Condition*. Princeton: Princeton University Press, 1991.

McGee, Patrick. *Paperspace: Style as Ideology in Joyce's Ulysses*. Lincoln: University of Nebraska Press, 1988.

McHugh, Roland. *Annotations to Finnegans Wake*. Baltimore: Johns Hopkins University Press, 1980.

———. *The Sigla of Finnegans Wake*. Austin: University of Texas Press, 1976.

McMillan, Dougald. *transition: The History of a Literary Era, 1927–1938*. London: Calder and Boyars, 1975.

Menand, Luke. *Discovering Modernism: T. S. Eliot and His Context*. New York: Oxford University Press, 1987.

Mercanton, Jacques. "The Hours of James Joyce." In *Portraits of the Artist in Exile: Recollections of James Joyce by Europeans*. Edited by Willard Potts. Seattle: University of Washington Press, 1979. Reprint. New York: Harcourt Brace Jovanovich, 1986.

Moi, Toril. *Sexual/Textual Politics: Feminist Literary Theory*. New York: Methuen, 1985.

Mondolfo, Vittoria L., and Margaret Hurley, eds. *Letters to Ibbotson, 1935–1952*. Orono, Me.: National Poetry Foundation, 1979.

Morse, J. Mitchell. "On Teaching *Finnegans Wake*." In *Twelve and a Tilly: Essays on the*

*Occasion of the Twenty-Fifth Anniversary of Finnegans Wake.* Edited by Jack P. Dalton and Clive Hart. London: Faber and Faber, 1966.

Naremore, James. *The World Without a Self: Virginia Woolf and the Novel.* New Haven: Yale University Press, 1973.

Nolde, John J. "Ezra Pound and the *Ta Hio*: The Making of a Confucian." *Paideuma* 15 (1986): 73–91.

Norris, Margot. *Joyce's Web: The Social Unraveling of Modernism.* Austin: University of Texas Press, 1992.

North, Michael. *The Political Aesthetic of Yeats, Eliot, and Pound.* Cambridge: Cambridge University Press, 1991.

———. "Where Memory Faileth: Forgetfulness and a Poem Including History." In *Ezra Pound: The Legacy of Kulchur.* Edited by Marcel Smith and William A. Ulmer. Tuscaloosa: University of Alabama Press, 1988.

Oppen, Mary. *Meaning A Life.* Santa Barbara, Calif.: Black Sparrow Press, 1978.

Parker, Andrew. "Ezra Pound and the 'Economy' of Anti-Semitism." *Boundary/2* 11 (1983): 103–28.

Patterson, Lee. "Introduction." *South Atlantic Quarterly* 91 (1992): 787–91.

Perl, Jeffrey M. *Skepticism and Modern Enmity: Before and After Eliot.* Baltimore: Johns Hopkins University Press, 1989.

Perloff, Marjorie. *The Futurist Moment: Avant-Garde, Avant Guerre, and the Language of Rupture.* Chicago: University of Chicago Press, 1986.

Poggioli, Renato. *The Theory of the Avant-Garde.* Cambridge, Mass.: Harvard University Press, 1968.

Poirier, Richard. *The Renewal of Literature: Emersonian Reflections.* New Haven: Yale University Press, 1988.

Potts, Willard. "Joyce's Notes on the Gorman Biography." *ICarbS* 4 (1981): 83–99.

Pound, Ezra. *ABC of Economics.* In *Selected Prose: 1909–1965.* Edited by William Cookson. New York: New Directions, 1973.

———. *ABC of Reading.* Norfolk, Conn.: New Directions, 1951.

———. Drafts for *ABC of Reading.* Beinecke Library, YCAL MSS 43, box 58, folder 2096.

———. *The Cantos of Ezra Pound.* New York: New Directions, 1981.

———. *The Exile* 3, 4 (1928).

———. *"Ezra Pound Speaking": Radio Speeches of World War II.* Edited by Leonard W. Doob. Westport, Conn.: Greenwood Press, 1978.

———. *Guide to Kulchur.* New York: New Directions, 1970.

———. "How to Read." In *Literary Essays of Ezra Pound.* Edited, with an introduction, by T. S. Eliot. Norfolk, Conn.: New Directions, 1954.

———. Typescript of "How to Read." Beinecke Library, YCAL MSS 43, box 97, folder 3599.

———. *Jefferson and/or Mussolini.* London: Stanley Nott, 1935.

———. *The Letters of Ezra Pound: 1907–1941.* Edited by D. D. Paige. New York: Harcourt, Brace, 1950.

———. *Literary Essays of Ezra Pound.* Edited, with an introduction, by T. S. Eliot. Norfolk, Conn.: New Directions, 1954.

———. *Polite Essays.* Norfolk, Conn.: New Directions, 1940.

———. *Pound/Zukofsky: Selected Letters of Ezra Pound and Louis Zukofsky.* Edited by Barry Ahearn. New York: New Directions, 1987.

———. *Prolegomena I.* le Beausset, France: To Publishers, 1932.

———. *Selected Prose: 1909–1965.* Edited by William Cookson. New York: New Directions, 1973.

————. *The Spirit of Romance*. New York: New Directions, 1968.

————. "T. S. Eliot." In *We Moderns*. New York: Gotham Book Mart, 1940.

————. "When Will School Books.......?" *Delphian Quarterly* 20 (1937): 16–24.

————. Translation and commentary. *Confucius: The Great Digest, The Unwobbling Pivot, The Analects*. New York: New Directions, 1969.

Rabaté, Jean-Michel. *James Joyce, Authorized Reader*. Baltimore: Johns Hopkins University Press, 1984.

————. *Language, Sexuality and Ideology in Ezra Pound's Cantos*. London: Macmillan, 1986.

Radin, Grace. *Virginia Woolf's "The Years": The Evolution of a Novel*. Knoxville: University of Tennessee Press, 1981.

Rainey, Lawrence S. "The Price of Modernism: Reconsidering the Publication of *The Waste Land*." *Yale Review* 78 (1989): 279–300.

Read, Forrest, ed. *Pound/Joyce: The Letters of Ezra Pound to James Joyce with Pound's Essays on Joyce*. London: Faber and Faber, 1967.

Redman, Tim. *Ezra Pound and Italian Fascism*. New York: Cambridge University Press, 1991.

Roe, Sue. *Writing and Gender: Virginia Woolf's Writing Practice*. New York: St. Martin's Press, 1990.

Rudge, Olga, ed. *"If This Be Treason."* Siena: Tipografia Nuova, 1948.

Ruotolo, Lucio. *The Interrupted Moment: A View of Virginia Woolf's Novels*. Stanford: Stanford University Press, 1986.

Sailer, Susan Shaw. "Conjunctions: Commentary and Text in *Finnegans Wake* II.2." *James Joyce Quarterly* 27 (1990): 793–802.

Sanders, Frederick K. *John Adams Speaking: Pound's Sources for the Adams Cantos*. Orono: University of Maine Press, 1975.

Schlack, Beverly Ann. "Virginia Woolf's Strategy of Scorn in *The Years* and *Three Guineas*." *Bulletin of the New York Public Library* 80 (1977): 146–50.

Schuster, Richard. "*Finnegans Wake* II.2, 'Night Lessons': The Talmud Another Source?" *James Joyce Quarterly* 27 (1990): 856–59.

Schwartz, Sanford. *The Matrix of Modernism: Pound, Eliot, and Early Twentieth-Century Thought*. Princeton: Princeton University Press, 1985.

Scott, Bonnie Kime. *Joyce and Feminism*. Bloomington: Indiana University Press, 1984.

Senn, Fritz. "Dynamics of Corrective Unrest." In *Joyce's Dislocutions: Essays on Reading as Translation*. Edited by John Paul Riquelme. Baltimore: Johns Hopkins University Press, 1984.

Sherry, Vincent. *Ezra Pound, Wyndham Lewis, and Radical Modernism*. New York: Oxford University Press, 1993.

Short, Robert S. "The Politics of Surrealism: 1920–36." *Journal of Contemporary History* 2 (1966): 3–25.

Showalter, Elaine. *A Literature of Their Own: British Women Novelists from Brontë to Lessing*. Princeton: Princeton University Press, 1977.

Sieburth, Richard. "In Pound We Trust: The Economy of Poetry/The Poetry of Economics." *Critical Inquiry* 14 (1987): 142–72.

Silver, Brenda R. "The Authority of Anger: *Three Guineas* as Case Study." *Signs: Journal of Women in Culture and Society* 16 (1991): 340–70.

————. Introduction to "'Anon' and 'The Reader': Virginia Woolf's Last Essays." *Twentieth-Century Literature* 25 (1979): 356–441.

————. "*Three Guineas* Before and After: Further Answers to Correspondents." In *Vir-*

ginia Woolf: A Feminist Slant. Edited by Jane Marcus. Lincoln: University of
    Nebraska Press, 1983.

———. *Virginia Woolf's Reading Notebooks*. Princeton: Princeton University Press, 1983.

———, ed. "'Anon' and the 'The Reader': Virginia Woolf's Last Essays." *Twentieth-
    Century Literature* 25 (1979): 356–441.

Slocum, John J., and Herbert Cahoon. *A Bibliography of James Joyce*. New Haven: Yale
    University Press, 1953.

Sollers, Philippe. "Joyce & Co." In *In the Wake of the Wake*. Edited by David Hayman and
    Elliott Anderson. Madison: University of Wisconsin Press, 1978.

Sontag, Raymond J. *A Broken World: 1919–1939*. New York: Harper & Row, 1971.

Spoerri, James Fuller. *Finnegans Wake by James Joyce: A Check List*. Evanston: North-
    western University Library, 1953.

Stein, Gertrude. *The Autobiography of Alice B. Toklas*. New York: Random House, 1961.

Stern, David. "Midrash and Indeterminacy." *Critical Inquiry* 15 (1988): 132–61.

Stock, Noel. *The Life of Ezra Pound: An Expanded Edition*. San Francisco: North Point
    Press, 1982.

———, ed. *"Verse Is a Sword: Unpublished Letters of Ezra Pound." X* 1 (1960): 258–65.

Stoppard, Tom. *Travesties*. New York: Grove Press, 1975.

Sultan, Stanley. *Eliot, Joyce and Company*. New York: Oxford University Press, 1987.

Terrell, Carroll F. *A Companion to the Cantos of Ezra Pound*. 2 vols. Berkeley: University
    of California Press, 1980, 1984.

Tindall, William York. *A Reader's Guide to Finnegans Wake*. 2d ed. New York: Farrar,
    Straus and Giroux, 1970.

Tribble, Evelyn B. *Margins and Marginality: The Printed Page in Early Modern England*.
    Charlottesville: University Press of Virginia, 1993.

Vico, Giambattista. *The New Science of Giambattista Vico*. Edited and translated by
    Thomas Goddard Bergin and Max Harold Fisch. Ithaca: Cornell University
    Press, 1948. Rev. ed. Ithaca: Cornell University Press, 1984.

White, Allon. *The Uses of Obscurity: The Fiction of Early Modernism*. London: Routledge
    and Kegan Paul, 1981.

Whittier-Ferguson, John. "The Voice Behind the Echo: Vladimir Dixon's Letters to
    James Joyce and Sylvia Beach." *James Joyce Quarterly* 29 (1992): 511–29.

Wilde, Oscar. *The Artist as Critic*. Edited by Richard Ellmann. Chicago: University of
    Chicago Press, 1969.

Woodward, Daniel H. "Notes on the Publishing History and Text of *The Waste Land*."
    *Papers of the Bibliographical Society of America* 58 (1964): 252–69.

Woolf, Virginia. "The Artist and Politics." In *The Moment and Other Essays*. New York:
    Harcourt, Brace, 1948.

———. *Between the Acts*. New York: Harcourt, Brace, 1941.

———. *The Death of the Moth and Other Essays*. New York: Harcourt, Brace, 1942.

———. *The Diary of Virginia Woolf*. 5 vols. Edited by Anne Olivier Bell. New York:
    Harcourt Brace Jovanovich, 1977–1984.

———. *The Essays of Virginia Woolf*. 3 vols. Edited by Andrew McNeillie. New York:
    Harcourt Brace Jovanovich, 1986–1988.

———. *Flush*. New York: Harcourt, Brace, 1933.

———. *Granite and Rainbow*. New York: Harcourt, Brace, 1958.

———. *Jacob's Room*. New York: Harcourt, Brace, 1922.

———. "The Leaning Tower." In *The Moment and Other Essays*. New York: Harcourt,
    Brace, 1948.

———. *The Letters of Virginia Woolf.* 6 vols. Edited by Nigel Nicolson and Joanne Trautmann. New York: Harcourt Brace Jovanovich, 1975–1980.

———. *Mrs. Dalloway.* New York: Harcourt, Brace, 1925.

———. *Orlando.* New York: Harcourt, Brace, 1928.

———. *The Pargiters: The Novel-Essay Portion of "The Years."* Edited and introduced by Mitchell A. Leaska. New York: New York Public Library and Readex Books, 1977.

———. *Roger Fry.* New York: Harcourt, Brace, 1940.

———. *A Room of One's Own.* New York: Harcourt, Brace, 1929.

———. *Three Guineas.* New York: Harcourt, Brace, 1938.

———. *To The Lighthouse.* New York: Harcourt, Brace, 1927.

———. *The Waves.* New York: Harcourt, Brace, 1931.

———. *The Years.* New York: Harcourt, Brace, 1937.

Yeats, William Butler. "Anima Hominis." In *Mythologies.* New York: Collier Books, 1969.

Zwerdling, Alex. "The Common Reader, the Coterie and the Audience of One." In *Virginia Woolf Miscellanies: Proceedings of the First Annual Conference on Virginia Woolf.* Edited by Mark Hussey and Vara Neverow-Turk. New York: Pace University Press, 1992.

———. *Virginia Woolf and the Real World.* Berkeley: University of California Press, 1986.

# INDEX

Maddox, Brenda, 26
Magalaner, Marvin, 32
Mahaffey, Vicki, 162n.66
Mailla, Father Joseph, de, 145
Malory, Sir Thomas, 110
Manganiello, Dominic, 18, 32
Marcus, Jane, 164n.19, 165n.36
Marcuse, Herbert, 30
Martin, Kingsley, 75
Martz, Louis, 140, 142
Masefield, John, 141
McAlmon, Robert, 49, 155n.51,
    156nn.53, 61
McCann, Phillip, 73
McCormick, Edith, 27, 29
McDiarmid, Lucy, 151n.3
McGann, Jerome 33, 155n.50
McGee, Patrick, 162n.67
McGreevy, Thomas, 45
McHugh, Roland, 10, 64, 67, 158n.19
McMillan, Dougald, 32, 34, 157nn.2,
    71
Menand, Luke, 152nn.31, 35
Milne, A. A., 124
Milton, John, 174n.90
*Modern Quarterly*, referendum on "Work
    in Progress," 37
Modernism
    aesthetics and/or politics, 9, 13, 14, 20,
        25, 28–30, 36–37, 111, 153,
        155n.42
    and apparatus 10, 117–18
    audience, 4, 6, 8, 14, 108, 131–32,
        150, 171n.46
    historically contingent term, 30–31
    pedagogy, 3, 12
    and textual contexts, 4, 5, 17–18
    *See also under individual authors*
Moi, Toril, 163n.6
Monroe, Harriet, 141, 146
Moore, Marianne, 9
Muir, Edwin, 140
Mussolini, Benito, 117, 124, 135–36,
    149–50, 166n.37, 172n.64,
    174n.102

Naremore, James, 164n.14
*New Age, The*, 143, 146
*New English Weekly*, 146
*New York Herald Tribune Books*, 123–25

1930s, 3, 4, 12–13, 14 (*see also under
    individual authors*)
Nolde, John, 169n.25
North, Michael, 117, 118, 155–56n.42,
    156–57n.70, 167n.5, 172n.68,
    174nn.90, 100, 175n.102
Norris, Margot, 29–30, 37, 154nn.20, 30

Oppen, George, 127–28, 170n.34
Oppen, Mary, 170n.34
Orage, A. R., 143, 173n.84
*Our Exagmination Round His Factifica-
    tion for Incamination of Work in
    Progress*, 13, 17, 41, 158n.14
    compared to "How to Read," 123–24
    cover of, *46*, 53, 124, 170n.31
    Joyce's attitude toward, 45–48
    ludic criticism in, 45, 48–49
    promoted by Joyce, 45–46
    textual history of, 45–47, 53
    "Two Letters of Protest" in, 49–51
    in "Work in Progress," 51, 54
    *See also* Joyce, works of, *Finnegans
        Wake*, "The Twelve"

Palgrave, Francis Turner, 126
Parker, Andrew, 172n.66
Patterson, Lee, 5, 151n.3
Paul, Elliot, 31, 53
Perl, Jeffrey, 11, 152n.35
Perloff, Marjorie , 155n.51, 157n.3,
    158n.10
Petitjean, Armand, 45, 48, 56, 157n.4
Phoenix Park, 160n.36
Pigott, Richard, 159–60n.36
*Poetry*, 141
Poirier, Richard, 7, 151n.11
Politics, 19–20
Por, Odon, 174n.97
Pound, Ezra
    addressing himself, 147–50
    as aesthete, 132
    and "Anon" (Woolf) 133
    as anthologist, 125, 139–46, 174n.88
    apparatus compared to Joyce's, 116,
        117, 121, 124, 129, 130, 134,
        135, 147, 148, 150 (*see also
        under Joyce; Woolf*)
    apparatus compared to Woolf's, 116,
        117, 121, 122, 129, 130,

Pound, Ezra (*continued*)
    133–134, 135, 147, 148, 150
    (*see also under Joyce*; *Woolf*)
  apparatus described, 14, 115–17, 119,
    121, 128, 134–37, 139,
    140–41, 145, 147, 149–50,
    173n.81
  apparatus, objections to, 115–16, 118,
    121, 122, 128, 146–47
  audience, 14, 77, 116–17, 124, 127,
    129, 130–34, 135–37, 139,
    141, 147–50, 153n.44, 170n.39,
    174n.96
  authority, 125, 134–35, 136–38, 142,
    144, 148, 173n.83
  and the avant-garde, 130
  "Bel Esprit" project, 168n.18
  book of the quarter club, 124, 170n.33
  Buddhists, 143
  China, 174n.87
  demotic author, 116, 124–25, 132–33
  *Dial* prize, 119, 168n.16
  Eliot's *Selected Essays* and Pound's crit-
    ical prose, 128, 172n.69
  *The Exile*, 123, 138, 172n.67
  fascism, 118, 133, 135, 148, 167n.5
  history, 123, 142, 144–45, 148, 150,
    168n.9, 172n.73
  idiogrammic method, 118, 138–39,
    167n.9, 168n.10
  incoherence, 118–20, 127, 128–30,
    133–34, 135–38, 148–49, 150,
    170n.38
  Jews, 123, 143
  in Joyce's dream of Molly Bloom, 73
  on Joyce's aesthetic experiments,
    162n.69
  pedagogy, 4, 14, 20, 116–17, 119–20,
    123, 124, 127–39, 140–41,
    145–46, 148–50, 169nn.21, 25,
    170n.35, 171n.53, 174n.100
  poetic "kinds" (melopoeia, phanopoeia,
    logopoeia), 127
  poetic style, 141–45
  politics, 20, 108, 116–19, 130,
    135–36, 145, 149, 168n.13,
    172n.68
  poststructuralist readings of, 172n.66
  prose style, 120–38, 145 (*see also*
    Lindberg, Kathryne)

scholarship, 125, 132
St. Elizabeths Hospital, 132
Taoist, Pound as, 174n.91
thirties, work of, 108, 116, 117, 118,
    122, 129, 133, 134, 135, 139,
    140, 141, 142, 145, 146, 147, 148
totalitarian treatises, 20, 174n.98
usury, 141
vanishing author, 113, 117–18, 138,
    167–68n.9, 172n.67
*The Waste Land* "Notes," Pound on, 6
weighing prose and poetry, 115, 116,
    117, 119–21, 133, 140–41,
    146, 168n.14
works of
  *ABC of Economics*: 14, 117, 134,
    136–39, 143; textual history of,
    171n.55
  *ABC of Reading*, 4, 14, 20, 116, 117,
    134–36, 138–39, 143, 144,
    145, 146, 147, 174n.89; drafts
    for, 20, 116, 153n.44; textual
    history of, 171n.55
  *Active Anthology*, 115
  *The Analects*, 169n.26
  *Cantos*, 14, 115–16, 117, 132,
    139–46, 172nn.73, 74,
    172–73n.75, 174n.91; *A Draft
    of XXX Cantos*, 171n.50,
    172n.74; Canto 36, 146; Canto
    37, 141, 143, 144, 145, 146,
    150; Canto 38, 146; Canto 42,
    145; Canto 45, 141, 142,
    173n.81; Canto 46, 141–43,
    173n.80; Canto 54, 143; Canto
    55, 143; Canto 60, 143; Canto
    62, 144; Canto 63, 144; Canto
    64, 144; Canto 68, 145; Canto
    70, 145; *Eleven New Cantos*,
    117, 145; *The Fifth Decade of
    Cantos*, 117, 141, 145, 146;
    *Cantos LII–LXXI*, 117, 145;
    *Section: Rock-Drill*, 169n.19
  *Carta da Visita*, 170n.38
  *Chung Yung*, 169n.26
  *Confucius, The Unwobbling Pivot,
    and The Great Digest*, 169n.29
  *Guide to Kulchur*, 14, 117, 119–20,
    134, 147–48, 149, 168n.10,
    174n.100

Thackeray, William Makepeace, 95,
    165n.32
Tindall, William York, 159n.28
Tiresias, 113
*transition*, 13, 18, 31–38, 44, 45
    frame for Joyce's work, 31, 32, 36, 41,
        42, 44, 45, 74
    "Homage to James Joyce," 49
    "INQUIRY ABOUT THE MALADY OF
        LANGUAGE," 44
    Joyce's influence in, 17–18, 31
    *"language of the night"* workshop, 44
Tribble, Evelyn, 151n.6

United States Foreign Broadcast Intelli-
    gence Service, 150

Van Buren, Martin, 141, 145, 146
Vico, Giambattista, 54, 59, 68,
    158–59n.22
vorticism, 139

Weaver, Harriet Shaw, 6, 27, 47, 53, 70,
    154n.18
Weston, Jessie, 117
White, Allon, 151n.11
Wilde, Oscar, 11, 65
Williams, William Carlos, 45
Womrath's Library and Bookshops, 124
Woodward, Daniel, 151n.7
Woolf, Leonard, 76, 93, 109
Woolf, Virginia
    anger, 81
    anonymity, 85, 94, 106–8, 110–14,
        115, 117, 166n.47
    apparatus and tyranny, 14, 89, 105
    apparatus compared to Joyce's, 77, 87,
        106, 107, 108, 110, 111, 112 (*see
        also under Joyce; Pound*)
    apparatus compared to Pound's, 77,
        108, 122 (*see also under Joyce;
        Pound*)
    apparatus described, 14, 77–78,
        79–80, 81–83, 87, 88–90,
        92–98, 99, 102–5, 106–8, 112,
        165n.30
    apparatus, objections to, 14, 89, 105,
        110
    audience, 14, 76, 77, 78, 79, 83–84,

    87–88, 91–92, 98–99, 108–12,
        133, 150, 166n.45
    authority, 79, 82, 83–84, 85–86,
        89–91, 94, 97–98, 102, 103–4,
        105, 107–8
    Christianity, case against in apparatus,
        96
    composition, disruptions of, 105, 106,
        110–14
    "facts," 14, 77–78, 79, 83, 86–87,
        88–89, 90–91, 94, 98–104,
        165nn.26, 35
    history, 78, 79, 80, 81, 86, 89, 94, 96,
        107, 163n.8
    "indifference," 17, 25, 76
    literary/cultural tradition, 77, 109, 113
    personae, 78–80, 82–83 (*see also*
        anonymity)
    photographs, 98–102, 165n.35 (*see also*
        "facts")
    politics, 14, 75–76, 77–78, 81, 85–86,
        91, 95–102, 105, 106, 107, 115,
        163n.3, 166n.40
    scholarship, 78–79, 81, 82, 83, 89,
        163–64n.12 (*see also* authority)
    "Society of Outsiders," 20, 25, 108
    suicide, 109, 166n.46
    thirties, work of, 76, 77, 85–86, 91,
        99, 102, 106, 108–9, 113, 122,
        133, 162n.1, 162–63n.2, 163n.3
    twenties, work of, 14, 77–78, 81, 84
    works of
        "Anon," 41, 110–14, 135, 166n.48;
            origins of apparatus, 111–12
        "Answers to Correspondents. *See
            Three Guineas*
        "Artist and Politics," 105, 166n.38
        *Between the Acts*, 78, 89, 110
        "Character in Fiction," 164n.21
        *Flush*, 163n.5, 165n.33
        "Here and Now." *See The Pargiters*
        history of English literature. *See*
            "Reading at Random"; "Anon"
        *Jacob's Room*, 164n.12
        "A Knock on the Door." *See Three
            Guineas*
        "Leaning Tower," 106, 133, 166n.41
        "Letter to an Englishman." *See Three
            Guineas*
        memoir of Julian Bell, 164n.17

"Miss Janet Case: Classical Scholar and Teacher," 85, 164n.17
"The Moths." *See The Waves*
*Mrs. Dalloway*, 88, 124
*Night and Day*, 86
"The Open Door." *See Three Guineas*
*Orlando*, 81, 82, 86, 163n.8
*The Pargiters*, 4, 14, 77, 78, 84–90, 91, 102, 106, 107, 113; textual history of, 164n.19 (*see also Three Guineas; The Years*)
"Professions for Women," 84, 164n.13
"The Reader," 166n.48
"Reading at Random," 110 (*see also* "Anon"; "The Reader")
*Roger Fry*, 78, 109
*A Room of One's Own*, 4, 14, 31, 77, 78–84, 85, 87, 88, 89, 91, 92, 93, 94–95, 100, 105–6, 107, 108; textual history of 163n.10
"A Sketch of the Past," 166
*Three Guineas*, 4, 14, 17, 25, 26, 31, 78, 82, 85, 86, 89, 90–107, 108, 113, 122; Leonard Woolf's reading of, 93; reception of 163n.11, 164n.24, 165nn.28, 30; textual history of, 75–77 (*see also The Pargiters; The Years*)
*To the Lighthouse*, 88
*The Waves*, 78, 83, 84–85, 86, 164n.14
"Why Art To-Day Follows Politics." *See* "Artist and Politics"
"Women and Fiction," 163n.10
Workers' Educational Association, speech to. *See* "The Leaning Tower"
*The Years*, 78, 89, 90; textual history of, 164n.20 (*see also Three Guineas; The Pargiters*)

Yeats, William Butler, 113, 135

Zukofsky, Louis, 128, 124, 170n.34
Zwerdling, Alex, 163nn.3, 4, 165nn.28, 30, 34, 166n.45